THE INVENTED REALITY

The Invented Reality

How Do We Know

What We Believe We Know?

Contributions to Constructivism

Edited and with commentary by

PAUL WATZLAWICK

W · W · NORTON & COMPANY

New York   *London*

The text of this book is composed in Palatino. Composition and manufacturing by the Maple-Vail Book Manufacturing Group.
Book design by Jacques Chazaud

Grateful acknowledgment is due the following copyright holders:
Jon Elster, "Active and Passive Negation," originally titled "Négation active et négation passive": © 1979. Archives Européennes de Sociologie, Paris.

Heinz von Foerster, "On Constructing a Reality," first published in *Environmental Design Research*, Vol. 2, W. F. E. Preiser (ed.), pp. 35–46: © 1973. Dowden, Hutchinson & Ross, Stroudsburg.

David L. Rosenhan, "On Being Sane in Insane Places," first published in *Science*, Vol. 179, pp. 250–258, January 19, 1973: © 1973. American Association for the Advancement of Science, Washington, D.C.

Gabriel Stolzenberg, "Can an Inquiry into the Foundations of Mathematics Tell Us Anything Interesting About Mind?," first published in *Psychology and Biology of Language and Thought—Essays in Honor of Erich Lenneberg*, pp. 221–269: © 1978. Academic Press, New York.

Illustrations 22 and 31: M. C. Escher, "Drawing Hands," M. C. Escher, "Print Gallery," both from Haags Gemeentmuseum, Den Haag: © Beeldrecht, Amsterdam.

Library of Congress Cataloging in Publication Data

Erfundene Wirklichkeit.
  The Invented reality.

  Includes indexes.
  Translation of: Die erfundene Wirklichkeit.
  1. Constructivism (Philosophy)—Addresses, essays, lectures. 2. Reality—Addresses, essays, lectures.
I. Watzlawick, Paul. II. Title.
BD331.E7413 1984   149   83–6258

ISBN 978-0-393-33347-3

W. W. Norton & Company, Inc.
500 Fifth Avenue, New York, N. Y. 10110
W. W. Norton & Company Ltd.
37 Great Russell Street, London WC1B 3NU
2 3 4 5 6 7 8 9 0

Contents

This is the creature that was not to be.
They knew it not; but all the same
They loved its gait, its poise, its name,
And in its eyes the light of sympathy.

Though it was not, their love had made it pure and free.
They always left for it a space
To outline it—and there, with quiet grace,
It raised its head and had no need to be.

It was not fed on corn
But on the possibility of being,
Which gave it strength to sprout a horn

Amid its forehead's snowy fur.
Thus in a virgin's mirror it was seen,
And came to life in it, and was in her.

Rainer Maria Rilke, *The Sonnets to Orpheus*
(translation by Ernst von Glasersfeld)

Every man's world picture is and always remains a construct of his mind and cannot be proved to have any other existence.

Erwin Schrödinger, *Mind and Matter*

Foreword

How *do we know what we believe we know?* This seemingly simple question involves three domains of thought that have concerned the human mind for thousands of years.

What we know is generally considered to be the result of our exploration and understanding of the real world, of the way things *really* are. After all, common sense suggests that this objective reality can be discovered. Consequently, the title of this book is nonsensical: An *invented* reality cannot— precisely because it is invented—be the true reality.

How we know is a far more vexing problem. To solve it, the mind needs to step outside itself, so to speak, and observe itself at work; for at this point we are no longer faced with facts that apparently exist independently of us in the outside world, but with mental processes whose nature is not at all self-evident. In this respect the title of this book is somewhat less nonsensical, for if *what* we know depends on *how* we came to know it, then our view of reality is no longer a true image of what is the case outside ourselves, but is inevitably determined also by the processes through which we arrived at this view.

But, then, what about the word *believe?* This is where the subject matter of this book takes its origin. It deals with a topic that was already known to the pre-Socratics, but which in our day is gaining increasing practical importance,

namely, the growing awareness that any so-called reality is—
in the most immediate and concrete sense—the *construction*
of those who believe they have discovered and investigated
it. In other words, what is supposedly found is an invention
whose inventor is unaware of his act of invention, who considers it as something that exists independently of him; the
invention then becomes the basis of his world view and
actions.

For many centuries the *what* and *how* of knowing have been
the subject of extensive philosophical pursuits, known,
respectively, to the expert as ontology (that branch of metaphysics that deals with the nature of being) and epistemology (the study of how we arrive at knowledge). For the third
aspect just mentioned, the "invention" of reality, a rather
unfortunate term, *constructivism*, is gaining acceptance—
unfortunate because, first, the word already has an established but somewhat different meaning in traditional philosophy; second, it refers to a short-lived movement in the arts
and especially the architecture of the Soviet Union during
the 1920s; and, third, it is ugly. If the brain child did not
already have this name, the pedestrian term *reality research*
would be preferable.

In this volume, experts from various fields explain how
scientific, social, individual, and ideological realities are
invented (constructed) as a result of the inevitable need to
approach the supposedly independent reality "out there"
from certain basic assumptions that we consider to be
"objective" properties of the real reality, while in actual fact
they are the consequences of our *search* for reality.

The book is thus a collection of essays on the subject of
constructivism. It is neither a thesis nor a comprehensive
textbook. A work of that kind would require a far more competent author and editor who, in a vast synthesis, would
have to follow the development of constructivism from the
days of antiquity to Giambattista Vico, Immanuel Kant,
David Hume, Eduard Zeller, Wilhelm Dilthey, Edmund
Husserl, Ludwig Wittgenstein and the Vienna Circle, Jean
Piaget, Erwin Schrödinger, Werner Heisenberg, George Kelly,
Nelson Goodman, and many other competent thinkers, to

say nothing of the great cyberneticians of our day and those poets and writers who, in their own way, have always known about these matters.

But this synthesis is not yet achieved; the bridges between these disciplines are not yet built.

What unites the contributing authors is their interest in the phenomena of constructivism and their willingness to describe them in this work. It will hardly surprise the reader to find that, in spite of their common subject matter, these contributions are like erratic blocks, very different in style and in their degrees of abstraction, and that they contain both contradiction and repetition. (For instance, the spirit of Epimenides, the Cretan, makes his ghostly appearance in more than one essay.) After all, these treatises have their origin in very different disciplines, and—except for the editor—only a few of the authors know some of the others personally.

I have written the commentaries as an introduction to the various chapters and in the hope that, read for themselves, they may constitute an essay on constructivism. I appeal to the reader's indulgence if so ambitious an enterprise can at best be only partly successful.

Finally, it should be understood that the commentaries do not necessarily reflect the views of the other contributors.

Villach, Austria
and Palo Alto, California   *Paul Watzlawick*

PART 1

Introduction

PAUL WATZLAWICK

*I*n the vast field of experimental psychology there exists a group
of tests that have special importance for the subject matter of
this book. They are called noncontingent reward experiments,
because their common feature is the absence of any causal connection between the subject's performance and the response of
the experimenter to his performance. This fact, called noncontin-
gency, is unknown to the subject.

In one of many such experiments that the psychologist Alex
Bavelas[1] conducted at Stanford University many years ago (but
unfortunately never published), the experimenter reads to the
subject a long list of number pairs (e.g., 31 and 80, 77 and 15).
After each pair the subject is supposed to say whether the two
numbers "fit" or not. Invariably the subject first wants to know
in what sense these numbers are supposed to "fit," and the experimenter explains that the task lies precisely in the discovery of
these rules. This leads the subject to assume that his task is one
of those usual trial-and-error experiments and that all he can
therefore do is start out with random "fit" and "do not fit"
responses. At first he is wrong every single time, but gradually
his performance begins to improve and the "correct" responses of
the experimenter increase. The subject thus arrives at a hypoth-

---

[1]Personal communication.

esis that, although not entirely correct, turns out to be more and more reliable.

What the subject does not know is that there is no immediate connection between his guesses and the experimenter's reactions. The latter gives his "correct" responses on the basis of the ascending half of a bell-shaped curve, that is, very rarely at first, and then with increasing frequency. This creates in the subject an assumption of the order underlying the relation between the number pairs that can be so persistent that he is unwilling to relinquish it even after the experimenter has told him that his responses were noncontingent. Some subjects are even convinced of having discovered a regularity that the experimenter was unaware of.

In the most concrete meaning of the word, the subject has thus invented a reality that he quite rightly assumes he has discovered. The reason for his conviction is that his image of that reality fits into the test situation. But this only means that it is not contradicted by the nature of the situation. It does not mean that it correctly reflects the (supposed) order governing the relationship between the number pairs. In an objective sense, there simply is no such order. And the laws of relationship that seem to exist between the numbers the subject may "discover" do not have a remote connection with the experimental arrangement; they more or less fit into the givens of the weird situation, but they certainly do not match its true nature.

The fundamental distinction between fitting and matching was postulated by Ernst von Glasersfeld, and it is one of the cardinal points of his Introduction to Radical Constructivism, the first essay of this book. In it he develops the provocative (and, on first reading, perhaps unacceptably radical) proposition that all we can ever know about the real world is what the world is not. This proposition and its practical, immediate consequences permeate not only von Glasersfeld's contribution, but the entire book. This being so, it may be useful to present it first by means of a metaphor.

A captain who on a dark, stormy night has to sail through an uncharted channel, devoid of beacons and other navigational aids, *will either wreck his ship on the cliffs or regain the safe, open sea beyond the strait. If he loses ship and life, his failure proves that the course he steered was not the right one. One may say that he discovered what the passage was* not. *If, on the other hand, he clears the strait, this success merely proves that he literally did not at any point come into collision with the (otherwise unknown) shape and nature of the waterway; it tells him nothing about how safe or how close to disaster he was at any given moment. He passed the strait like a blind man. His course* fit *the unknown topography, but this does not mean that it* matched *it—if we take matching in von Glasersfeld's sense, that is, that the course matched the real configuration of the channel. It would not be too difficult to imagine that the* actual *geographical shape of the strait might offer a number of safer and shorter passages.*

Constructivism in its pure, radical sense is incompatible with traditional thinking. As different as most philosophical, scientific, social, ideological, or individual world images may be from one another, they still have one thing in common: the basic assumption that a real reality exists and that certain theories, ideologies, or personal convictions reflect it (match it) more correctly than others.

The question then arises as to how such realities are constructed. This is the subject of the second contribution to this introductory part: Heinz von Foerster's by now classic lecture On Constructing a Reality, originally given in 1973. In it the internationally renowned cybernetician and biomathematician investigates the various steps of this process from first premises, that is, from the realization that the environment, as we perceive it, is our invention, to the neurophysiological mechanisms of these perceptions and to the ethical and aesthetic implications of these constructs. What needs to be stressed here is his concise refutation of the apparently justified objection that the constructivist view is nothing but a reiteration of an age-old philosophical fallacy, solipsism, *namely, the claim that there is no reality outside my mind, but that all human perception and experience—the world, heaven, hell, and everything else—is only in my head, that I (ego solus ipsus) alone exist.*

ERNST VON GLASERSFELD

An Introduction to Radical Constructivism *

> The gods have certainty, whereas to us
> as men conjecture [only is possible].
> Alcmaeon[1]

Preliminary Remarks

WITHIN THE LIMITS of one chapter, an unconventional way of thinking can certainly not be thoroughly justified, but it can perhaps be presented in its most characteristic features and anchored here and there in single points. There is, of course, the danger of being misunderstood. In the case of constructivism there is the additional risk that it will be discarded at first sight, because, like skepticism—with which it has certain features in common—it might seem too cool and critical, or simply incompatible with ordinary common sense. The proponents of an idea, as a rule, explain its nonacceptance differently from the way their critics and opponents do. Being myself much involved, it seems to me that the resistance met in the eighteenth century by Giambattista Vico, the first true constructivist, and by Silvio Ceccato and Jean Piaget in the more recent past is not so much due to inconsistencies or gaps in their argumentation as to the justifiable suspicion that constructivism intends to undermine too large a part of the traditional view of the world.

---

*An original contribution.

[1]From *Ancilla to the Pre-Socratic Philosophers* [5]. Diels, of whose work this is a translation, uses the German word *erschliessen*, which, beyond "to infer" and "to conjecture," also means "to unlock"—hence my use of the key metaphor, p. 6ff below.

Indeed, one need not enter very far into constructivist thought to realize that it inevitably leads to the contention that man—and man alone—is responsible for his thinking, his knowledge, and therefore also for what he does. Today, when behaviorists are still intent on pushing all responsibility into the environment, and sociobiologists are trying to place much of it into genes, a doctrine may well seem uncomfortable if it suggests that we have no one but ourselves to thank for the world in which we appear to be living. This is precisely what constructivism intends to say—but it says a good deal more. We build this world for the most part unawares, simply because we do not know how we do it. This ignorance is quite unnecessary. Radical constructivism maintains—not unlike Kant in his *Critique*—that the operations by means of which we assemble our experiential world can be explored, and that an awareness of this operating (which Ceccato in Italian so nicely called *consapevolezza operativa*) [4]* can help us do it differently and, perhaps, better.

This introduction, I repeat, will be limited to the exposition of a few aspects. The first section deals with the relation between knowledge and that "absolute" reality that is supposed to be independent of all experience, and I shall try to show that our knowledge can never be interpreted as a picture or representation of that real world, but only as a key that unlocks possible paths for us (see Alcmaeon's fragment).

The second section outlines the beginnings of skepticism and Kant's insight that, because our ways of experiencing are what they are, we cannot possibly conceive of an unexperienced world; it then presents some aspects of Vico's constructivist thought.

The third section explicates some of the main traits of the constructivist analysis of concepts. Some of the many ideas I have taken over from Piaget as well as from Ceccato will be outlined and only sparsely supported by quotations. Piaget's work has greatly influenced and encouraged me during the seventies, and before that the collaboration with Ceccato had provided direction and innumerable insights to my think-

---

*Bracketed numbers refer to sources at end of the essays.

ing. But for constructivists, all communication and all understanding are a matter of interpretive construction on the part of the experiencing subject, and therefore, in the last analysis, I alone can take the responsibility for what is being said in these pages.

I

The history of philosophy is a tangle of isms. Idealism, rationalism, nominalism, realism, skepticism, and dozens more have battled with one another more or less vigorously and continuously during the twenty-five centuries since the first written evidence of Western thought.

The many schools, directions, and movements are often difficult to distinguish. In one respect, however, any ism that wants to be taken seriously must set itself apart from all those that are already established: It must come up with at least *one* new turn in the theory of knowledge. Often this is no more than a rearrangement of well-known building blocks, a slight shift in the starting point, or the splitting of a traditional concept. The epistemological problem—how we acquire knowledge of reality, and how reliable and "true" that knowledge might be—occupies contemporary philosophy no less than it occupied Plato. The ways and means of the search for solutions have, of course, become more varied and complicated, but the basic question has, almost without exception, remained the same. The way that question was put at the very beginning made it impossible to answer, and the attempts that have since been made could not get anywhere near a solution to the problem.

The philosopher of science Hilary Putnam has recently formulated it like this: "It is impossible to find a philosopher before Kant (and after the pre-Socratics) who was *not* a metaphysical realist, at least about what he took to be *basic* or unreducible assertions" [18]. Putnam explains that statement by saying that, during those 2,000 years, philosophers certainly disagreed in their views about what *really* exists, but their conception of truth was always the same, in that it was tied to the notion of objective validity. A metaphysical realist, thus, is one who insists that we may call something "true" only if it corresponds to an independent, "objective" reality.[2]

On the whole, even after Kant the situation did not change. There were some who tried to take his *Critique of Pure Reason* seriously, but the pressure of philosophical tradition was overwhelming. In spite of Kant's thesis that our mind does not derive laws from nature, but imposes them on it [9], most scientists today still consider themselves "discoverers" who unveil nature's secrets and slowly but steadily expand the range of human knowledge; and countless philosophers have dedicated themselves to the task of ascribing to that laboriously acquired knowledge the unquestionable certainty which the rest of the world expects of genuine truth. Now as ever, there reigns the conviction that knowledge is knowledge only if it reflects the world as it is.[3]

The history of Western epistemology cannot, of course, be described adequately and fairly in a few pages. Given the limits of this essay, it will have to suffice if I pick out the main point in which the constructivism I am proposing differs *radically* from the traditional conceptualizations. This radical difference concerns the relation of knowledge and reality. Whereas in the traditional view of epistemology, as well as of cognitive psychology, this relation is always seen as a more or less picturelike (iconic) correspondence or match, radical constructivism sees it as an adaptation in the functional sense.

In everyday English, this conceptual opposition can be brought out quite clearly by pitting the words *match* and *fit* against one another in certain contexts. The metaphysical realist looks for knowledge that *matches* reality in the same sense as you might look for paint to match the color that is already on the wall you have to repair. In the epistemolo-

---

[2]"Am Anfang der Erkenntnis steht die Wahrheitsfrage. Ihre Einführung macht das menschliche Erkennen zu einem Wissensproblem."

[3]In *Begründung, Kritik und Rationalität* Spinner provides an excellent comprehensive survey of the thinkers and their arguments that have attacked that still widespread notion, and he documents the general bankruptcy of conventional epistemology [23].

gist's case it is, of course, not color that concerns him, but some kind of "homomorphism," which is to say, an equivalence of relations, a sequence, or a characteristic structure—something, in other words, that he can consider *the same,* because only then could he say that his knowledge is *of* the world.

If, on the other hand, we say that something *fits,* we have in mind a different relation. A key fits if it opens the lock. The fit describes a capacity of the key, not of the lock. Thanks to professional burglars we know only too well that there are many keys that are shaped quite differently from our own but which nevertheless unlock our doors. The metaphor is crude, but it serves quite well to bring into relief the difference I want to explicate. From the radical constructivist point of view, all of us—scientists, philosophers, laymen, school children, animals, and indeed, any kind of living organism—face our environment as the burglar faces a lock that he has to unlock in order to get at the loot.

This is the sense in which the word *fit* applies in the Darwinian and neo-Darwinian theories of evolution. Unfortunately, Darwin himself used the expression *survival of the fittest.* In doing this, he prepared the way for the misguided notion that, on the basis of his theory, one could consider certain things fitter than fit, and that among those there could even be a fittest.[4] But in a theory in which survival is the *only* criterion for the selection of species, there are only two possibilities: Either a species fits its environment (including the other species) or it does not; that is, either it survives or it dies out. Only an external observer who introduces other criteria (e.g., the economy, simplicity, or elegance of the method of surviving), only an observer who deliberately posits values beyond survival, could venture comparative judgments about those items that have already manifested their fitness by surviving.

In this one respect the basic principle of radical construc-

---

[4]C. F. von Weizsäcker, during a symposium in Bremen (1979), drew attention to the fact that in the German evolutionary literature *fit* is often translated as *tüchtig,* which has the flavor of "prowess" and therefore leads to talk of "the best" or "the toughest."

tivist epistemology coincides with that of the theory of evolution: Just as the environment places constraints on the living organisms (biological structures) and eliminates all variants that in some way transgress the limits within which they are possible or "viable," so the experiential world, be it that of everyday life or of the laboratory, constitutes the testing ground for our ideas (cognitive structures). This applies to the very first regularities the infant establishes in its barely differentiated experience; it applies to the rules with whose help adults try to manage their commonsense world; and it applies to the hypotheses, the theories, and the so-called "natural laws" that scientists formulate in their endeavor to glean from the widest possible range of experiences lasting stability and order. In the light of further experience, regularities, rules of thumb, and theories either prove themselves reliable or they do not (unless we introduce the concept of probability, in which case we are explicitly relinquishing the condition that knowledge must be *certain*).

In the history of knowledge, as in the theory of evolution, people have spoken of "adaptation" and, in doing so, have generated a colossal misunderstanding. If we take seriously the evolutionary way of thinking, it could never be that organisms or ideas adapt to reality, but that reality, by *limiting what is possible,* inexorably annihilates what is not fit to live. In phylogenesis, as in the history of ideas, "natural selection" does not in any positive sense select the fittest, the sturdiest, the best, or the truest, but it functions negatively, in that it simply lets die whatever does not pass the test.

The comparison is, of course, stretched a little too far. In nature, a lack of fitness is invariably fatal; philosophers, however, rarely die of their inadequate ideas. In the history of ideas it is not a question of survival, but one of "truth." If we keep this in mind, the theory of evolution can serve as a powerful analogy: The relation between viable biological structures and their environment is, indeed, the same as the relation between viable cognitive structures and the experiential world of the thinking subject. Both structures *fit*—the first because natural accident has shaped them that way, and the second because human intention has formed them to attain the ends they happen to attain, ends that are the explanation, prediction, or control of specific experiences. More important, still, is the epistemological aspect of the analogy. In spite of the often misleading assertions of ethologists, the structure of behavior of living organisms can never serve as a basis for conclusions concerning an "objective" world, that is, a world as it might be prior to experience.[5] The reason for this, according to the theory of evolution, is that there is no causal link between that world and the survival capacity of biological structures or behaviors. As Gregory Bateson has stressed, Darwin's theory is based on the principle of constraints, not on the principle of cause and effect [1]. The organisms that we find alive at any particular moment of evolutionary history, and their ways of behaving, are the result of cumulative *accidental* variations, and the influence of the environment was and is, under all circumstances, limited to the elimination of nonviable variants. Hence the environment can at best be held responsible for extinction, but never for survival. That is to say, an observer of evolutionary history may indeed establish that everything that has died out must in some way have transgressed the range of the viable and that everything he finds surviving is, at least for the time being, viable. To assert this, however, evidently constitutes a tautology (what survives lives) and throws no light whatever on the objective properties of that world that manifests itself in negative effects alone.

These considerations fit the basic problem of the theory of knowledge equally well. Quite generally, our knowledge is useful, relevant, viable, or however we want to call the pos-

---

[5] Jakob von Uexküll, for example, in his *Streifzüge durch die Umwelten von Tieren und Menschen* (with Georg Kriszat, 1933; reprinted 1970, Fischer, Frankfurt am Main) shows very elegantly that each living organism, because of its own properties, determines an individual environment. Only an independent, wholly extraneous being that does not experience the world but knows it unconditionally and immediately could speak of an "objective" world. For this reason, attempts, such as that by Lorenz, to explain the human concepts of space and time as an "adaptation" but to consider them also as aspects of ontological reality result in a logical contradiction (see Konrad Lorenz, 1941, Kants Lehre vom Apriorischen im Lichte gegenwärtiger Biologie, *Blätter für Deutsche Philosophie*, 15, 94–125).

itive end of the scale of evaluation, if it stands up to experience and enables us to make predictions and bring about or
avoid, as the case may be, certain phenomena (i.e., appearances, events, experiences). If knowledge does not serve that
purpose, it becomes questionable, unreliable, useless, and is
eventually devaluated as superstition. That is to say, from
the pragmatic point of view, we consider ideas, theories, and
"laws of nature" as structures that are constantly exposed to
our experiential world (from which we derived them), and
either they hold up or they do not. Any cognitive structure
that serves its purpose in our time, therefore, proves no more
and no less than just that—namely, given the circumstances
we have experienced (and determined *by* experiencing them),
it has done what was expected of it. Logically, this gives us
no clue as to how the "objective" world might be; it merely
means that we know *one* viable way to a goal that we have
chosen under specific circumstances in our experiential world.
It tells us nothing—and cannot tell us anything—about how
many other ways there might be or how that experience that
we consider the goal might be connected to a world *beyond*
our experience. The only aspect of that "real" world that
actually enters into the realm of experience is its constraints,
or, as Warren McCulloch, one of the first cyberneticists, so
dramatically said, "to have proved a hypothesis false is indeed
the peak of knowledge" [14].

Radical constructivism, thus, is *radical* because it breaks
with convention and develops a theory of knowledge in which
knowledge does not reflect an "objective" ontological reality,
but exclusively an ordering and organization of a world constituted by our experience. The radical constructivist has
relinquished "metaphysical realism" once and for all and
finds himself in full agreement with Piaget, who says, "Intelligence organizes the world by organizing itself" [17].

For Piaget, organization is always the result of a necessary
interaction between conscious intelligence and environment, and because he considers himself primarily a philosopher of biology, he characterizes that interaction as
"adaptation." With that, too, I agree, but after what was said
in the preceding pages about the process of evolutionary

selection, it should be clear that the adaptive fit must never be interpreted as a correspondence or homomorphism. With regard to the basic question, how cognitive structures or knowledge might be related to an ontological world beyond our experience, Piaget's position is somewhat ambiguous. Frequently one has the impression that, in spite of his massive contributions to constructivism, he still has a hankering for metaphysical realism. In that, of course, he is not alone. Donald Campbell, who has provided an excellent survey of proponents of "evolutionary epistemology" since Darwin, writes, "The controversial issue is the conceptual inclusion of the real world, defining the problem of knowledge as the fit of data and theory to that real world" [3]. In his conclusion he then declares that the evolutionary epistemology, which he and Karl Popper represent, "is fully compatible with an advocacy of the goals of realism and objectivity in science." But the theory of which he provided an extremely lucid exposition points in the opposite direction [22].

In this first section, I have tried to show that the notion of correspondence or match between knowledge and reality, a notion that is indispensable for realism, cannot possibly be derived from, let alone substituted for, the evolutionary notion of "fit." In the second section I shall provide at least an approximate account of the links between radical constructivism and the history of epistemology, from which one may see that this constructivism is not quite as radical as it appears at first sight.

II

Doubts concerning the correspondence between knowledge and reality arose the moment a thinking individual became aware of his own thinking. Already Xenophanes, one of the earliest of the pre-Socratics, said that no man has ever seen certain truth, nor will there ever be one who knows about the gods and the things of the world, "for if he succeeds to the full in saying what is completely true, he himself is nevertheless unaware of it; opinion (seeming) is fixed by fate upon all things" [6].

Something that could be "seen" would have to *be there* before a glance can fall upon it—and knowledge thus becomes a reflection or picture of a world that is there, that is, exists, before any consciousness sees it or experiences it in any other way. The stage was set, and with it the dilemma that has determined Western epistemology ever since the sixth century B.C. "Metaphysical realism" [18] given that scenario, is not one philosophical stance among others, but it is inherently predetermined as the only possible one. As Maturana has made particularly clear, "the a priori assumption that objective knowledge constitutes a description of that which is known . . . begs the questions '*What is to know?* and *How do we know?*' " [15] By taking for granted that knowledge must reflect reality, traditional epistemology has created for itself a dilemma that was as inevitable as it was unsolvable.

If knowledge is to be a description or image of the world as such, we need a criterion that might enable us to judge when our descriptions or images are "right" or "true." Thus, with the scenario in which man is born into a ready-made independent world as a "discoverer" with the task of exploring and "knowing" that reality in the truest possible fashion, the path of skepticism is there from the outset. The notion of "appearance" and "semblance" that, according to Xenophanes, is attached to all human knowledge, was elaborated and applied above all to perception by Pyrrho's school and, later, by Sextus Empiricus; and the unanswerable question as to whether, or to what extent, any picture our senses "convey" might correspond to the "objective" reality is still today the crux of the entire theory of knowledge. Sextus used, among other things, an apple as an example. To our senses it appears smooth, scented, sweet, and yellow, but it is far from self-evident that the real apple possesses these properties, just as it is not at all obvious that it does not possess other properties as well, properties that are simply not perceived by our senses [21].

The question is unanswerable because, no matter what we do, we can check our perceptions only by means of other perceptions, but never with the apple as it might be *before* we perceive it. The skeptics' argument made the philosopher's life difficult for some 2,000 years [19]. Then Kant added a second, even more troublesome argument. By considering space and time aspects of our way of experiencing, he shifted them out of reality into the realm of the phenomenal, and in doing so he made questionable not only the sensory properties but also the "thinghood" of the apple. Thus not only are the apple's smoothness, scent, sweetness, and color doubtful, but we can no longer be sure that there actually exists an object such as we experience it, separated from the rest of the world as a unitary whole or "thing."

This second doubt is indeed more serious in its consequences than that concerning the reliability of our senses: It undermines any representation of objective structure in the real world and thus inevitably raises the questions as to why and, above all, *how* it comes about that we search for and can also find a structure in our experiential world when such a structure may not be given by reality. In other words, if Kant's statement is correct and our experience can teach us nothing about the nature of things in themselves [10] how, then, can we explain that we nevertheless experience a world that is in many respects quite stable and reliable?

This is the main question with which radical constructivism attempts to deal, and the answer it suggests was prepared, at least in its main lines, by Giambattista Vico in 1710, more than half a century before Kant:

> As God's truth is what God comes to know as he creates and assembles it, so human truth is what man comes to know as he builds it, shaping it by his actions. Therefore science (*scientia*) is the knowledge (*cognitio*) of origins, of the ways and the manner how things are made. [25]

Vico's battle cry, *"Verum ipsum factum"*—the truth is the same as the made (*factum* and *fact* both come from the Latin *facere*, to make!)—has been quoted quite frequently since Vico was rediscovered in our century as a cultural historian and philosopher of history. His revolutionary epistemological ideas, however, are rarely mentioned, let alone explicated. According to him, the only way of "knowing" a thing is to have

made it, for only then do we know what its components are
and how they were put together. Thus God knows his creation, but we cannot; we can know only what we ourselves
construct. Vico even uses the word *operation* and thus
preempts the main term launched by constructivists such as
Dewey, Bridgman, Ceccato, and Piaget in our century.

Vico, of course, still tries to establish a connection between
human cognitive construction and God's creation. Reading
his treatise on metaphysics, one gets the impression that he
occasionally gets frightened of his own ideas. Although the
theory of knowledge he has developed is logically closed
because man's knowledge is seen as man's construction and
does not (and could not) require God's ontological creation,
Vico is reluctant to stress that independence. Because of this
reluctance, his picture of the world could be seen as a counterpart to Berkeley's metaphysics. For Berkeley, the principle
"esse est percipi" (to be is to be perceived) does the same trick
as Vico's statement that God knows everything because he
has made everything. For both, ontology is assured through
God's activities. Vico, however, also opens another way
toward ontology that I find much more acceptable because it
does not involve any form of rational realism. He suggests
that mythology and art approach the real world by means of
symbols. They, too, are *made*, but the interpretation of their
meaning provides a kind of knowledge that is different from
the rational knowledge of construction.

For us, the important difference between Vico and Berkeley, as well as later idealists, is that Vico considers man's
rational knowledge and the world of rational experience
simultaneous products of man's cognitive construction [26].
Thus Vico's "knowledge" is what today we might call an
awareness of the operations that result in our experiential
world. Though Berkeley says "that all the choir of heaven
and furniture of earth, in a word all those bodies which com-
pose the mighty frame of the world, have not any subsis-
tence without a mind, their *being* is to be perceived or
known," [2] and thus presupposes the activity of the intellect, his accent always lies on the *being*, whereas Vico invari-

ably stresses human *knowledge* and its construction.[6]

There can be no doubt that Vico's explicit use of the word *facere* and his constant reference to the composing, the putting together, and, in short, the active construction of all knowledge and experience come very much closer to Piaget's genetic epistemology and to modern constructivism in general than did Berkeley. Nowhere does this become clearer than in a statement with which Vico anticipated the epistemological attitude of some of today's philosophers of science: "Human knowledge is nothing else but the endeavour to make things correspond to one another in shapely proportion" [29].

Our main question was how it might come about that we experience a relatively stable and reliable world in spite of the fact that we are unable to ascribe stability, regularity, or any other perceived property to an objective reality. Vico does not answer this question; rather, he makes it superfluous and meaningless. If, as he says, the world that we experience and get to know is necessarily constructed by ourselves, it should not surprise us that it seems relatively stable. To appreciate this, it is necessary to keep in mind the most fundamental trait of constructivist epistemology, that is, that the world which is constructed is an experiential world that consists of experiences and makes no claim whatsoever about "truth" in the sense of correspondence with an ontological reality. Hence Vico's position is in this respect similar to that of Kant, who says, "Nature, therefore . . . is the collective conception of all objects of experience" [11]. For Kant, it is the "raw material of sensory impressions" that "the mind's activity . . . processes so that it becomes knowledge of objects that we call experience" [12]. In other words, experience as well as all objects of experience are under all circumstances the result of *our* ways and means of experiencing and are necessarily

---

[6]Berkeley's *Treatise* and Vico's *De Antiquissima* were both published in 1710 and are in some ways remarkably parallel, yet the authors knew nothing of one another. They met a few years later in Naples but, to my knowledge, there is no record of the discussions that—it would seem inevitable—they must have had.

structured and determined by space and time and the other categories derived from these. The processing of the raw material in Kant's system is governed *automatically* by space and time (without which *no* experience would be possible) and the other categories that, for that very reason, are called a priori. The a priori, therefore, might be considered the technical description of the organism's experiential capability. The a priori describes the framework within which such an organism operates, but it does not tell us what the organism does, let alone why it does it. "A priori" is tantamount to "built in" or "innate," and Kant's justification of it leads, albeit in a roundabout fashion, to God and to a Platonic mythology of ideas. In this respect, Vico is more modern and more prosaic. Of the category of causality, for instance, he says, "If true means to have been made, then to prove something by means of its cause is the same as causing it" [27]. This notion (which has been rediscovered, no doubt without any knowledge of Vico, by the modern constructivist mathematicians) has, as Vico realized, a remarkably wide range of application.

Causes thus originate in the putting together of individual elements; that is, they originate from an experiencer's active operating, such that, for instance, "the determinate (i.e., causally determined) form of the object springs from the order and the composition of elements" [28].[7] Quite generally this means that the world we experience is, and must be, as it is, because *we* have put it together in that way. While the way in which that composition takes place is determined by the a priori for Kant, there are no immutably built-in principles in Vico's system that determine our ways of experiencing, thinking, and constructing. Instead, such constraints as we encounter spring from the history of our construction, because at any moment whatever has been done limits what can be done now [20].

To sum up Vico's thought, the construction of knowledge,

---

[7]George A. Kelly, founder of the psychology of personal constructs, independently came to the same conclusion: "To the living creature, then, the universe is real, but it is not inexorable unless he chooses to construe it that way" (*A Theory of Personality*. W. W. Norton, New York, p. 8).

for him, is not constrained by the goal of (impossible) corre-spondence with an "objective" reality that can neither be experienced nor known. It is, however, constrained by con-ditions that arise out of the material used, which, be it con-crete or abstract, always consists of the results of prior construction. With this idea of consistency within certain restraints that replaces the iconic notion of "truth," Vico, without knowing it, anticipated the basic principle of *viabil-ity* in the constructivist theory of knowledge.

As elegant as his system is, it still leaves open two ques-tions: First. what are the conditions under which a new con-struct will be considered compatible with what has already been constructed? Second, why should any organism under-take the task of cognitive construction? The third section will describe an attempt to answer these questions.

III

In traditional theories of knowledge, the activity of "knowing" is taken as a matter of course, an activity that requires no justification and which functions as an initial constituent. The knowing subject is conceived of as a "pure" entity in the sense that it is essentially unimpeded by biological or psychological conditions. The radical construc-tivist epistemology quite deliberately breaks that conven-tional framework and commits what professional phil-osophers, more or less disparagingly, dismiss as "psychol-ogism." The deliberations that have led me to this somewhat iconoclastic step derive from what was said in the first two sections as soon as one considers them jointly.

First, there is the realization that knowledge, that is, what is "known," cannot be the result of a passive receiving, but originates as the product of an active subject's activity. This activity is, of course, not a manipulating of "things in them-selves," that is, of objects that could be thought to possess, prior to being experienced, the properties and the structure the experiencer attributes to them. We therefore call the activity that builds up knowledge "operating," and it is the operating of that cognitive entity which, as Piaget has so succintly formulated, organizes its experiential world by organizing itself. Epistemology thus becomes the study of *how* intelligence operates, of the ways and means it employs to construct a relatively *regular* world out of the flow of its experience. The function of the intellect, however, has always been a matter that interested psychology—and the greater the emphasis put on active operating, the more psychological the investigation becomes. If, besides, a developmental view is taken and phylogenetic or ontogenetic concepts are applied, we are decidedly in the area of "genetic epistemology," an area that metaphysical realists take great pains to avoid, because in their view the theory of knowledge must on no account be adulterated by biological or physiological considerations [16].

If, however, as Alcmaeon already suggested, the human activity of knowing cannot lead to a certain and true picture of the world, but only to conjectural interpretation, then that activity can be viewed as the creating of keys with whose help man unlocks paths toward the goals he chooses. This means that the second question we asked at the end of the preceding section, namely, why a cognitive activity should take place, is inextricably connected with the first one—because the success of a key does not depend on finding a lock into which it might fit, but solely on whether or not it opens the way to the particular goal we want to reach.

Constructivism necessarily begins with the (intuitively confirmed) assumption that all cognitive activity takes place within the experiential world of a goal-directed consciousness. Goal directedness, in this context, has, of course, nothing to do with goals in an "external" reality. The goals that are involved here arise for no other reason than this: 'A cognitive organism evaluates its experiences, and because it evaluates them, it tends to repeat certain ones and to avoid others. The products of conscious cognitive activity, therefore, always have a purpose and are, at least originally, assessed according to how well they serve that purpose. The concept of purposiveness, however, presupposes the assumption that it is possible to establish regularities in the experiential world. Hume's argument describes the situation perfectly: "For all Inferences from Experience suppose, as their Foundation, that the future will resemble the past. . . . If there be any Suspicion, that the Course of Nature may change, and that the past may be no Rule for the future, all Experience becomes useless, and can give rise to no Inferences or Conclusions" [8]. This belief is inherent in everything we consider alive.

The concept of "nature," for Hume no less than for Kant, was the totality of the objects of experience [11]. That is to say, whatever we infer from our experience—that is, whatever we call *inductive*—necessarily concerns our experience and not that mythical experiencer-independent world of which metaphysical realists dream.

The second insight the constructivist approach allows us to formulate concerns the nature of the regularities that a cognitive organism finds or, rather, produces in its experiential world. In order to claim of anything whatever that it is regular, constant, or in any sense *invariant*, a comparison has to be made. That is to say, something that has already been experienced is put in relation to a second experience which, in the experential sequence, does not coincide with the first experience. This "putting in relation," irrespective of whether the comparison yields similarity or difference, will give rise to one of two essentially different concepts: equivalence and individual identity. The confusion of these two mutually incompatible concepts is greatly enhanced by the fact that, in English, the word *same* is quite indiscriminately used for both. The confusion, however, is a conceptual one, because in other languages that originally provided two distinct expressions (e.g., in German, *das Gleiche* and *dasselbe*; in Italian, *stesso* and *medesimo*) present-day usage is no less indiscriminate. Yet if we want to understand one of the most elementary building blocks of cognitive construction, we must clearly distinguish the two concepts involved.

As Piaget has shown, the concepts of equivalence and individual identity are not given a priori (innate), but have to be built up; and every "normal" child does, in fact, build them up within the first two years of life [17]. The development of a representational capability is crucial in this achievement. On the one hand, it is the capability of representing to oneself a past perception or experience that makes possible the comparison between it and a present experience; and on the other hand, this same capability of representation makes it possible for us to consider repeated perceptions, and especially groups of repeated perceptions, as *objects* and to place them into a space that is independent of the subject's own motion and into a time independent of the subject's own stream of experience. Hand in hand with this development, there arise two possible ways of comparing. Two experiential items can always be "externalized" as two mutually independent objects; but two experiential items can also be considered two experiences of one and the same individually "existing" object. This distinction does not depend on the result of a comparison between the two experiences, but is determined by the conceptual character of the two items being compared. If that comparison leads to a verdict of "sameness," we have either two objects that are equivalent with respect to the properties examined in the comparison, or *one* object which has remained unchanged during the interval between the two experiences. If, instead, the comparison leads to a verdict of "difference," we have either two objects with different properties or one object that has *changed* since our preceding experience of it.

In our everyday practice of experience, we do, of course, establish contexts that propel us toward one or the other conceptualization, respectively, without consciously having to choose between equivalence and individual identity each time. I have shown elsewhere that there are cases of indecision and how we then try to determine individual identity by the more or less plausible demonstration of some form of continuity [7]. In the present context, I merely want to stress that any such continuity in the existence of an individual object is under all circumstances the result of operations carried out by the cognizing subject and can never be explained as a given fact of objective reality.

No one uses these conceptual possibilities more skillfully than the professional magician. During a performance he may, for instance, request a spectator's ring, toss the ring across the room to his assistant, and then let the stunned spectator find his ring in his own coat pocket. The magic consists in directing the spectators' perception in such a way that they unwittingly construct an individual identity between the first experience of the ring and the experience of the thrown object. Once this has been done, it would indeed require magic to transfer the ring from the assistant to the spectator's pocket. Another case is that of the red ribbon that the magician cuts into little pieces and then—literally with a flick of his hand—produces once more as one whole piece.

A similar, often cited example is the movie film that, depending on the conditions of perception, we see as a sequence of individually different images or as *one* continuously moving image. Irrespective of any "real" horse that may or may not have trotted somewhere at some time and been filmed while doing so, when the film is presented to us, we ourselves must construct the motion by constituting a *continuous* change of one horse from the succession of images. The fact that we do this unconsciously cannot alter the fact that we have to do it in order to perceive the motion.

No less constructed are the judgments of sameness and difference in the realm of perceptual objects. As I indicated above, "sameness" is always the result of an examination with regard to specific properties. Two eggs may be considered the same because of their shape, size, or color, or because they come from the same hen, but there will be a pungent difference between them if one was laid yesterday and the other six weeks ago. A field mouse and an elephant are different in many ways, but they will be considered the same whenever we want to distinguish mammals from other animals. Finally, all eggs, all animals, and indeed all objects that I have ever seen or imagined are the same in the one respect that I have isolated them as bounded, unitary objects in the total field of my experience. In these cases, as in all conceivable ones, it should be clear that the criteria by means of which sameness or difference is established are criteria which are created and chosen by the judging, experiencing subject and cannot be ascribed to an experiencer-independent world.

For an understanding of radical constructivism, it is even

more important to appreciate the subject's active operating
that gives rise to regularities and invariances in the experiential world. Both regularity and constancy presuppose
repeated experience, and repetition can be established only
on the basis of a comparison that yields a judgment of
sameness. Sameness, however, as we have seen, is always
relative: Objects, and experiences in general, are the "same"
with respect to the properties or components that have been
checked in a comparison. Hence an experience that consists,
for instance, of the elements a, b, and c can be considered the
same as an experience consisting of a, b, c, and x, as long as
x is not taken into account. This, in fact, is the principle of
assimilation. In a context in which only the components or
properties a, b, and c matter, every object that contains a, b,
and c is acceptable. Indeed, no such object will be discrimin-
able from other objects that also contain a, b, and c, as long
as no other elements are included in the comparison. The
situation, however, changes if an object, in spite of the fact
that it manifests a, b, and c, turns out to behave in a way that
is different from the behavior that, on the basis of prior experience, is expected of a–b–c objects. If this happens, it causes
a disturbance (perturbation) that can lead to the examination
of other properties or components. This opens the way toward
a discrimination of the disturbing object (i.e., the object that
is no longer acceptable) on the basis of some hitherto disregarded element x. We then have an instance of the principle
of *accommodation*, the mainstay of Piaget's theory within the
framework of action schemes and of his analysis of cognitive
development. Here I merely want to emphasize that in this
principle, too, the concept of "fit" is incorporated, because
here, too, it does not matter what an object might be like in
"reality" or from an "objective" point of view; what matters
is exclusively whether or not it performs or behaves in the
way that is expected of it, that is, whether or not it fits.

If repetition can be constructed on the basis of such com-
parisons, it should be clear that the same holds for all kinds
of regularities. All concepts that involve repetition are
dependent on a particular point of view, namely, *what* is
being considered, and with respect to *what* sameness is

demanded. Given that the raw material of the experiential world is sufficiently rich, an assimilating consciousness can construct regularities and order even in a chaotic world. The extent to which this will succeed depends far more on the goals and the already constructed starting points than on what might be given in a so-called "reality." But in our experience, which is always determined by the goals we have chosen, we always tend to ascribe the obstacles we meet to a mythical reality rather than to the way in which we operate.

A bricklayer who builds exclusively with bricks must sooner or later come to the conclusion that wherever there is to be an opening for a door or window, he has to make an arch to support the wall above. If this bricklayer then believes he has discovered a law of an absolute world, he makes much the same mistake as Kant when he came to believe that all geometry had to be Euclidean. Whatever we choose as building blocks, be it bricks or Euclid's elements, determines limiting constraints. We experience these constraints from the "inside," as it were, from the brick or the Euclidean perspective. We never get to see the constraints of the world, with which our enterprises collide. What we experience, cognize, and come to know is necessarily built up of our own building blocks and can be explained in no other way than in terms of our ways and means of building.

Summary

Language inexorably forces us to present everything as a sequence. The three sections of this essay, thus, will have to be read one after the other, but this inevitable succession should not be understood as a logically necessary order. What is contained in each of these sections could be outlined only very approximately as independent themes, because, in constructivist thought, each is so closely interwoven with the other principal themes that, presented separately, each would seem to be little more than a finger exercise. Singly, the arguments I have presented here certainly cannot create a new way of thinking about the world; if they can do that at all, it will be through the fabric of their interrelations.

The conceptual analysis shows, on the one hand, that a consciousness, no matter how it might be constituted, can "know" repetitions, invariances, and regularities only as the result of a comparison; on the other hand, it shows that there must always be a decision preceding the comparison proper, whether the two experiences to be compared should be considered occurrences of one and the same object or of two separate ones. These decisions determine what is to be categorized as "existing" unitary objects and what as relationships between them. Through these determinations, the experiencing consciousness creates *structure* in the flow of its experience; and this structure is what conscious cognitive organisms experience as "reality"—and since this reality is created almost entirely without the experiencer's awareness of his or her creative activity, it comes to appear as given by an independently "existing" world.

This view is not particularly new. Skeptics have tended toward it ever since Pyrrho, and the theoretical physicists of our time come close to it in their own terms (they have to ask more and more often whether they are discovering laws of nature or whether it is not, rather, their sophisticated preparation of experimental observations that forces nature into a preconceived hypothesis). However, as long as we remain, in our innermost belief, "metaphysical realists" and expect that knowledge (the scientific as well as the everyday) provide a "true" picture of a "real" world that is supposed to be independent of any knower, the skeptic cannot but seem a pessimist and spoilsport because his arguments perpetually draw attention to the fact that no such "true" knowledge is possible. The realist may, of course, remain a realist in spite of this and say that the skeptic's arguments can be disregarded simply because they contradict common sense. If, however, he takes these arguments seriously, the realist must retreat to some form of subjective idealism, and this retreat inevitably leads to solipsism, that is, to the belief that there exists no world at all apart from the conceiving mind of the subject.

On the one hand, this situation seems inevitable because of the unimpeachable logic of the skeptical arguments; on the other hand, we are intuitively convinced and find constant experiential confirmation that the world is full of obstacles that we do not ourselves deliberately place in our way. To resolve the situation, then, we must find our way back to the very first steps of our theories of knowledge. Among these early steps there is, of course, the definition of the relationship between knowledge and reality, and this is precisely the point where radical constructivism steps out of the traditional scenario of epistemology. Once knowing is no longer understood as the search for an iconic representation of ontological reality, but, instead, as a search for *fitting* ways of behaving and thinking, the traditional problem disappears. Knowledge can now be seen as something that the organism builds up in the attempt to order the as such amorphous flow of experience by establishing repeatable experiences and relatively reliable relations between them. The possibilities of constructing such an order are determined and perpetually constrained by the preceding steps in the construction. This means that the "real" world manifests itself exclusively there where our constructions break down. But since we can describe and explain these breakdowns only in the very concepts that we have used to build the failing structures, this process can never yield a picture of a world which we could hold responsible for their failure.

Once this has been fully understood, it will be obvious that radical constructivism itself must not be interpreted as a picture or description of any absolute reality, but as a possible model of knowing and the acquisition of knowledge in cognitive organisms that are capable of constructing for themselves, on the basis of their own experience, a more or less reliable world.

REFERENCES

1. Bateson, Gregory. Cybernetic explanation. *American Behaviorist* 10, 1967, 29–32.
2. Berkeley, George. *A Treatise Concerning the Principles of Human Knowledge*. Open Court, La Salle, Illinois, 1963, p. 32.
3. Campbell, Donald T. Evolutionary epistemology. In *The Philosophy of*

Karl Popper (P. A. Schilpp, ed.). Open Court, La Salle, Illinois, 1974, p. 449.

4. Ceccato, Silvio. *Un tecnico fra i filosofi,* Vols. 1 and 2. Marsilio, Mantua, 1964/1966.
5. Freeman, Kathleen. *Ancilla to the Pre-Socratic Philosophers.* Harvard University Press, Cambridge, Massachusetts, 1948, p. 40.
6. Freeman (1948), p. 33.
7. Glasersfeld, Ernst von. Cybernetics, experience, and the concept of self. In *A Cynbernetic Approach to the Assessment of Children: Toward a More Humane Use of Human Beings* (M. N. Ozer, ed.). Westview Press, Boulder, Colorado, 1979.
8. Hume, David. *An Enquiry Concerning Human Understanding.* Washington Square Press, New York, 1963, p. 47.
9. Kant, Immanuel (1783). *Prolegomena zu jeder künftigen Metaphysik. Werke,* Vol. 4. Konigliche Preussische Akademie der Wissenschaften, Berlin, 1911, p. 294.
10. Kant (1783), p. 295.
11. Kant (1783), p. 295.
12. Kant, Immanuel. *Kritik der reinen Vernunft,* 2nd ed. *Werke,* Vol 3, Königliche Preussische Akademie der Wissenschaften, Berlin, 1911, p. 27.
13. Kelly, George A., *A Theory of Personality: The Psychology of Personal Constructs,* W. W. Norton, New York, 1963.
14. McCulloch, Warren S. *Embodiments of Mind.* MIT Press, Cambridge, Massachusetts, 1965, p. 154.
15. Maturana, Humberto. *Biology of Cognition* (Report 9.0). Biological Computer Laboratory, Urbana, Illinois, 1970, p. 2.
16. Mays, Wolfe. The epistemology of Professor Piaget. *Minutes of the Aristotelian Society,* December 7, 1953, 54–55.
17. Piaget, Jean. *La Construction du réel chez l'enfant.* Delachaux et Niestlé, Neuchâtel, 1937, p. 311.
18. Putnam, Hilary. *Reason, Truth and History.* Cambridge University Press, Cambridge, 1981.
19. Richards, John, and Glasersfeld, Ernst von. The control of perception and the construction of reality. *Dialectica* 33, 1979, 37–58.
20. Rubinoff, Lionel. Vico and the verification of historical interpretation. In *Vico and Contemporary Thought* (G. Tagliacozzo, M. Mooney, and D. P. Verene, eds.). Humanities Press, Atlantic Highlands, New Jersey, 1976.
21. Sextus Empiricus. *Outlines of Pyrrhonism* (translated by R. G. Bury). Heinemann, London, 1967, pp. 57, 94–95.
22. Skagestad, Peter. Taking evolution seriously: Critical comments on D. T. Campbell's evolutionary epistemology. *Monist* 61, 1978, 611–621.
23. Spinner, Helmut F. *Begründung, Kritik und Rationalität,* Vol. 1. Vieweg, Braunschweig, 1977, p. 61.
24. Uexküll, Jacob von, *Streifzüge durch die Umwelten von Tieren und Menschen,* Fischer, Frankfurt am Main, 1970.
25. Vico, Giambattista. (1710). *De antiquissima Italorum sapientia.* Stamperia de' Classici Latini, Naples, 1858, Chapter I, Section 1, pp. 5–6.
26. Vico (1710), Chapter I, Section III, p. 2.
27. Vico (1710), Chapter III, Section I, p. 2.
28. Vico (1710), Chapter III, Section I, p. 3.
29. Vico (1710), Chapter VII, Section III, p. 5.

HEINZ VON FOERSTER

On Constructing a Reality*

Draw a distinction!

G. Spencer Brown [1]

The Postulate

I AM SURE YOU remember the plain citizen Jourdain in
Molière's *Le Bourgeois Gentilhomme* who, nouveau riche,
travels in the sophisticated circles of the French aristocracy
and who is eager to learn. On one occasion his new friends
speak about poetry and prose, and Jourdain discovers to his
amazement and great delight that whenever he speaks, he
speaks prose. He is overwhelmed by this discovery: "I am
speaking Prose! I have always spoken Prose! I have spoken
Prose throughout my whole life!"

A similar discovery has been made not so long ago, but it
was neither of poetry nor of prose—it was the environment
that was discovered. I remember when, perhaps ten or fifteen years ago, some of my American friends came running
to me with the delight and amazement of having just made a
great discovery: "I am living in an Environment! I have always
lived in an Environment! I have lived in an Environment
throughout my whole life!"

However, neither M. Jourdain nor my friends have as yet
made another discovery, and that is when M. Jourdain speaks,

*This article is an adaptation of an address given on April 17, 1973, to the
Fourth International Environmental Design Research Association Con-
ference at the College of Architecture, Virginia Polytechnic Institute,
Blacksburg, Virginia.

may it be prose or poetry, it is he who invents it, and, likewise, when we perceive our environment, it is we who invent it.

Every discovery has a painful and a joyful side: painful, while struggling with a new insight; joyful, when this insight is gained. I see the sole purpose of my presentation to minimize the pain and maximize the joy for those who have not yet made this discovery; and for those who have made it, to let them know they are not alone. Again, the discovery we all have to make for ourselves is the following postulate.

The Environment as We Perceive It Is Our Invention. The burden is now upon me to support this outrageous claim. I shall proceed by first inviting you to participate in an experiment; then I shall report a clinical case and the results of two other experiments. After this I will give an interpretation, and thereafter a highly compressed version of the neurophysiological basis of these experiments and my postulate of before. Finally, I shall attempt to suggest the significance of all that to aesthetical and ethical considerations.

Experiments

The Blind Spot. Hold book with right hand, close left eye, and fixate star of Figure 1 with right eye. Move book slowly back and forth along line of vision until at an appropriate distance (from about 12 to 14 inches) round black spot disappears. With star well focused, spot should remain invisible even if book is slowly moved parallel to itself in any direction.

Figure 1

This localized blindness is a direct consequence of the absence of photo receptors (rods or cones) at that point of the retina, the "disk," where all fibers leading from the eye's light-sensitive surface converge to form the optic nerve.

Clearly, when the black spot is projected onto the disk, it cannot be seen. Note that this localized blindness is not perceived as a dark blotch in our visual field (seeing a dark blotch would imply "seeing"), but this blindness is not perceived at all, that is, neither as something present, nor as something absent: Whatever is perceived is perceived "blotchless."

Scotoma. Well-localized occipital lesions in the brain (e.g., injuries from high-velocity projectiles) heal relatively fast without the patient's awareness of any perceptible loss in his vision. However, after several weeks motor dysfunction in the patient becomes apparent, for example, loss of control of arm or leg movements of one side or the other. Clinical tests, however, show that there is nothing wrong with the motor system, but that in some cases there is substantial loss (Fig. 2) of a large portion of the visual field (*scotoma*) [9]. A suc-

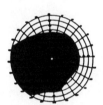 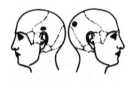 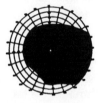

Figure 2

cessful therapy consists of blind-folding the patient over a period of one to two months until he regains control over his motor system by shifting his "attention" from (nonexistent) visual clues regarding his posture to (fully operative) channels that give direct postural clues from (proprioceptive) sensors embedded in muscles and joints. Note again absence of perception of "absence of perception," and also the emergence of perception through sensorimotor interaction. This prompts two metaphors: Perceiving is doing, and If I don't see I am blind, I am blind; but if I see I am blind, I see.

Alternates. A single word is spoken once into a tape recorder and the tape smoothly spliced (without click) into a loop. The word is repetitively played back with high rather than low volume. After one or two minutes of listening (from 50 to 150 repetitions), the word clearly perceived so far abruptly changes into another meaningful and clearly perceived word: an "alternate." After ten to thirty repetitions of this first alternate, a sudden switch to a second alternate is perceived, and so on [6]. The following is a small selection of the 758 alternates reported from a population of about 200 subjects who were exposed to a repetitive playback of the single word *cogitate: agitate, annotate, arbitrate, artistry, back and forth, brevity, ça d'était, candidate, can't you see, can't you stay, Cape Cod you say, card estate, cardiotape, car district, catch a tape, cavitate, cha cha che, cogitate, computate; conjugate, conscious state, counter tape, count to ten, count to three, count yer tape, cut the steak, entity, fantasy, God to take, God you say, got a date, got your pay, got your tape, gratitude, gravity, guard the tit, gurgitate, had to take, kinds of tape, majesty, marmalade.*

Comprehension.[1]   Into the various stations of the auditory pathways in a cat's brain microelectrodes are implanted that allow a recording (electroencephalogram) from the nerve cells first to receive auditory stimuli (cochlea nucleus, CN) up to the auditory cortex [10]. The cat so prepared is admitted into a cage that contains a food box whose lid can be opened by pressing a lever. However, the lever–lid connection is operative only when a short single tone (here C_6, which is about 1000 hertz) is repetitively presented. The cat has to learn that C_6 "means" food. Figures 3–6 show the pattern of nervous activity at eight ascending auditory stations and at four consecutive stages of this learning process [10]. The cat's behavior associated with the recorded neural activity is for "random search" in Figure 3, "inspection of lever" in Figure 4, "lever pressed at once" in Figure 5, and "walking straight toward lever (full comprehension)" in Figure 6. Note that no tone is perceived as long as this tone is uninterpretable (Figs. 3,4; pure noise), but the whole system swings into action with the appearance of the first "beep" (Figs. 5,6; noise becomes signal), when sensation becomes comprehensible, when *our* perception of "beep, beep; beep" is in the *cat's* perception "food, food, food."

---

[1]Literally, *con* = together; *prehendere* = to seize, grasp.

Figures

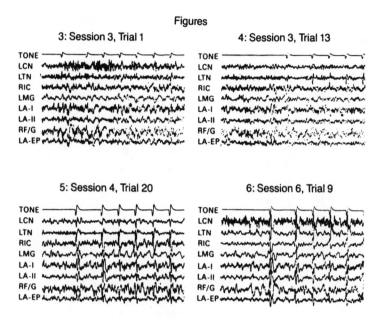

3: Session 3, Trial 1

4: Session 3, Trial 13

5: Session 4, Trial 20

6: Session 6, Trial 9

Interpretation

In these experiments I have cited instances in which we see or hear what is not "there," or in which we do not see or hear what is "there" unless coordination of sensation and movement allows us to "grasp" what appears to be there. Let me strengthen this observation by citing now the "principle of undifferentiated encoding":

> The response of a nerve cell does *not* encode the physical nature of the agents that caused its response. Encoded is only "how much" at this point on my body, but not "what."

Take, for instance, a light-sensitive receptor cell in the retina, a "rod" that absorbs the electromagnetic radiation originating from a distant source. This absorption causes a change in the electrochemical potential in the rod, which will ultimately give rise to a periodic electric discharge of some cells higher up in the postretinal networks (see below, Fig. 15), with a period that is commensurate with the intensity of the radiation absorbed, but without a clue that it was electromagnetic radiation that caused the rod to discharge. The same is true for any other sensory receptor, may it be the taste buds, the touch receptors, and all the other receptors that are associated with the sensations of smell, heat and cold, sound, and so on: They are all "blind" as to the quality of their stimulation, responsive only as to their quantity.

Although surprising, this should not come as a surprise, for indeed "out there" there is no light and no color, there are only electromagnetic waves; "out there" there is no sound and no music, there are only periodic variations of the air pressure; "out there" there is no heat and no cold, there are only moving molecules with more or less mean kinetic energy, and so on. Finally, for sure, "out there" there is no pain.

Since the physical nature of the stimulus—its *quality*—is not encoded into nervous activity, the fundamental question arises as to how does our brain conjure up the tremendous variety of this colorful world as we experience it any moment while awake, and sometimes in dreams while asleep. This is the "problem of cognition," the search for an understanding of the cognitive processes.

The way in which a question is asked determines the way in which an answer may be found. Thus it is upon me to paraphrase the "problem of cognition" in such a way that the conceptual tools that are today at our disposal may become fully effective. To this end let me paraphrase ($\rightarrow$) "cognition" in the following way:

cognition $\rightarrow$ computing a reality

With this I anticipate a storm of objections. First, I appear to replace one unknown term *cognition*, with three other terms, two of which, *computing* and *reality*, are even more opaque than the definiendum, and with the only definite word used here being the indefinite article *a*. Moreover, the use of the indefinite article implies the ridiculous notion of other realities besides "the" only and one reality, our cherished Environment; and finally I seem to suggest by "computing" that everything, from my wristwatch to the galaxies, is merely computed, and is not "there." Outrageous!

Let me take up these objections one by one. First, let me

remove the semantic sting that the term *computing* may cause in a group of women and men who are more inclined toward the humanities than to the sciences. Harmlessly enough, computing (from *com-putare*) literally means to reflect, to contemplate (*putare*) things in concert (*com*), without any explicit reference to numerical quantities. Indeed, I shall use this term in this most general sense to indicate any operation (not necessarily numerical) that transforms, modifies, rearranges, orders, and so on, observed physical entities ("objects") or their representations ("symbols"). For instance, the simple permutation of the three letters A,B,C, in which the last letter now goes first—C,A,B—I shall call a computation; similarly the operation that obliterates the commas between the letters—CAB—and likewise the semantic transformation that changes CAB into *taxi*, and so on.

I shall now turn to the defense of my use of the indefinite article in the noun phrase *a reality*. I could, of course, shield myself behind the logical argument that solving for the general case, implied by the a, I would also have solved any specific case denoted by the use of *the*. However, my motivation lies much deeper. In fact, there is a deep hiatus that separates the *the* school of thought from the *a* school of thought in which, respectively, the distinct concepts of "confirmation" and "correlation" are taken as explanatory paradigms for perceptions. The *the* school: My sensation of touch is *confirmation* for my visual sensation that here is a table. The *a* school: My sensation of touch in *correlation* with my visual sensation generate an experience that I may describe by "here is a table."

I am rejecting the *the* position on epistemological grounds, for in this way the whole problem of cognition is safely put away in one's own cognitive blind spot: Even its absence can no longer be seen.

Finally one may rightly argue that cognitive processes do not compute wristwatches or galaxies, but compute at best *descriptions* of such entities. Thus I am yielding to this objection and replace my former paraphrase by

cognition → computing descriptions of a reality

Neurophysiologists, however, will tell us [4] that a description computed on one level of neural activity, say, a projected image on the retina, will be operated on again on higher levels,and so on, whereby some motor activity may be taken by an observer as a "terminal description," for instance, the utterance, "Here is a table." Consequently, I have to modify this paraphrase again to read

cognition → computing descriptions of ⌐
‸_____|

where the arrow turning back suggests this infinite recursion of descriptions of descriptions, etc. This formulation has the advantage that one unknown, namely, "reality," is successfully eliminated. Reality appears only implicit as the operation of recursive descriptions. Moreover, we may take advantage of the notion that computing descriptions is nothing else but computations. Hence

cognition → computations of ⌐
‸_____|

In summary, I propose to interpret cognitive processes as never-ending recursive processes of computation, and I hope that in the following *tour de force* of neurophysiology I can make this interpretation transparent.

Neurophysiology

Evolution. In order that the principle of recursive computation be fully appreciated as being the underlying principle of all cognitive processes—even of life itself, as one of the most advanced thinkers in biology assures me [5]—it may be instructive to go back for a moment to the most elementary— or as evolutionists would say, to very "early"—manifestations of this principle. These are the "independent effectors," or independent sensorimotor units, found in protozoa and metazoa distributed over the surface of these animals (Fig. 7). The triangular portion of this unit, protruding with its tip from the surface, is the sensory part; the onion-shaped portion, the contractile motor part. A change in the chemical

Figure 7

concentration of an agent in the immediate vicinity of the sensing tip, and "perceptible" by it, causes an instantaneous contraction of this unit. The resulting displacement of this or any other unit by change of shape of the animal or its location may, in turn, produce perceptible changes in the agent's concentration in the vicinity of these units, which, in turn, will cause their instantaneous contraction, and so on. Thus we have the recursion

$$\rightarrow \text{change of sensation} \rightarrow \text{change of shape}$$

Separation of the sites of sensation and action appears to have been the next evolutionary step (Fig. 8). The sensory and motor organs are now connected by thin filaments, the "axons" (in essence degenerated muscle fibers having lost their contractility), which transmit the sensor's perturbations to its effector, thus giving rise to the concept of a "signal": See something here, act accordingly there.

The crucial step, however, in the evolution of the complex organization of the mammalian central nervous system (CNS) appears to be the appearance of an "internuncial neuron," a

Figure 8

Figure 9

cell sandwiched between the sensory and the motor unit (Fig. 9). It is, in essence, a sensory cell, but specialized so as to respond only to a universal "agent," namely, the electrical activity of the afferent axons terminating in its vicinity. Since its present activity may affect its subsequent responsivity, it introduces the element of computation in the animal kingdom and gives these organisms the astounding latitude of nontrivial behaviors. Having once developed the genetic code for assembling an internuncial neuron, to add the genetic command *repeat* is a small burden indeed. Hence, I believe, it is now easy to comprehend the rapid proliferation of these neurons along additional vertical layers with growing horizontal connections to form those complex interconnected structures we call "brains."

The Neuron. The neuron, of which we have more than 10 billion in our brain, is a highly specialized single cell with three anatomically distinct features (Fig. 10): (1) the branch-like ramifications stretching up and to the side, the "dendrites"; (2) the bulb in the center housing the cell's nucleus, the "cell body"; and (3), the "axon," the smooth fiber stretching downward. Its various bifurcations terminate on dendrites of another (but sometimes—recursively—on the same) neuron. The same membrane that envelops the cell body forms also the tubular sheath for dendrites and axon, and causes the inside of the cell to be electrically charged

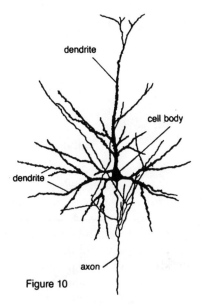

dendrite

cell body

dendrite

axon

Figure 10

against the outside with about ¹/₁₀ of a volt. If in the dendritic region this charge is sufficiently perturbed, the neuron "fires" and sends this perturbation along its axon to its termination, the synapses.

Transmission.   Since these perturbations are electrical, they can be picked up by "microprobes," amplified and recorded. Figure 11 shows three examples of periodic discharges from a touch receptor under continuous stimulation, the low frequency corresponding to a weak stimulus, the high frequency to a strong stimulus. The magnitude of the discharge is clearly everywhere the same, the pulse frequency representing the stimulus intensity, but the intensity only.

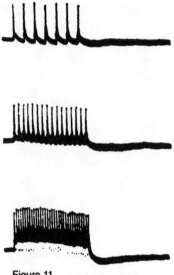

Figure 11

Synapse. Figure 12 sketches a synaptic junction. The afferent axon (Ax), along which the pulses travel, terminates in an end bulb (EB), which is separated from the spine (sp) of a dendrite (D) of the target neuron by a minute gap (sy), the "synaptic gap." (Note the many spines that cause the rugged appearance of the dendrites in Fig. 10.) The chemical composition of the "transmitter substances" filling the synaptic gap is crucial in determining the effect an arriving pulse may have on the ultimate response of the neuron: Under certain circumstances it may produce an "inhibitory effect" (cancellation of another simultaneously arriving pulse), in others a "facilitory effect" (augmenting another pulse to fire the neuron). Consequently, the synaptic gap can be seen as the "microenvironment" of a sensitive tip, the spine, and with this interpretation in mind we may compare the sensitivity of the CNS to changes of the *internal* environment (the sum total of all microenvironments) to those of the *external* environment (all sensory receptors). Since there are only 100 million sensory receptors, and about 10,000 billion synapses in our nervous system, we are 100 thousand times more receptive to changes in our internal than in our external environment.

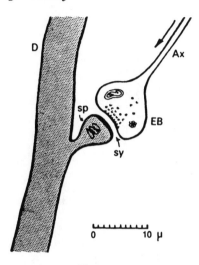

Figure 12

The Cortex. In order that one may get at least some perspective on the organization of the entire machinery that computes all perceptual, intellectual, and emotional experiences, I have attached Figure 13 [7], which shows a magnified section of about 2 square millimeters of a cat's cortex by a stain-

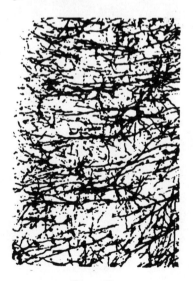

Figure 13

ing method that stains only cell body and dendrites, and of those only 1% of all neurons present. Although you have to imagine the many connections among these neurons provided by the (invisible) axons, and a density of packing that is 100 times that shown, the computational power of even this very small part of a brain may be sensed.

Descartes.   This perspective is a far cry from that held, say, 300 years ago [2]:

> If the fire A is near the foot B [Fig. 14], the particles of this fire, which as you know move with great rapidity, have the power to move the area of the skin of this foot that they touch; and in this way drawing the little thread, c, that you see to be attached at base of toes and on the nerve, at the same instant they open the entrance of the pore, d,e, at which this little thread terminates, just as by pulling one end of a cord, at the same time one causes the bell to sound that hangs at the other end. Now the entrance

Figure 14

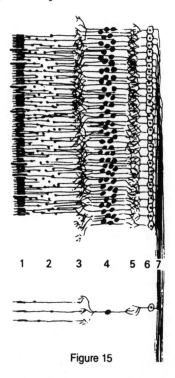

1   2   3   4   5 6 7

Figure 15

of the pore or little conduit, d,e, being thus opened, the animal spirits of the cavity F, enter within and are carried by it, partly into the muscles that serve to withdraw this foot from the fire, partly into those that serve to turn the eyes and the head to look at it, and partly into those that serve to advance the hands and to bend the whole body to protect it.

Note, however, that some behaviorists of today still cling to the same view [8], with one difference only, namely, that in the meantime Descartes' "animal spirit" has gone into oblivion.

Computation.   The retina of vertebrates, with its associated nervous tissue, is a typical case of neural computation. Figure 15 is a schematic representation of a mammalian retina and its postretinal network. The layer labeled 1 represents the array of rods and cones, and layer 2 the bodies and nuclei

of these cells. Layer 3 identifies the general region where the
axons of the receptors synapse with the dendritic ramifications of the "bipolar cells" (4) which, in turn, synapse in layer
5 with the dendrites of the ganglion cells" (6), whose activity
is transmitted to deeper regions of the brain via their axons,
which are bundled together to form the optic nerve (7). Computation takes place within the two layers labeled 3 and 5,
that is, where the synapses are located. As Maturana has
shown [3] it is there where the sensation of color and some
clues as to form are computed.

Form computation: Take the two-layered periodic network
of Figure 16, the upper layer representing receptor cells sensitive to, say, "light." Each of these receptors is connected to
three neurons in the lower (computing) layer, with two excitatory synapses on the neuron directly below (symbolized by
buttons attached to the body) and with one inhibitory synapse (symbolized by a loop around the tip) attached to each
of the two neurons, one to the left and one to the right. It is
clear that the computing layer will not respond to uniform
light projected on the receptive layer, for the two excitatory
stimuli on a computer neuron will be exactly compensated
by the inhibitory signals coming from the two lateral receptors. This zero response will prevail under strongest and
weakest stimulations as well as for slow or rapid changes of
the illumination. The legitimate question may now arise:
"Why this complex apparatus that doesn't do a thing?"

Consider now Figure 17, in which an obstruction is placed
in the light path illuminating the layer of receptors. Again all
neurons of the lower layer will remain silent, except the one
at the edge of the obstruction, for it receives two excitatory
signals from the receptor above, but only one inhibitory signal from the sensor to the left. We now understand the
important function of this net, for it computes any spatial
variation in the visual field of this "eye," independent of the
intensity of the ambient light and its temporal variations,
and independent of place and extension of the obstruction.

Although all operations involved in this computation are
elementary, the organization of these operations allows us to
appreciate a principle of considerable depth, namely, that of

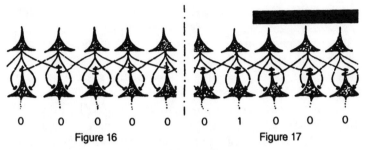

Figure 16   Figure 17

the computation of abstracts, here the notion of "edge."

I hope that this simple example is sufficient to suggest to you the possibility of generalizing this principle in the sense that "computation" can be seen on at least two levels, namely, (1) the operations actually performed and (2) the organization of these operations represented here by the structure of the nerve net. In computer language (1) would again be associated with "operations," but (2) with the "program." As we shall see later, in "biological computers" the programs themselves may be computed on. This leads to the concepts of "metaprograms," "meta-metaprograms," and so on. This, of course, is the consequence of the inherent recursive organization of those systems.

Closure. By attending to all the neurophysiological pieces, we may have lost the perspective that sees an organism as a functioning whole. In Figure 18 I have put these pieces together in their functional context. The black squares labeled *N* represent bundles of neurons that synapse with neurons of other bundles over the (synaptic) gaps indicated by the spaces between squares. The sensory surface (SS) of the organism is to the left, its motor surface (MS) to the right, and the neuropituitary (NP), the strongly innervated master gland that regulates the entire endocrinal system, is the stippled lower boundary of the array of squares. Nerve impulses traveling horizontally (from left to right) ultimately act on the motor surface (MS) whose changes (movements) are immediately sensed by the sensory surface (SS), as suggested by the "external" pathway following the arrows. Impulses traveling vertically (from top to bottom) stimulate the neuropituitary (NP), whose activity releases steroids into the synaptic gaps, as suggested by the wiggly terminations of the lines following the arrow, and thus modify the *modus operandi* of all synaptic junctures, hence the *modus operandi* of the system as a whole. Note the double closure of the system that now recursively operates not only on what it "sees," but on its operators as well. In order to make this twofold closure even more apparent I propose to wrap the diagram of Figure 18 around its two axes of circular symmetry until the artificial boundaries disappear and the torus (doughnut) in Figure 19

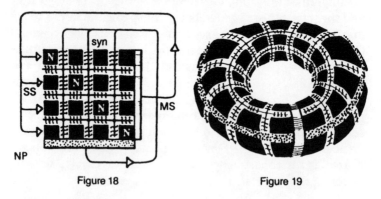

Figure 18   Figure 19

is obtained. Here the "synaptic gap" between the motor and sensory surfaces is the striated meridian in the front center, the neuropituitary the stippled equator. This, I submit, is the functional organization of a living organism in a (dough)nut shell.

The computations within this torus are subject to a nontrivial constraint, and this is expressed in the postulate of cognitive homeostais:

> The nervous system is organized (or organizes itself) so that it computes a stable reality.

This postulate stipulates "autonomy," that is, "self-regulation," for every living organism. Since the semantic structure of nouns with the prefix *self-* becomes more transparent when this prefix is replaced by the noun, *autonomy* becomes synonymous with *regulation of regulation*. This is precisely what the doubly closed, recursively computing torus does: It regulates its own regulation.

Significance

It may be strange in times like these to stipulate autonomy, for autonomy implies responsibility: If I am the only one who decides how I act, then I am responsible for my action. Since the rule of the most popular game played today is to make someone else responsible for *my* acts—the name of the game is "heteronomy"—my arguments make, I understand, a most unpopular claim. One way of sweeping it under the rug is to dismiss it as just another attempt to rescue "solipsism," the view that this world is only in my imagination and the only reality is the imagining "I." Indeed, that was precisely what I was saying before, but I was talking only about a single organism. The situation is quite different when there are two, as I shall demonstrate with the aid of the gentleman with the bowler hat (Fig. 20).

He insists that he is the sole reality, while everything else appears only in his imagination. However, he cannot deny that his imaginary universe is populated with apparitions that are not unlike himself. Hence he has to concede that they themselves may insist that they are the sole reality and everything else is only a concoction of their imagination. In that case their imaginary universe will be populated with apparitions, one of which may be *he*, the gentleman with the bowler hat.

According to the principle of relativity, which rejects a hypothesis when it does not hold for two instances together, although it holds for each instance separately (Earthlings and Venusians may be consistent in claiming to be in the center of the universe, but their claims fall to pieces if they should ever get together), the solipsistic claim falls to pieces when besides me I invent another autonomous organism. However, it should be noted that since the principle of relativity is not a logical necessity—nor is it a proposition that can be proven to be either true or false—the crucial point to be rec-

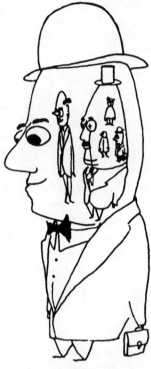

Figure 20

ognized here is that I am free to choose either to adopt this principle or to reject it. If I reject it, I am the center of the universe, my reality is my dreams and my nightmares, my language is monologue, and my logic monologic. If I adopt it, neither I nor the other can be the center of the universe. As in the heliocentric system, there must be a third that is the central reference. It is the relation between Thou and I, and this relation is *identity*:

reality = community

What are the consequences of all this in ethics and aesthetics?

The ethical imperative: Act always so as to incrase the number of choices.

The aesthetical imperative: If you desire to see, learn how to act.

REFERENCES

1. Brown, G. S. *Laws of Form*. Julian Press, New York, 1972, p. 3.
2. Descartes, R. *L'Homme*. Angot, Paris, 1664. Reprinted in *Oeuvres de Descartes*, Vol. 11. Adam and Tannery, Paris, 1957, pp. 119–209.
3. Maturana, H. R. A biological theory of relativistic colour coding in the primate retina. *Archivos de Biología y Medicina Experimentales, Suplemento 1*, 1968.
4. Maturana, H. R. Neurophysiology of cognition. In *Cognition: A Multiple View* (P. Garvin, ed.). Spartan Press, New York, 1970, pp. 3–23.
5. Maturana, H. R. *Biology of Cognition*. University of Illinois, Urbana, Illinois, 1970.
6. Naeser, M. A., and Lilly, J. C. The repeating word effect: Phonetic analysis of reported alternatives. *Journal of Speech and Hearing Research*, 1971.
7. Sholl, D. A. *The Organization of the Cerebral Cortex*. Methuen, London, 1956.
8. Skinner, B. F. *Beyond Freedom and Dignity*. A. Knopf, New York, 1971.
9. Teuber, H. L. Neuere Betrachtungen über Sehstrahlung und Sehrinde. In *Das Visuelle System* (R. Jung and H. Kornhuber, eds.). Springer, Berlin, 1961, pp. 256–274.
10. Worden, F. G. EEG studies and conditional reflexes in man. In *The Central Nervous System and Behavior* (Mary A. B. Brazier, ed.). Josiah Macy, Jr., Foundation, New York, 1959, pp. 270–291.

PART 2

Effect or Cause?

PAUL WATZLAWICK

Post hoc, ergo propter hoc.

*T*he aesthetic and ethical imperatives postulated by Heinz von
Foerster at the conclusion of his essay strike us as unusual.
*They appear obscure as long as their core concept—autonomy,
self-regulation, or self-reference—is not yet part of our thinking.
But since this concept inseparably permeates our view of reality
(and therefore of this book), some introductory remarks and elabo-
rations are required.*

*Probably the most universally accepted construction of reality
rests on the supposition that the world cannot be chaotic—not
because we have any proof for this view, but because chaos would
simply be intolerable. Of course, we listen to the arguments of
the theoretical physicists and nod in agreement: There is no "certain" relation between cause and effect, there are only degrees of
probability; time does not necessarily run from the past to the
present and into the future; space is not infinite but curves back
upon itself. However, none of this changes our everyday assumptions about the world and our lives by one iota. The two "languages"—ours and the physicists'—are too different, and even
the best translator fails. The physicists convincingly explain that
they have mathematical proof for the correctness of their world
view. But since these proofs (even if we could follow the language
of mathematics in which they are expressed) relate to a world that
is unimaginable in terms of our thinking and experiencing, we*

continue to live as if effect necessarily followed cause. And we have little trouble finding overwhelming proof for the conviction that event A, through its occurrence, becomes the cause of event B, that B therefore is the effect of A, that without A there could be no B, that B's occurrence in turn becomes the cause of C, and so on. From Aristotle to Descartes and Newton into the most recent past, thinking in terms of three-dimensional space and of the uni-directional progress of time has been the scaffold of scientific as well as social constructions of reality. It may be assumed that the model of a linear causality also accounts for the occidental con-cepts of responsibility, justice and guilt, morals, ethics, aesthet-ics, and, above all, objective truth and falsehood.

Chaos erupts when and where—in von Glasersfeld's sense—this construction no longer fits. Nietzsche once remarked that whoever has a why of living will endure almost any what, and this may explain our incessant need to construct a viable why, a model of the world that answers at least the most urgent questions of existence. When this attempt fails, we fall headlong into despair, madness, or the terrifying experience of nothingness.

But even where this linear model of causality holds, it holds only until someone opens our eyes to its internal inconsistency. After reading Riedl's essay on the consequences of causal think-ing (the first contribution to this chapter), it becomes somewhat difficult to go back to one's earlier view of causality, except at the price of massive self-deception. And there lies the rub: We laugh about Riedl's example of the boy and the chamber pot, but by the time we get to his description of the pigeons in the Skinner box, we no longer feel like laughing. Where is the experimenter who could identify for us the absurdities out of which we have constructed our world?

Riedl critically examines the proposition Post hoc ergo prop-ter hoc *(After this, therefore because of this), the quintessence of causal thinking through which the concept of time is introduced into the classic deterministic construction of the world. In simpler words, in this reality the effect of a cause must follow that cause; it cannot occur simultaneously with, let alone precede, its cause.*

This is how common sense sees it. After all, what is involved here amounts to an if–then sequence, or so it seems; and in this view of the world it seems equally impossible that an effect should become its own cause.

To repeat, closely associated with our experience of time is the idea of a linear, unidirectional movement—from cause to effect and from the past to the present. However, even the most trivial everyday experience may flatly contradict these commonsensical "fact." Consider the phenomenon of the vicious circle, in which the sequence of events is not rectilinear, but in which the effect may feed back on its own cause. This happens in nearly every marital conflict that turns and turns on itself in the same vicious manner, whose starting point is beyond recall and, even if recalled, no longer matters. We have already encountered these circular, self-reflexive sequences in von Foerster's essay (p. 48), where he defines cognition as "computations of computations of computations. . . ." Once established, such a circle is beyond beginning and end, and beyond cause and effect.

All this is still very cerebral and abstract. Let us look for some more practical examples:

Around the middle of the eighteenth century, when James Watt began to work on the design of a steam-driven engine, "experts" pointed out to him that the contraption would never work. To be sure, by forcing steam into one end of the cylinder the piston could be pushed to the other end—say, from right to left. But with this, the movement had apparently come to an end, for in order to push the piston back to the right end of the cylinder, it was obviously necessary to shut the right-side steam valve and introduce steam from the left side. In other words: The back-and-forth movement of the piston required a spiritus rector *outside the machine, or—more prosaically—an operator who opened and closed the valves at the right moments. This, of course, was incompatible with the idea of an independently functioning machine. Watt had a solution to this problem that nowadays seems obvious, but which then was not: He put the movement of the piston in the service of* its own regulation *by having the move-*

ment itself effect the opening and closing of the steam valves. Thus the movement of the piston became the cause of the functioning of the valves; in turn, this effect on the valves became the cause of the movement of the piston. For Watt's contemporaries, whose thinking was linear in terms of a "one-way street" from cause to effect, the circular causality of this feedback arrangement (its self-regulation) seemed "paradoxical."

Of course, the steam engine is still an array of purely physical, concrete components. But the nature of self-reflexiveness or self-reference becomes much more complex when it begins to involve the human realm and when at least part (if not all) of the dynamics are no longer merely a matter of physics, but extend into the social and behavioral sciences. Here emotional and psychological factors of our experience of the world come into play. Their nature is far more difficult to grasp than a mechanical array. Convictions, traditions, hopes, prejudices, and above all certain adamant assumptions have the strange ability to generate—self-reflexively—their own practical proof and justification. These so-called self-fulfilling prophecies defy our traditional if–then thinking by turning effect into cause. They are the subject of the second contribution to this chapter.

Self-fulfilling prophecies alter the seemingly firm, objective frame of our reality, and it is therefore more than a mere play of words to associate them with altered states of the mind. After all, the meaning of the ancient term ecstasy meant precisely a "standing outside" the frame of mind that was considered normal. But what if the frame itself is a self-fulfilling prophecy? Madness would then be a construction (or a "manufacture," in Thomas Szasz's [2] terms), and the traditional forms of its treatment might then—self-reflexively—turn out to be the cause of the supposed illness. Half a century ago the Viennese writer and critic Karl Kraus hinted at this possibility in his bitter aphorism according to which psychoanalysis is the illness whose cure it considers itself to be.

As is known, the traditional psychiatric criterion for a person's sanity or insanity is the degree of his "reality adaptation." This criterion tacitly assumes that there is such a thing as a real, objective reality and that it is open to our scrutiny and understanding. It goes without saying that the irruption of constructivist thinking into the orthodoxy of this view of reality is producing severe repercussions in that discipline and its institutions that are considered competent for the diagnosis and treatment of madness.

Early in 1973 the psychologist David Rosenhan published in Science, *the highly respected journal of the American Association for the Advancement of Science, a paper with the title "On Being Sane in Insane Places." It had the effect of a scientific bomb, and it is reprinted here as the third contribution to this chapter. Rosenhan's interest at the time was, to be sure, of a sociopsychological nature, yet what he presents is eminently constructivistic. Through a research design of elegant simplicity, he was able to show that certain psychiatric diagnoses—unlike the diagnoses in all other medical specialties—do not so much* define *as* create *a pathological condition. Once such a diagnosis has been made, a reality is invented whereby even so-called normal behavior is seen as somehow disturbed. From this point on, the process acquires its own momentum and can no longer be controlled by the patient or the other participants in the construction of this reality. The diagnosis produces the pathological condition; the condition makes necessary the existence of those institutions in which it can be treated; the milieu of the institution (the mental hospital) causes the very helplessness and depersonalization of the patient, which—self-reflexively—confirms the "correctness" of the diagnosis. The outcome is a self-fulfilling prophecy that eventually even the patient accepts as real, and he fashions his life accordingly.* [1]

Rosenhan's study is a small sample of the universal tragicomedy of interpersonal relations to whose construction we all contribute—whether actively or passively does not seem to make

---

[1]As can be imagined, Rosenhan's report triggered strong reactions and criticisms. They can be found, together with his reply, in his article "The Contextual Nature of Psychiatric Diagnosis" [1], published in 1975 and containing an extensive bibliography.

much difference, since plus ça change, plus c'est la même chose. *Who knows how many scientific, social, and personal contexts operate on the same mechanisms that Rosenhan describes for psychiatry? Who knows if we are not, all of us, and in a much more immediate sense than postulated by Freud, the descendants of Oedipus Rex in that, like him, we manage to fulfill a particular prophecy through our attempts to avoid it? Since antiquity this peculiar reversal of having effect rule cause—rather than vice versa—has been considered the core element of tragedy.*

But if tragedy, drama, and ultimately all literature are fictitious descriptions of reality, and if reality (long before all description) is itself a fiction, then literature—very much in von Foerster's sense—is the description of a description, and literary research the description of a description of a description. This particular form of self-reflexiveness is the essence of Rolf Breuer's concluding contribution to this chapter. In the first pages he alters and widens the frame in which most of us habitually experience theater and literature; for if, as Breuer shows throughout Beckett's novels, subject and object ultimately interpenetrate each other, if in the final analysis the invention and its inventor are inseparable, then end and beginning paradoxically merge into one—a unity symbolized since time immemorial by the Ouroborus, the snake that bites its tail.

REFERENCES

1. Rosenhan, David L. The contextual nature of psychiatric diagnosis. *Journal of Abnormal Psychology* 5, 1975, 462–474.
2. Szasz, Thomas S. *The Manufacture of Madness.* Dell, New York, 1970.

RUPERT RIEDL

The Consequences of Causal Thinking*

I T IS LATE in the day and the shadows have fallen. The house we enter is unknown to us, but the situation is familiar. It is too dark in the entrance hall to read the name plates. Where is the light switch? There—three buttons. It's probably the top one. We push it and immediately jump back: For as long as the finger was on the switch, a bell shrilled through the whole house (and then the fluorescent light flickers on as well). Embarrassing! It must have been the doorbell (or did we also cause the light to come on?). A door opens behind us. Have we roused the tenants too ? But no! It is the front door. "Excuse me," says the person coming in, "I thought the door was already locked." Did he then cause the bell to ring and did we turn on the light after all? Apparently. But why do we expect to be the cause of an unexpected coincidence, namely, the simultaneous occurence of the touching of the switch and the sound of the bell? Or the coincidence of the bell and the door, although here we must consider the purpose and intent of the entering person. In other words, how can our expectations of cause and purpose be accounted for or justified?

Unteachable Teachers

What logic or reason can we call upon? Is there some basic necessity, an inevitable way of reasoning in what guides our

---

*An original contribution, translated by Ursula Berg Lunk.

actions and expectations? We can examine that with a few (less trivial) examples: first, that connection we experience as deterministic in the sense of a causal nexus.

We hide a horn under a parked car and cover the wire that runs from the horn to our observation post with some sand in the gutter. We decide to honk the horn as long as the driver sits in the car with the door closed. Now the driver comes; he unlocks the car, opens the door, gets in, closes the door. The horn honks; the driver immediately opens the door (the door is the cause of the honking!) and the sound stops. The driver looks up and down the street (if not the door, what else could it be?), gets back in, closes the door. The horn honks; the driver opens the door (it's the door after all!)—the sound stops. The driver gets out, looks about, walks around the car (what is it?), raps the roof (what for?), shakes his head, gets in, closes the door. The horn honks. The driver jumps out. He stands, looking bewildered. An idea hits him! He expectantly closes the door from the outside. The horn is silent. Aha! The driver gets in the car and closes the door. The horn honks—he jumps out! He gestures his disgust and resignation. The whole process is repeated, but faster this time. Now the driver opens the hood (?), closes it; then he tries the trunk (what am I looking for?). Then he tries his own horn (!): It sounds different (!?). Now he starts talking to people on the street. The whole thing is repeated with various suggestions from everyone. Somebody goes for a gas station attendant, and so on. The humanity of the experimenter ends the scene. He is showered with disapproval and reprimands.

How could a door then lead to the spontaneous assumption that it is the cause for the honking of the horn? Has this ever happened before? Of course not. But the very fact that it has not forces the driver to seek an explanation.

And now for an example of that connection, in which we experience a certain purpose, a finality nexus.

People are getting on a streetcar in Vienna. Among the passengers is a working-class woman with her young son. The boy has an enormous bandage wrapped around his head. (How dreadful! What happened to him?) People give up their seats to the afflicted pair. The bandaging is not a professional job, it was obviously done at home and in a hurry; they must be on their way to the hospital (people secretly search the child's face for an explanation, and the bandage for traces of blood). The little boy whines and fusses (signs of sympathy from everyone). The mother seems unconcerned (how inappropriate!); she even shows signs of impatience (that is amazing). The little one begins to fidget; his mother pushes him back in his seat. The passengers' attitude changes from discrete observation to manifest concern. (The mother's behavior is disgraceful!) The boy cries and tries to climb the bench on which they are sitting. His mother pulls him back so roughly that even the bandage begins to shake. (The poor child! This is terrible!) The passengers' mood turns to open confrontation. The mother is criticized, but for her part rejects all interference. Now she is criticized again and more openly. Thereupon she tells them to mind their own business and questions the competence of all those who criticized her. (That is too much! An outrage to human decency!) Emotions run high, and things get noisy and turbulent. The child is bawling; his mother, red-faced and furious, declares she is going to show us what is the matter and begins (to everybody's horror) tearing off the whole bandage. What appears is a metal chamber pot that the little Don Quixote has pushed so tightly on his head that it is stuck; they are on their way to get help from the nearest plumber. People get off the streetcar in great embarrassment.

How could a few rags around the boy's head lead to the spontaneous assumption of a serious accident, when all other indications were against it?

The Impossibility of Rational Argumentation

How do we account for our tendency (whenever we are in the dark) to predict causes and purposes, that is, causality and finality, in spite of the fact that we are often mistaken, that we misread the purpose and see the sequence of cause and effect the wrong way around; in spite of the fact that we have often, for instance, taken a glove stretcher for a pair of pliers, a compressor for a generator, the wheel of a river mill for that of a paddle steamer; in spite of the fact that we have mistaken someone who cannot get the key out of the keyhole for one who cannot unlock the door, carpet thieves for delivery men, or art thieves for restorers of paintings?

What justifies our assumption that the tides are caused by the moon's orbit, the market by the buying public, and the behavior of laboratory rats by their experimenter? For it turns out that the earth's tides slow down the moon's orbit, that market and industry manipulate the buyer, and that the rat's behavior repertoire determines the experimenter's procedure [18].

But we should be wary not only of prejudice and error. Following the inquiry of the Scottish philosopher David Hume [5], we should realize that the *because* in the sentences with which we argue an assumed cause is itself not explainable. In fact, if we believe Hume, the "because" (the *propter hoc*) is itself not verifiable, only the "when this, then that" (the *post hoc*). Therefore, as Hume says, one can never say, "The stone gets warm because the sun shines," but merely, "Whenever the sun shines, the stone gets warm." Causality, Hume argued in 1739–1740 in his *Treatise on Human Nature*, may not be a part of nature at all, and therefore probably nothing more than a "need of the human mind." He rejects all metaphysical, beyond-sense experience and explanations.

All this made a deep impression on Immanuel Kant, who was thirteen years younger than Hume. So impressed was he that he traced his ancestors (Cant) to Scotland, mistakenly as we know today. But he was not mistaken in the insight that reasonable thinking is impossible without the expectation of causality and finality. Kant testified to their necessity in Königsberg in his great critical works—causality in *The Critique of Pure Reason* [6] and finality in *The Critique of Judgement* [7]. He demonstrated that these *a prioris* could not be explained as a prerequisite for all reasons, even by reason itself. And that's how it stood for 200 years—at first from Hume's *Treatise* in 1739–1740 to Konrad Lorenz's *Kant's Lehre vom Apriorischen im Lichte gegenwärtiger Biologie* [11], published in 1940 (at the University of Konigsberg, of all places), and the second time from Kant's *Critique* of 1781 to our time.

But what happens to the verification of our assumption of causation when expectation, although recognized as necessary, cannot be verified by reason? It has remained unverified. So our expectation that there are such things as causality and finality may be a need, but at the same time a totally erroneous expectation of the human mind. Traditional epistemology cannot explain its own foundation; it takes evolutionary epistemology to do that.

The Natural History of Causal Expectations

Evolutionary epistemology generally regards the evolution of organisms as a process of accumulating knowledge [19]. This makes us observers of a procedure that took place almost exclusively outside of us, and in so many strains of organisms that it lends itself to scientifically objective and comparative study. The successful accumulation of knowledge by the herditary material, that is, the genetic memory, depends on exactly repeating the new knowledge, the new success, in the next generation, or upon experimenting with slight variations within the scope of this new knowledge. One could say the unchanged primary form contains the "expectation" of being successful with what had brought success before; the changed mutant contains an attempt (albeit a blind one) at improvement. Selection determines success or failure. The rate of success is necessarily small, but this principle extracts nonetheless all relevant, and for the organism accessible, natural laws from the environment in order to permanently incorporate their guidelines for the construction and operation of that species in the form of structures and functions. This principle is based on the constancy of nature [17].

But even at this early stage it is clear that the same problem in the natural world can give rise to many different solutions. Comparing our eye with that of a bee, or the wing of an eagle with that of a butterfly, shows how totally different the structure may be.

Sensibility develops in this way, as do stimuli, conductors for stimuli, nerve cells, switches, and feedback loops, as, for example, our unconditioned reflexes. In this way, a mere puff of air on the cornea regulates the reflex of the eyelid, the protective closing of the eye. In the same way a change of tension in the patellar tendon regulates the stretch of the leg muscles in order to ensure automatic walking.

All this is still learned "genetically," "invented" gradually by individual mutants, propagated in the species by their success, and faithfully conserved in their memory.

Only now does creative, individual learning begin—with, let us say, the conditioned reflex. If, for example, the experimenter regularly shines a light just before he guides a puff of air toward the subject's cornea, the eye soon begins to close after the stimulus of the light alone. This preapplied, conditioned stimulus functions in place of, and in anticipation of, the puff of air, the unconditioned stimulus. The advantage lies in a faster reaction, in time to prevent a possible disturbance. And this evolutional advantage was the reason that individual learning prevailed wherever these conditions had developed.

Even unconditioned reflexes are based not only on the constancy of nature, but also on the continuance of the coincidences, that is, on the connection or concurrence of their characteristics and occurrence. The puff of air on the cornea causes the eye to expect imminent danger, and sudden increased tension in the patellar tendon is a warning that we will collapse and fall unless the extensor muscle contracts strongly and quickly enough. This faith in dependable and constant coincidences of characteristics in this world is now utilized further by creative, individual learning. Whenever a coincidence is repeated often enough to be confirmed, it is "expected" that this coincidence will keep on recurring, so that it can then be used in making useful predictions. When, in the conditioned reflex of the eyelid, the conditioned stimulus, the light, is taken as the precursor of the puff of air, it is of course the experimenter who has constructed a coincidence, one that does not exist in nature, in the environment of the organism. One can hardly expect that a flash of light in the eye is always followed by a disturbing puff of air. Clearly there are limitations to this learning principle, and we can see why an organism is programmed to unlearn in a short time what it has learned if the expected coincidence repeatedly fails to be confirmed. But in general and under natural conditions it will prove more successful to expect that coincidences that have already been repeated will occur again than not to do so. This is the simple "experience" that has again been built into the biological program.

In certain significant cases a perceived coincidence can even become unforgettable and subsequently unalterable. This is the phenomenon called imprinting. For example, the pattern perceived by a nestling of a certain age will from then on invariably be interpreted as its parents, whether it be the experimenter, a stuffed dog, or even a toy train. In nature, of course, this error is practically impossible, since during the critical time period only the parents, and never a stuffed dog, appear at the nest.

In other significant cases an inherent trigger mechanism is built in that assures that a certain signal is always followed by a prompt and straightforward reaction—for instance, heightened attention, alarm, or instant flight. It is obviously much wiser to turn to flight or safety in a flash when there is a sudden rustling close by or a bang in the quiet of the night than to engage in lengthy speculations.

There are programs such as these that do not depend on the reconfirmation of coincidences but cause an immediate reaction—presumably whenever the disadvantages of a false alarm are less than the possible damage caused by failing to react promptly. Only by the repeated nonoccurrence of the expected habituation can the reaction be dampened for a limited time.

There are additional programs by which need satisfaction may come to be reliably expected: Organisms are forever on the move trying to satisfy their variously evolved needs for shelter, food, companionship, and mates. This is what we call need behavior, or appetency. Conditioned appetencies also exist. If we regularly ring a dinner bell just before feeding a dog, he will begin to salivate at the sound of the bell alone, just as our own mouths water when we are hungry and hear the description of a fine meal. If the dog is taken off the leash, we will see him jump around the bell, barking and wagging his tail, performing the whole social repertoire of begging for food. We might say that he takes the bell for the source of food.

There is evidence that we human beings have inherited an abundance of such archaic programs. The expectation that coincidences are unlikely to be accidental has become part of us in such a general way that we suppose a direct connection in almost every coincidence. Konrad Lorenz, in his "Altenberger Kreis," describes how such programs can be the cause of the most fantastic hypotheses. Imagine, he said, a hotel room in a strange city. The wind keeps banging a shutter, and when a church clock starts striking in the same rhythm, the expectation rises inescapably that one must be the cause of the other. Once the secret origins of such delusions are recognized, they can be observed again and again, and it is surprising how often we are influenced by them. And now it becomes clear why we first thought we were the cause of the ringing bell when our finger touched the light switch, and later thought it was the person entering behind us, as well as why the car door was taken for the cause of the honking horn, and the child's bandages as a signal that led us to expect an injury.

With the capacity of the more complex nervous systems and their memory—their ability to store information and recall it—evolution took the next decisive step. It created the "central representation of space," the ability to close one's eyes and reflect on the contents of memory, to recall what is stored in memory and contemplate it. Consciousness was born. And the evolutional advantage is again so significant that it prevails wherever these conditions exist. The advantage lies in the fact that instead of risking one's own skin, one need only risk a mental experiment; the hypothesis, Lorenz [12] says, can perish in place of its owner.

The hereditary programs that influence our conscious expectation are now also becoming evident; they are our hereditary patterns of perception. They determine the mental representations and expectations with which we approach the world in which we live. To be sure, these programs become evident only when and where they demonstrably and stupidly mislead us. Whenever they guide us correctly, they seem wise and almost self-evident—a system of instructions apparently guided by reason. Brunswik called their interaction our ratiomorphological apparatus. This apparatus represents the achievement of our unpremeditated common sense, and its task is to give us solid guidance not only in judging the most essential features of this world, but also in making the right decisions about the thousand small choices of everyday life, saving us from getting bogged down in constant rumination and speculation.

Two simple examples of such modes of perception are our innate patterns of conceiving of space and time. A brief review of these patterns will show the limitations of such guidance, for it is their very inadequacy (caused by insufficient concordance with reality) that was exposed by Einstein.

Time, you will agree, seems to us like a stream. It flows past us, comes from an unknown source, never runs backward, and disappears—no one knows where. Time is only experienced in one dimension, like a stream of water from a faucet, whose movement is unequivocal, irreversible. We do not know in which mountain range the stream began, nor in which ocean it will end. We are just as much at a loss in our understanding of time; we cannot tell where time begins or where it finds its end.

We experience space, on the other hand, in three dimensions; it is Euclidean, as termed in geometry, and we perceive it as similar to the three planes of a box or the boundaries of a room. But as soon as we ask how the boundaries of space, the boundaries of our universe, are to be imagined, we are out of our depth. We can only imagine a space of this kind inside another space, without being able to imagine an end.

Actually, both modes of perception are greatly oversimplified. For this world, as Einstein taught us, contains a space–time continuum, also known as a four-dimensional space, curved back onto itself. Although physics unquestionably proved it to exist, it can never be conceived of by the human mind. This continuum permits the theory, for example, that

if we could see as far as we liked, and in whichever direction
of the compass, we would eventually always see the back of
our head.

These examples should warn us that our modes of perception can only be rough approximations of the structure of
this world. They were selected long ago for our animal ancestors, their environment, and the problems facing them. For
their purposes a simple form of perception was sufficient.
Even for the microcosm we human beings inhabit, the old
modes of perception of space and time suffice, because we
would have to travel almost with the speed of light to experience the error ourselves.

Our perception of causes, on the other hand, influences us
directly here on our planet. Not only is it responsible for a
currently unbridgeable split in our image of the world, but it
has also brought us a sociological and environmental malaise
from which we clearly have not been able to extricate ourselves [18]. This is what makes our example useful.

The Superstition About Causes

You will recall, in the experiment on conditioned appetencies, that the dog seemed to take the bell for the source of
food. To be more exact, he behaved toward the bell exactly
as a subordinate wolf in a pack behaves toward a dominant
one when he is begging for a share of the kill, with a show
of "subservience" and "flattery." And this program, built in,
functions only through the ritual of tail wagging, barking,
whining, and jumping, with a lowering of the head and chest
and exposure of the throat to the dominant wolf, who may
not be touched except gently with a paw. Of course we do
not know what a dog is thinking when he is begging, but
since he sometimes begs when he is dreaming, he might have
some concept, if only a very simple one, of what he is doing.
And since he behaves toward the bell as he does toward the
leader of a pack, he might have in both cases the concept of
a "when–then" connection. The coincidence of food and bell
gives rise to the expectation of a necessary or, as we say,
causal connection.

Our very similar "when–then" expectation must therefore have been imprinted long ago into our ancestors in the animal kingdom as a consistent program that worked most of the time and proved again and again to be important for the survival.

Of course we all know that bells are not ordinarily the source of food. But how forcibly that same mechanism of individual, creative learning can lead to superstition and how far back in the animal kingdom this originates must still be demonstrated.

B. F. Skinner placed individual pigeons into what are now called "Skinner boxes." One can look into these boxes, but the bird inside receives only those messages deliberately conveyed by the experimenter. Skinner put a number of pigeons into as many of these boxes and set up his experiment so that a mechanism released a food pellet into each box at regular intervals. Pigeons, however, and this is not always taken into consideration, are not merely reacting robots; they have their appetencies and programs and are constantly engaged in some activity: They strut, they look around, they preen their feathers, and so on. Consequently the appearance of the pellet always coincides with *some* movement. And now it is only a matter of time until the pellet coincides several times with the same movement. From then on a curious learning process begins. The respective movement is associated with getting food, and so this movement—let us say a step to the left—is now made more often. The coincidence therefore becomes more frequent. The pigeon is increasingly confirmed in its "expectation" that there is a connection between food and this movement, until finally there is practically definitive evidence that this particular and now constantly performed movement is followed by food. For if the pigeon does nothing but turn to the left, every food pellet must bring reward and confirmation. The result is a large group of crazy pigeons; one constantly circles to the left, another keeps spreading its right wing, a third swings its head endlessly from side to side. The "prophecy" of a causal connection fulfills itself. To what degree we humans become the victims of such "self-fulfilling prophecies" will be the subject of subsequent considerations (see also p. 95 ff in this volume). The roots of this superstition are hereditary and deep-seated.

Is there one of you who has never knocked on wood so as not to tempt your luck with too hopeful an expectation? Some people are even droll enough to knock on their own heads when there is nothing made of wood within reach. And we have to admit that the action works, for in most cases the reversal of our luck never materializes!

This brings us very close to conscious reflection. Earlier we touched upon the evolutionary advantage that resulted from this consciousness, namely, the advantage of transferring the risk of extinction from the individual to his hypothesis. This substitution in the realm of thought is undoubtedly one of the most significant achievements of evolution, but the subsequent pitfalls of this progress should not be overlooked. All resulting disastrous errors have the same origin: A verification in the realm of thought is mistaken for an actually and successfully accomplished verification in the real world.

Something like another world has arisen, a theoretical world in addition to the observable one [22]. And who decides when these worlds are in conflict? Do we find the truth through our deceptive senses or in our unreliable consciousness? And here is the beginning of man's dilemma: the schism in his world that is particularly painful because it divides the unity of his own self into body and soul, mind and matter. This is the root of the conflict that has been part of the history of civilization for two and a half milennia, the conflict between rationalism and empiricism, idealism and materialism, science and the humanities, causal and objective interpretation, hermeneutics and scientism.

But the schism reaches even farther back than our history; documentation of this dilemma exists from more than 40 million years ago.

The History of Causal Reasoning

On Mount Circeo on the Tyrrhenian coast of Italy there is a cave that contains the skull of a Neanderthal man. The severed head, impaled on a stick, was buried within a circle of stones. The opening at the back of the head had been forcibly enlarged to expose the brain. It was probably eaten by the man's clan—it has been found that other primitive people also butchered a family member so that by jointly eating the brain his name could be used again for a newborn child. After all, they might reason, where else would one find a name? As another example, in the Zagros mountains in Iraq there are Neanderthal graves that contain such a quantity of pollen that there can be no doubt that bodies were buried with lychnis, mallows, and grape hyacinths. Were these plants thought to have healing powers that would help the dead come back to life? We do not know. But we can see that procedures were invented that were presumably recognized by the entire tribe.

In Swiss mountain caves Neanderthal man practiced the cult of bear worship as do certain tribes, even today, in the Arctic who believe that bears are mediators between man and his gods, and who carry out elaborate rituals to pacify the bear after they have eaten him. For nothing happens simply by chance, and threatening portent looms everywhere, in the dark as in the invisible. And who would deny that appeasements can be successful?

Many different tribes still bury their dead for reasons other than piety. Rather, they try to hinder the ghost's return by covering the grave with stones, because, as everyone knows, the dead have the disconcerting habit of appearing in people's dreams in the most realistic and ghastly fashion. Weapons and provisions are also put into the grave in the hope of appeasing the dead and improving their chances of traveling far away.

The unknown is interpreted by analogy with familiar purposes and powers. "This makes the unknown explicable," Klix says. "The uncertainty of knowledge is replaced by the certainty of faith. Animistic thinking fills the gaping holes in the knowledge of the causes of natural phenomena. It creates confidence . . . where otherwise there would be nothing but confusion and perplexity" [8].

What today we call cause and effect was generally regarded

in terms of guilt and subsequent atonement. Therefore nego-
tiations seemed advisable. Greek culture is familiar with this
ancient concept. And we even ask ourselves whose "fault" it
is that the car does not start, although we already have a feeling that the spark plugs are wet.

The "wild thinking" [10] of primitive people like our
ancestors operated with virtually arbitrary analogies and
transferred the innate concept of powers and purposes to
whatever was felt to be in need of an explanation.

In some Indian tribes pregnant women are not allowed to
eat squirrels, because, obviously, the squirrels' bodies have
a tendency to disappear into dark burrows, whereas a birth
is supposed to bring a body out into the light. Pregnant Hopi
women, on the other hand, have to eat squirrels as often as
possible because, just as obviously, these animals have a
facility for finding their way out of dark burrows, which is
exactly the process of a birth. I myself was scolded many times
when I was a child, until I finally learned that at dinner my
left hand was supposed to be on the table next to my plate.
My children, growing up in the United States, were scolded
just as often, until they learned that this hand belonged under
the table on their laps. Looking for an anthropological reason, I have come up with only one explanation that satisfied
our American friends: Keeping the left hand on the table prevents the European from following his natural inclination to
put it on the knee of the lady next to him.

The oldest cosmogonies are very constructive for the study
of early concepts of causality. Our own concept goes back to
the Greeks' prephilosophical theogonies, which are in turn
based on the Kumarbi epic. This story of the creation of the
universe, examined by Schwabl [20], shows approximately
the following sequence of events: Emerging from the original
Chaos are Erebus, the underworld, and Nyx, his sister, night.
Aether and Hemera, ether and day, are descended from them.
Chaos, Eros, and Gaea (the broad-breasted earth) are the pri-
mal powers. Gaea gives birth to the mountains, Pontos (the
sea), and Uranos (heaven). From her union with Uranos
sprang the Titans, Cyclôpês, and the Hekatoncheires (three
giants with fifty heads and a hundred arms). Uranos, how-

ever, hates his children, forces them back into the earth, and does not let them out into the light. Gaea, suffering greatly from this constriction, forges a sickle and urges her children to take revenge. All are filled with great fear; only Kronos, one of the Titans, is willing. Gaea gives him the serrated sickle and hides him, and when Uranos comes, leading the night, and embraces Gaea, Kronos separates the pair with his serrated iron. Uranos' severed penis falls into the ocean; its white foam will give rise to Aphrodite. Drops of blood fall on the earth, and Gaea gives birth to the Erinyes, the Giants, and the human Nymphs. The Titans are now able to come forth from the earth. Kronos forms a union with his sister Rhea, but he devours all the children she bears in order to prevent them from banishing him, as was prophecied by Uranos and Gaea. When Rhea gives birth to Zeus in a cave on Crete, she therefore gives Kronos a rock wrapped in a diaper, which he devours in place of the child. In this way the Greek father of the gods was preserved. What a turmoil of highly "visceral" or, shall we say, human (?) intentions, impregnations, banishments, and deceptions created and explained this world.

This is what all cosmogonies have in common. The expectation of intentions and causes comes before every being and becoming. And theological and ontological thinking is closely related to cosmogony; "Greek philosophy," Schwabl says, "is in its beginnings really nothing more than cosmogony and representation of the unfolding of phenomena in the universe. Proceeding from the cleansing of the mythological concept of life there follows the more and more subtle refinement of thought and with it the refinement of science."

The ancient concept of causality reached its highest form in Aristotle, who postulated four different classes of causes such as those involved in building a house. First a *causa efficiens* is required, the cause of the incentives or driving power, whether it be labor or capital; then the *causa materialis,* the cause of the construction material, for power alone has never built a house. The *causa formalis* is required next, the blueprint that allows the selection and arrangement of the materials. This, too, is confirmed by our everyday experience, for no house is built by the material alone, no matter how much

of it is unloaded. And finally Aristotle postulates the effect of
a *causa finalis*, of a purpose; somebody must have the intention of building a house. In modern times only the univer-
sality of the purpose cause has been seriously challenged.
Marx concedes a purpose to the architect, but not to the bee.
But even this was proven incorrect, for it is clear that even
the bee, the spider, or the gypsy moth has the injunction to
act for the preservation of the species firmly built into its
genetic memory.

So where do we go from here? The exegetes of early scho-
lasticism already asked themselves this question. Why four
different causes? Should there not be one original cause preceding all the others and generating them? Thus began, a
thousand years ago, the search for the original cause. This
search is still in progress.

The Discovery of the Original Cause

The exegetes of Aristotle soon agreed: By the cause of all
causes the master could only have meant the *causa finalis*. For
experience teaches us every day that first we have to have an
intention, for instance, to build a house, before it makes any
sense to worry about money, materials, and plans. And does
not this intention determine everything else—plans, materials, and financial expenditure?

But what is much more important is that we see a purposefully ordered universe, that there is meaning in all relationships in nature—in the bee, lion, and eagle, in the sowing,
growing, and ripening, and in the seasons. And this chain
of purposes—each the consequence of a still higher one—
must surely terminate in the universal purpose of harmony
in the whole world. Since such a final purpose must be outside or above this world, it could only be the ultimate purpose of the world's creator. The *causa finalis* found its last
and supreme formulation in the *causa exemplaris* of theology.
Who would want to exclude himself from the exalted view of
the philosophers? And indeed, no one did. Christianity was
too deeply enmeshed in the world view of the Middle Ages
to allow any doubts about the harmony of the plan of crea-

tion. The mythological figure of Doctor Faustus (probably Georg Faust of Knittlingen) was nothing more than a warning example, a necromancer trafficking with the devil, which, figuratively speaking, he still is.

This medieval philosophy did not realize that the other problems of the web of causes were not resolved, only excluded. An artificial world was constructed, a world without a sense for consequences. Nobody could foresee that some day (namely, March 22, 1762) Voltaire would hear about the Inquisition's absurd murder of the linen merchant Calas and put the whole power of this pen into action against fanaticism and baseness, right in the era of Enlightenment and just before the French Revolution. Nobody could predict that the young theologian Hegel, rooted in the Enlightenment, would move on to become a romantic idealist and would develop, out of self-awareness and the idea of an ultimate "world spirit," a principle of dialectics so precarious that Marx [13] could turn this entire philosophy into its opposite. Nobody predicted that the reliance on absolute ultimate causes would rob man absolutely of any authority that could be called upon for mediation between these contrasting world views.

In the Renaissance, on the other hand, Galileo began to experiment with the free fall. And although, as the physicist Pietschmann [15] says, everyone can see that in an autumnal forest no two leaves fall in quite the same way, Galileo developed the laws of gravity. The concept was a Promethean "measuring the course of the stars," and he began by setting himself the task of "making measurable that which is not measurable." What does this mean? It means an incomparably more precise prognostication of a very narrow range of real occurrences in this world, but at the price of the exclusion and ignoring of all others. To exclude the effect of weight, Galileo experimented with heavy objects; to exclude form, he used balls; and to avoid air resistance, he chose the inclined plane. And what remains in formulating the prognosis and the laws can only be energy, Aristotle's *causa efficiens*. Material and form are forgotten and purposes have disappeared altogether. The result is tremendous, first a scientific and then technical, industrial, and military revolution of civilization, the beginning of the immense power of man.

Again it was not recognized that other dimensions of causal relationships were not resolved, but only excluded. It was not and is still not recognized that energy alone is not the answer. It was impossible to see oneself as the sorcerer's apprentice. Nobody could foresee that some day (namely, February 8, 1939) Einstein, in a letter to Roosevelt, would give the impetus for the development of the first atomic bomb. Nobody predicted that it would become impossible for us to extricate ourselves from the vicious circle of technocracy, progress, arms buildup, power, and fear. Nobody was able to foresee that this would be the consequence of the supposed measurability of efficiency, production, communication, and even intelligence. Nobody could foresee that an explanation of the world, derived from energy and chance events, will have to deny the existence of all purposes, that it will even strip man and his civilization of all meaning.

Divided Philosophies

The division of these conflicting interpretations stands to this day. Interpreting the world from the point of view of its purposes became the method of the humanities, especially the art of explication or hermeneutics as formulated by Dilthey [2]. Interpretation from the viewpoint of forces or energy became the method of the sciences, the so-called scientism. The latter operates with causality, the former with finality. It is assumed that causal relations influence the present from the past, whereas final relations affect the present from the future; for does not the future house influence today's preparations? The division of these philosophies is firmly established. There is no negotiation across its boundaries, and whoever tries it must be prepared for the wrath of both sides.

This gives the division the characteristics of exclusivity, and it is expected that one be committed either to the finality or the causality convenant, with the injunction to reject the other. And each covenant has its own long-established doctrines, dogmas, and tenets of scientific conduct that the opposition declares to be inadmissable while it immunizes its own position against any possible challenge.

All this in spite of the fact that these seemingly mutually exclusive interpretations are mirror images of each other, and in spite of the fact that purposes as well as causality influence the present from the past, for the house that I imagine to be finished in ten years actually exists in my head now. If I open a savings account for it tomorrow, a decision from yesterday will influence my actions tomorrow.

This mirrorlike relationship becomes visible if one considers the hierarchical layers of the world's structure. Without question, elementary particles make up atoms, which make up molecules, biological molecules, cells, tissue, and organs. These again make up individuals, societies, and cultures. If one asks for an explanation for a chicken's flight muscle, for example, one will find that its structure and performance can be traced back to those of its cells, their biological molecules, atoms, and elementary particles; but an understanding of its form and function comes from its purpose in the wing; the form and position of the wing from the bird, the bird from its species, and the species from its environment. In just the same way the understanding of a man hauling bricks comes from the building of a wall, this from the construction of a house, the construction from the traditions of his group and its civilization.

And yet the division remains, even though the effects of energy as well as those of purpose are immediately apparent, although it is equally obvious that the expectations of their effects are solidly built into every human being, every civilization, as its hereditary mode of perception. What prevents us from uniting both philosophies is what Kant called our "indolent reasoning," which persuades us to go the easier route of excluding alternatives, although uniting them would be less of a challenge to our thinking than the fusion of our concepts of space and time. I have presented the solution of this riddle more thoroughly elsewhere [18,19]. Here we are more concerned with the consequences.

Varieties of Obscurantism

As was to be expected, concepts of a highly spectral nature are now appearing wherever an attempt is made to reach a unified explanation with the help of one of the causality concepts. And not surprisingly, phantoms of the causal and the final world, idealistic and materialistic ghosts, will be found to rise against each other.

Let us begin with the materialistic, the causality phantoms. Among the venerable representatives of this ghostly circle is the robot, "man as machine," first published in 1745 by the French Army physician La Mettrie [9], as a precursor to Enlightenment. The author was promptly banished for his materialism and just as promptly taken up by Frederic II and made a member of the Berlin Academy. This phantom never left center stage; on the contrary, it has given rise to a whole spirit world of related spooks when it comes to problems of the science of living organisms. The rule is that a materialistic phantom is followed by an idealistic one, and vice versa—quite a ghostly dance. But as entertainment, it turned out to be poor—too much melodrama in the small theaters of life.

Let us note a few examples from the next two and a half centuries: Roux discovered causal processes in embryonic development; there follow the mechanics of development and also its counter-phantom vitalism. The old animal psychology has its roots in this finalist camp, and as counter-phantom we have Skinner and behaviorism, which regards the animal as a reacting automaton. Morphology, that is, the science of biological structure, attracted the German Idealism, and as its counterreaction there arose the numerical taxonomy of Sokal and Sneath, who believed they could classify organisms without any background knowledge. Modern genetics gave rise to its "central dogma," which will not allow the idea of a transfer of information from the body structures to the genetic material. With the onset of an understanding of the effects of chance in all aspects of organic evolution, Monod [14] expected us humans to finally admit to our own meaninglessness.

The method behind this movement was exceedingly successful. This "scientism," as it arose with Galileo, has fundamentally changed our world. Its concept of causes is based on the expectation that all phenomena can be understood by reducing them to their parts; this is called "pragmatic reductionism." With it one explains the mind through the physiology of the brain, which in turn is explained by the conduction of stimuli through nerve cells, the nerve impulses, these again by the transport of molecules to their circuits, and these through the kinetics of chemical reactions and finally the orbits of electrons of the elements involved, in other words, from the properties of the elementary particles. The interpretation of scientism, moreover, contains the assumption that this is all there is to it; it excludes any other causes. This is the error of "ontological reductionism," which does not recognize that with any dissection it has destroyed the relationship in the system as a whole. It throws out the baby with the bath water. It does not take into account that although a brain thinks, it makes no sense to say that a brain cell thinks, that a nerve transmits stimuli, but that a wandering molecule is far from being a conduction. "You have the parts and all the sections," as Goethe predicted, "but unfortunately you lack the mental connections." Mind thus either does not exist at all, it is merely an anthropomorphic overestimation of the significance of molecular transports, or it is considered a reality, as Rensch [16] represents it. But then an ever smaller piece of mind would have to be contained in every cell, molecule, quantum, and quark. As an explanation of the world, therefore, this theory clearly cannot be right. Absolute scientism leads only to scientific obscurantism.

In this situation one would hope that the concept of purposes avoids these mistakes. Did not Aristotle himself set the final cause before all the others? Does not purpose come before every action we decide upon? So, as long as one holds to purpose, one can hardly lose that which is most essential for an interpretation of the world, but again it turns out, here, too, the essential element gets lost.

Driesch [3], in contrast to Roux, found embryos that compensate for injuries inflicted on them. This means that the whole knows where it is going; it has an inherent goal, an entelechy, that cannot be explained by energy alone. Therefore one will have to assume a goal-oriented life force, as does Bergson [1], an "élan vital." Long ago Goethe explained the prototype, the construction plans of organisms, by an "esoteric" principle. Should this "inner principle" not be construed as something mysterious and spiritual? And the philosophy that followed, German Idealism, with Fichte, Hegel, and Schelling, which sees the world only as "participating in the general matrix of being," was this philosophy not justified in considering morphology (idealistically the origin of forms) as the realization of ideas? An absolute consciousness, the ultimate world purpose, existing beyond the universe, was surely to be expected if the world was created for consciousness, and matter for the purpose of life. Considering the goal orientation in every aspect of organic evolution, Teilhard de Chardin [21] sees all human beings, notwithstanding all the atrocities we commit, on a divinely ordained course, a path leading to the creator himself.

The method behind this finalism and idealism was not entirely without success either. Not only did it give rise to a multitude of fantastic, metaphysical systems, but it also sees itself, as Dilthey recommends, as "hermeneutics," the art of explication, as a tool for the humanities. For where should the understanding of texts, intentions, and actions in history and culture come from if not from their purposes? But what is explained by Driesch's entelechy? And Bergson's "élan vital" does not make us understand living organisms any better than an "élan locomotive" would explain the nature of a steam engine. As the exclusive interpretation of the world, the concept of purpose in the macrocosm must depend on the ultimate purposes of the creator, inexplicable to us and beyond our universe. In the microcosm it must postulate premeditated purposes in the molecules and particles, which also preclude any possibilities of understanding. As an interpretation of the world, this theory clearly cannot be right either. Absolute hermeneutics lead only to humanistic obscurantism.

Society's Dilemma

One might protest, however, with some justification, that unadulterated disciples of scientism and finalism hardly exist anymore and probably never have existed. Every proponent of scientism will be guided by purposes, and every finalist will respect the laws of causality, if only by being careful around fire or by avoiding the effect of a thrown rock. One may also suggest that the branches of natural science and the humanities have not been separated without thought or reason, for it did turn out that in the one progress comes with scientism, and that the other prospers with hermeneutics. But in reality the practice of this division says only that we are getting used to the split in the interpretation of the world, that we have accepted the schizophrenia of fragmented man, the opposition of body and soul, mind and matter.

This schism pervades all elements of civilization. We are not just engaged in an academic dispute; our whole world is divided. Two-sided perceptions, just as one-sided ones, lead from the contradictions of half-true causes to the social dilemmas in which we all find ourselves, individuals as well as the whole society. This dilemma is guided by the schism in the scientific concept of the world, gives it a basis in society, and is in turn defined by it recursively.

Intelligence, some people say, is innate. All creatures have their predetermined purpose; therefore there is little one can do for the stupid. It follows that society needs an elite to guide its course, and, indeed, there are political elites everywhere competing for the consent of the masses, in parties as well as in politburos. But others say that intelligence is a causal product of the environment, and therefore any failure in developing it is the fault of education. And thus egalitarian schools crop up everywhere, and the task of finding the right and necessary expertise becomes the responsibility of committees. The consequences of both positions are known only too well, and they interfere with each other in the most bewildering way.

Teaching ethics, some say, is the responsibility of the family, for it represents the purpose of life. Schools are for the three R's. For why should a teacher decide what kind of morality is to be passed on to my child? We responsible parents, not some neighborhood collective, should watch over the moral development of our precious progeny. And so drunkards and hoodlums have a causal influence on their children's development and thereby pass on their traditions. Teaching ethics, the others say, can therefore only be formulated by the community, because only the community contains the causal determinants of the conditions of future life. For how should yesterday's parents know about what is needed in the future? And so the voters commission the party of their choice to appoint the experts who in turn announce to the school principals what the purpose of the masses' education is, and—even more important—what cannot be taught under any circumstances. Now cause and effect have two diametrically opposed ends, which, however, meet in the middle and cancel each other out.

Economy and business, some say, are dependent on the consumer. He is king because what he doesn't want, business can't get rid of. The goal of commerce is to satisfy the customer. What is hushed up is that business has good reasons to manipulate the consumer in order to have an advantage over the competition. But others are of the opinion that the goal of commerce is the development of society. But what must be the goal of society has already been decided by the ideologists. What is hushed up here is that their goals do not coincide with the goals of society, unless society is manipulated accordingly. In order to remove the contradictions in these sociocapitalistic achievement societies, the competing industries on both sides are forced to run a suicidal course in their effort to survive. Partial causes are on collision course. The result is the disaster of unchecked growth and abused environment.

Justice, according to natural law, is based on the idea of law. It would definitely be wrong to concede unlimited powers to some sovereign. Therefore one must rely on an inherent idea of justice. But to be safe, it seems advisable to make sure that it is firmly planted in human consciousness. But, say the legal positivists, laws have nothing to do with justice; they obviously comprise only what the sovereign expects, or what people think he expects. And so the sovereign has an interest in making his subjects think he has a perfectly natural right to everything he expects. Such half-truths have always enabled us to trace all those mass catastrophies caused by battles for power—the so-called turning points of history—back to the idea of honor and morality.

Some people declare that society's goal is the freedom of the individual. If an individual has the advantage of special circumstances, be they physical or financial, and whether he came by them through inheritance or chance, the others must respect the additional freedom his money or strength give him. The origin of progress, social Darwinism tells us, is based on the success of the fittest. This goes to show, others say, that this cannot be true; rather, the opposite is the case: The goal of progress is a certain form of society, a society based on egalitarian principles. To bring about this form of society, there arose a new class of potentates. For human beings are equal, but if they are not, Che Guevara says, society has the responsibility of compensating the incompetents for their undeserved fate by increased expenditure. The competents fear that this would create a society of incompetents. And the question arises, Is the individual or society the main concern of civilization? Which decision maker can we turn to in this conflict about ultimate purposes? There is none. And so we end up with an ever-growing arms buildup, with peace based on ever-increasing fear.

"The human mind," Jay Forrester [4] says, "is unable to understand human social systems." This is true. Our innate conceptions were selected to cope with the modest causal environment of our animal ancestors. But they are inadequate for dealing with the responsibilities our current technocracy presumes in this world. Our one-dimensional causal thinking is unqualified to find a solution. Society therefore constructs social truths and causes that alternately cancel each other out, and the decision is still in the hands of that blind power which, let us admit it, fills us all with fear.

REFERENCES

1. Bergson, Henry L. *Creative Evolution* (translated by Arthur Mitchell). Modern Library, New York, 1944.
2. Dilthey, Wilhelm. *Einleitung in die Geisteswissenschaften.* Teubner, Stuttgart, 1933.

3. Driesch, Hans A. E. *Philosophie des Organischen*. Engelmann, Leipzig, 1909.
4. Forrester, J. "Behavior of social systems." In *Hierarchically Organized Systems in Theory and Practice* (P. Weiss, ed.). Hafner, New York, 1971.
5. Hume, David. *Enquiries Concerning Human Understanding and Concerning the Principles of Morals*. Clarendon Press, Oxford, 1975.
6. Kant, Immanuel. *Kant's Critique of Pure Reason* (translated by F. Max Müller). MacMillan, London, 1881.
7. Kant, Immanuel. *Kant's Critique of Judgement* (translated by J. H. Bernard), 2nd ed. MacMillan, London, 1913.
8. Klix, Friedhart. *Erwachendes Denken*. VEB Deutscher Verlag der Wissenschaften, Berlin, 1980.
9. La Mettrie, Julien Offray de. *L'Homme Machine*. In *Oeuvres philosophiques*. D'E. Luzac, Leyden, 1748.
10. Lévi-Strauss, Claude. *The Savage Mind*. Weidenfeld and Nicolson, London, 1966.
11. Lorenz, Konrad. Kants Lehre vom Apriorischen im Lichte gegenwartiger Biologie. *Blätter für Deutsche Philosophie* 15, 1941, 94–125.
12. Lorenz, Konrad. *Behind the Mirror* (translated by Ronald Taylor). Harcourt Brace Jovanovich, New York, 1977.
13. Marx, Karl, and Engels, Friedrich. *The German Ideology* (R. Pascal, ed.). International Publishers, New York, 1939.
14. Monod, Jacques. *Chance and Necessity* (translated by Austryn Wainhouse). Knopf, New York, 1971.
15. Pietschmann, Herbert. *Das Ende des naturwissenschaftlichen Zeitalters*. Zsolnay, Vienna, 1980.
16. Rensch, Bernhard. *Biophilosophy* (translated by C. A. M. Sym). Columbia University Press, New York, 1971.
17. Riedl, Rupert. *Die Strategie der Genesis*. Piper, Munich, 1976.
18. Riedl, Rupert. Über die Biologie des Ursachen-Denkens. In *Mannheimer Forum 78/79* (H. von Dithfurth, ed.). Boehringer, Mannheim, 1979.
19. Riedl, Rupert. *Biology of Cognition*. Wiley, London, 1983.
20. Schwabl, H. Weltschopfung. In *Paulys Realenzyklopädie der klassischen Altertumswissenschaften, Supplement*, Vol. 9. Druckenmüller, Stuttgart, 1958.
21. Teilhard de Chardin, Pierre. *Man's Place in Nature* (translated by René Hague). Harper and Row, New York, 1966.
22. Watzlawick, Paul. *How Real Is Real?* Random House, New York, 1976.

PAUL WATZLAWICK

Self-Fulfilling Prophecies*

A SELF-FULFILLING PROPHECY is an assumption or prediction that, purely as a result of having been made, causes
the expected or predicted event to occur and thus confirms
its own "accuracy." For example, if someone assumes, for
whatever reason, that he is not respected, he will, because of
this assumption, act in such a hostile, overly sensitive, suspicious manner that he brings about that very contempt in
others which "proves" again and again his firmly entrenched
conviction. This mechanism may be commonplace and well
known, but it is based upon a number of facts that are by no
means part of our everyday thinking and which have a profound significance for our view of reality.

In our traditional cause-and-effect thinking we usually see
event B as the result of a preceding, causal event (A)—which
in turn has, of course, its own causes, just as the occurrence
of B produces its own sequel of events. In the sequence $A \rightarrow$
B, A is therefore the cause and B its effect. The causality is
linear, and B follows A in the course of time. Accordingly, in
this causality model, B can have no effect on A, because this
would mean a reversal of the flow of time: The present (B)
would have to exert a backward effect on the past (A).

Matters stand differently in the following example: In March
1979, when the newspapers in California began to publish

---

*An original contribution, translated by Ursula Berg Lunk.

sensational pronouncements of an impending, severe gasoline shortage, California motorists stormed the gas stations
to fill up their tanks and to keep them as full as possible. This
filling up of 12 million gasoline tanks (which up to this time
had on the average been 75% empty) depleted the enormous
reserves and so brought about the predicted shortage practically over night. The endeavor to keep the fuel containers
as full as possible (instead of getting gas when the tank was
almost empty, as had been done before) resulted in endless
lines and hours of waiting time at the gas stations, and
increased the panic. After the excitement died down, it turned
out that the allotment of gasoline to the state of California
had hardly been reduced at all.

Here the customary cause-and-effect thinking breaks down.
The shortage would never have occurred if the media had not
predicted it. In other words, an event that had not yet taken
place (i.e., an event in the future) created an effect in the
present (the storming of the gas stations), which in turn
caused the predicted event to become reality. In this sense it
was the future—not the past—that determined the present.

The objection could be raised that all of this is neither
astonishing nor unheard of. Are not almost all human decisions and actions largely dependent on the evaluation of their
probable effects, advantages, and dangers (or at least should
they not be)? Does not the future therefore always play a part
in the present? Significant as these questions may be, they
do not seem to make much sense here. Whoever tries, usually on the basis of earlier experience, to evaluate the future
effect of his decision, normally intends the best possible outcome. The specific action tries to take the future into consideration, and subsequently proves to be true or false, correct
or incorrect; but it does not have to have any influence whatever on the course of events. However, an action that results
from a self-fulfilling prophecy itself produces the requisite
conditions for the occurrence of the expected event, and in
this sense *creates* a reality which would not have arisen without it. The action that is at first neither true nor false produces a fact, and with it its own "truth."

Here are examples of both perspectives: If someone begins

to suffer from headaches, sneezes, and shivers, he will, on the basis of past experience, assume that he is coming down with a cold; and if his diagnosis is correct, he can, with aspirin, hot drinks, and bedrest, favorably influence the (future) course of the illness by these means in the present. By doing so, he has correctly grasped a causal sequence that had at first been totally independent of him, and exerted a partial influence on it.

A fundamentally different sequence results from the practice of collecting taxes in certain countries. Since the revenue agency assumes *a priori* that no citizen will ever truthfully declare his income, the tax rate is dictated more or less arbitrarily. The revenue offices rely largely on the information of their assessment agents, who take into consideration such vague factors as a person's standard of living, his real estate property, the fur coats of his wife, the make of his car, and so forth. To the income, "ascertained" in this way, there is then added a certain percentage that is supposed to make up for any undeclared income, because—as we said—it is assumed *a priori* that the taxpayer cheats. This assumption, however, produces the situation in which a truthful declaration of income becomes unacceptable even for an honest taxpayer, and in which dishonesty is practically made a necessity if one wants to escape unfair taxes. Again an assumption believed to be true creates the assumed reality, and again it is irrelevant whether the assumption was originally true or false. And so we see that the difference lies in the fact that, in the example of the head cold, a development that is already taking place in the present is acted upon as best as is possible, and its course is influenced in this way in the present; whereas in the examples of the gasoline shortage and the income tax the course of events is induced by the very measures which are undertaken as a (supposed) reaction to the expected event in question. Therefore what is supposed to be a *reaction* (the effect) turns out to be an action (the cause); the "solution" produces the problem; the prophecy of the event causes the event of the prophecy.

This singular reversal of cause and effect is particularly obvious in interpersonal conflicts, where the phenomenon of the so-called *punctuation* of a sequence of events is invariably present. Making use of an example that has already been employed elsewhere [29], we will imagine a married couple struggling with a conflict that they both assume to be basically the other's fault, while their own behavior is seen only as a *reaction* to that of their partner. The woman complains that her husband is withdrawing from her, which he admits, but because he sees his silence or his leaving the room as the only possible reaction to her constant nagging and criticizing. For her this reasoning is a total distortion of the facts: His behavior is the *cause* of her criticism and her anger. Both partners are referring to the same interpersonal reality but assign to it a diametrically opposed causality. The following diagram, Figure 21, may illustrate this discrepancy, although it postulates—unavoidably but wrongly—a starting point that does not really exist, because the behavior pattern between the two people has been repeating itself for a long time, and the question of who started it has long since become meaningless.

The arrows with the solid lines represent the behavior of the husband ("withdraws"), and the dotted lines that of the wife ("nags"). The husband dissects ("punctuates") the whole of the pattern into the triads 2–3–4, 4–5–6, 6–7–8, and so on, and so sees the interpersonal reality as one in which his wife nags (cause) and he *therefore* withdraws from her (effect). From her point of view, however, it is his cold passivity (cause) that causes her nagging (effect); she criticizes him *because* he withdraws from her, and therefore punctuates the pattern into the triads 1–2–3, 3–4–5, 5–6–7, and so on. With this opposed punctuation, both have literally brought about two contradictory realities and—what is perhaps even more important—two self-fulfilling prophecies. The two modes of behavior, which are seen subjectively as a reaction to the behavior of the partner, cause this very behavior in the other and "therefore" justify one's own behavior.

It goes without saying that self-fulfilling prophecies in an interpersonal context can also be used deliberately and with a specific intent. The dangers of this practice will be discussed later on. As an example here let me only mention the

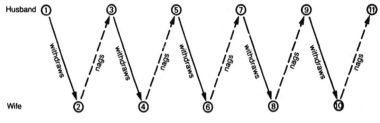

Figure 21

well-known method of former matchmakers in patriarchal societies, who had the thankless task of awakening a mutual interest in two young people, who possibly cared nothing for each other, because their families had decided that for financial reasons, social standing, or other similarly impersonal motives, the two would make a good couple. The matchmaker's usual procedure was to talk with the young man alone and ask him whether he had not noticed how the girl was always secretly watching him. Similarly, he would tell the girl that the boy was constantly looking at her when her head was turned. This prophecy, disguised as a fact, was often quickly fulfilled. Skilled diplomats also know this procedure as a negotiating technique.[1]

Everyday experience teaches us that only few prophecies are self-fulfilling, and the above examples should explain

---

[1]The following untrue story is a further illustration: In 1974, Secretary of State Kissinger, who is on one of his innumerable mediating missions in Jerusalem, is on his way back to the hotel after a private, late-evening stroll. A young Israeli stops him, introduces himself as an economist out of work, and asks Kissinger to help him find a job through his numerous connections. Kissinger is favorably impressed by the applicant and asks him whether he would like to be the vice-president of the Bank of Israel. The young man thinks of course that Kissinger is making fun of him, but the latter promises quite seriously that he will manage the matter for him. Next day Kissinger calls Baron Rothschild in Paris: "I have a charming young man here, a political economist, talented, going to be the next vice-president of the Bank of Israel. You have to meet him; he would be a jewel of a husband for your daughter." Rothschild growls something that does not sound like total rejection, whereupon Kissinger immediately calls the president of the Bank of Israel: "I have a young financial expert here, brilliant fellow, exactly the stuff to make a vice-president for your bank, and most of all—imagine *that*—he is the future son-in-law of Baron Rothschilds's."

why: Only when a prophecy is believed, that is, only when it is seen as a fact that has, so to speak, already happened in the future, can it have a tangible effect on the present and thereby fulfill itself. Where this element of belief or conviction is absent, this effect will be absent as well. To inquire how the construction or acceptance of such a prophecy comes to be would go far beyond the scope of this essay. (An extensive study of the social, psychological, and physiological effects of self-fulfilling prophecies was published in 1974 by Jones [14].) Too numerous and various are the factors involved—from the realities one fabricates for oneself during the course of the so-called noncontingent reward experiments [27] mentioned on p. 13, to such oddities as the (perhaps unverified, but not improbable) assertion that since Bernadette had a vision of the Virgin Mary in February of 1858, only pilgrims, but not a single inhabitant of Lourdes, found a miraculous cure there.

Of this story one can say, *se non è vero, è ben trovato,* since it helps to build a bridge from our previous, somewhat trivial reflections to manifestations of self-fulfilling prophecies that have a deeper human as well as scientific significance.

The oracle had prophesied that Oedipus would kill his father and marry his mother. Horrified by this prediction, which he undoubtedly believed to be true, Oedipus tries to protect himself from the impending doom, but the precautionary measures themselves lead to the seemingly inescapable fulfillment of the oracle's dictum. As is known, Freud used this myth as a metaphor for the incestuous attraction for the opposite sex inherent in every child, and the consequent fear of retaliation on the part of the parent of the same sex; and he saw in this key constellation, the Oedipus conflict, the fundamental cause of later neurotic developments. In his autobiography [17] the philosopher Karl Popper refers back to a self-fulfilling prophecy that he had already described two decades earlier and which he called the Oedipus *effect:*

> One of the ideas I had discussed in *The Poverty* [*of Historicism*] was the influence of a prediction upon the event predicted. I had called this the "Oedipus effect," because the oracle played a most

important role in the sequence of events which led to the fulfil-
ment of its prophecy. (It was also an allusion to the psychoana-
lysts, who had been strangely blind to this interesting fact, even
though Freud himself admitted that the very dreams dreamt by
patients were often coloured by the theories of their analysts;
Freud called them "obliging dreams.")

Again we have the reversal of cause and effect, past and
future; but here it is all the more critical and decisive because
psychoanalysis is a theory of human behavior that hinges on
the assumption of a linear causality, in which the past determines the present. And Popper points to the significance of
this reversal by explicating further:

> For a time I thought that the existence of the Oedipus effect dis-
> tinguished the social from the natural sciences. But in biology
> too—even in molecular biology—expectations often play a role
> in bringing about what has been expected.

Similar quotations, referring to the effect of such "unscientific" factors as simple expectations and assumptions in the
sciences, could be collated in abundance—the book in hand
is itself intended as such a contribution. In this connection
one might recall, for instance, Einstein's remark in a talk with
Heisenberg: "It is the theory that determines what we can
observe." And in 1959 Heisenberg himself says, "We have
to remember that what we observe is not nature in itself, but
nature exposed to our method of questioning" [11]. And more
radical still, the philosopher of science Feyerabend: "Not
conservative, but anticipatory suppositions guide research"
[7].

Some of the most carefully documented and elegant investigations of self-fulfilling prophecies in the area of human
communication are associated with the name of the psychologist Robert Rosenthal of Harvard University. Of particular
interest here is his book with the appropriate title *Pygmalion
in the Classroom* [19], in which he describes the results of his
so-called Oak School experiments. They concerned a primary
school with 18 women teachers and over 650 students. The
self-fulfilling prophecy was induced in the members of the

faculty at the beginning of a certain school year by giving the students an intelligence test whereby the teachers were told that the test could not only determine intelligence quotients, but could also identify those 20% of the students who would make rapid and above-average intellectual progress in the coming school year. After the intelligence test had been administered, but before the teachers had met their new students for the first time, they received the names (indiscriminately picked from the student list) of those students who supposedly, on the basis of the test, could be expected with certainty to perform unusually well. The difference between these children and the others thus existed solely in the heads of their particular teacher. The same intelligence test was repeated at the end of the school year for all students and showed *real* above-average increases in the intelligence quotients and achievements of these "special" students, and the reports of the faculty proved furthermore that these children distinguished themselves from their fellow students by their behavior, intellectual curiosity, friendliness, and so on.

Saint Augustine thanked God that he was not responsible for his dreams. Nowadays we do not have this comfort. Rosenthal's experiment is only one, although especially clear example of how deeply and incisively our fellow human beings are affected by our expectations, prejudices, superstitions, and wishful thinking—all purely mental constructions, often without the slightest glimmer of actuality—and how these discoveries erode our comfortable conviction of the surpassing importance of heredity and innate characteristics. For it hardly needs to be expressly emphasized that these constructions can have negative as well as positive effects. We are not only responsible for our dreams, but also for the reality created by our hopes and thoughts.

It would, however, be a mistake to assume that self-fulfilling prophecies are restricted to human beings. Their effects reach deeper, into prehuman stages of development, and are in this sense even more alarming. Even before Rosenthal carried out his Oak School experiment, he reported in a book [18] published in 1966 a similar experiment with rats that was repeated and confirmed by many scholars in the following years. Twelve participants in a laboratory course in experimental psychology were given a lecture on certain studies that purported to prove that good or bad test achievements of rats (for instance, in learning experiments in labyrinth cages) can become innate by selective breeding. Six of the students then received thirty rats whose genetic constitution allegedly made them especially good, intelligent laboratory subjects, while the other six students were assigned thirty rats of whom they were told the opposite, namely, that they were animals whose hereditary factors made them unsuitable for experiments. In fact and truth, the sixty rats were all of the same kind, the one that has always been used for such purposes. All sixty animals were then trained for exactly the same learning experiment. The rats whose trainers believed them to be especially intelligent did not just do better from the very outset, but raised their achievements far above that of the "unintelligent" animals. At the end of the five-day experiment the trainers were asked to evaluate their animals subjectively, in addition to the noted results of the experiments. The students who "knew" that they were working with unintelligent animals expressed themselves accordingly, that is, negatively, in their reports, whereas their colleagues, who had experimented with rats of supposedly above-average talents, rated their charges as friendly, intelligent, ingenious, and the like, and mentioned furthermore that they had often touched the animals, petted them, and even played with them. When we consider the surpassing role rat experiments play in experimental psychology and especially in the psychology of learning, and how often inferences are drawn from them to human behavior, these inferences now seem somewhat questionable.

Rats are known to be very intelligent animals, and the students' reports suggest that in the way they handled their animals, they literally "handed" them their assumptions and expectations. But the results of another research project, reported in 1963 by the research team Cordaro and Ison [5], suggest that it is not only a matter of such direct influence. In this project the laboratory subjects were earthworms (*planaria*), who are of great interest for the student of evolution and of behavior alike, in that they are the most primitive form of life possessing the rudiments of a brain. The supposition therefore suggested itself that these worms were capable of training of the simplest kind, as, for instance, a change in direction (to the left or to the right) upon arriving at the crossbeam of a T-shaped groove arrangement. Experiments of this kind began in several American universities in the late fifties. As in the rat experiments, Cordaro and Ison caused the experimenters to believe that they were working with especially intelligent or especially incapable worms, and even here, at this primitive stage of development (which, moreover, left little room for emotional attachment), there grew from the conviction, once it was established, objectively discernible and statistically significant differences in the experimental behavior of the planaria.[2]

For the very reason that these experiments undermine our basic concepts, it is all too easy to shrug them off and return to the comfortable certainty of our accustomed routines. That, for instance, test psychologists ignore these extremely disturbing results and continue to test people and animals with unmitigated tenacity and scientific "objectivity" is only a small example of the determination with which we defend ourselves when our world view is being threatened. The fact that we are responsible to the world in its entirety and to a much higher degree than is dreamed of in our philosophy is

---

[2]Here I will briefly mention an interesting sequel to these experiments: For reasons irrelevant to our topic, several researchers [15] studied the fascinating theory that at the planaria's primitive stage of development, information stored in a worm's ribonucleic acid (RNA) could possibly be directly transferred to other worms. For this purpose they fed untrained animals their already successfully trained fellow worms. Even we laymen can imagine the sensation among experts when the training of the worms provided with such food actually turned out to be much easier and faster. The euphoria lasted for a short while until the experiments, repeated under more rigorous controls, showed themselves to be inconclusive, and serious doubts arose concerning the transferability of intelligence through ground meat. The suspicion suggests itself, but was, as far as I know, never proven, that the original results were due to self-fulfilling prophecies, similar to those whose effect on the worms were already known. (The analogy, however, to the superstition of certain African tribes that eating a lion's heart will confer the lion's courage cannot be dismissed out of hand.)

for the present almost unthinkable; but it can penetrate our consciousness through a better understanding of the processes of human communication—a study that will encompass many disciplines that heretofore have been either considered as being quite independent of each other or not considered at all. Rosenhan's contribution to this book (p. 117 ff.) illuminates the alarming possibility that at least some so-called mental illnesses are nothing but constructions, and that the psychiatric institutions actually contribute to the constructions of those realities that are supposed to be treated therein. The chronic problem that still plagues modern psychiatry is that we have only the vaguest and most general concepts for the definition of mental health, while for the diagnosis of abnormal behavior there exist catalogs perfected to the last detail. Freud, for instance, used the concept of the ability to love and work as a basic criterion for mature emotional normalcy (a definition that does not do justice to a Hitler, on the one hand, or to the proverbial eccentricities of men of genius, on the other). The other medical specialties work with definitions of pathology that refer to certain deviations from fairly well-known normal functions of the healthy organism. Quite irrationally, in psychiatry it is just the opposite. Here pathology is considered the known factor, whereas normalcy is seen as difficult to define, if it is definable at all. This opens the floodgates to self-fulfilling diagnoses. There is a great number of very definite patterns of behavior that in the terminology of psychiatry are so tightly associated with certain diagnostic categories (again I refer to Rosenhan) that they virtually function like Pavlovian buzzers, not only in the thinking of the psychiatrist but also in the family environment of the patient. An attempt to show how certain specific forms of behavior take on the meaning of pathological manifestations on the basis of their cultural and societal significance, and how these manifestations in turn become self-fulfilling prophecies, would go beyond the scope of this essay. Of the already quite extensive literature on this topic, *The Manufacture of Madness* [26] by Thomas Szasz is particularly notable. Suffice it to say that an essential part of the self-fulfilling effect of psychiatric diagnoses is based on our unshakable conviction that everything that has a name must *therefore* actually exist. The materializations and actualizations of psychiatric diagnoses probably originate largely from this conviction.

"Magic" diagnoses, in the actual sense of the word, have of course been known for a very long time. In his classic paper "Voodoo Death" [4], the American physiologist Walter Cannon described a number of mysterious, sudden, and scientifically difficult to explain deaths that followed curses, evil spells, or the breaking of moral taboos. A Brazilian Indian, cursed by a medicine man, is helpless against his own emotional response to this death sentence and dies within hours. A young African hunter unknowingly kills and eats an inviolably banned wild hen. When he discovers his crime, he is overcome with despair and dies within twenty-four hours. A medicine man in the Australian bush points a bone with magic properties at a man. Believing that nothing can save him, the man sinks into lethargy and prepares to die. He is saved only at the last moment, when other members of the tribe force the witch doctor to remove the spell.

Cannon became convinced that voodoo death exists as a phenomenon,

> characteristically noted among aborigines—among human beings so primitive, so superstitious, so ignorant, that they feel themselves bewildered strangers in a hostile world. Instead of knowledge, they have fertile and unrestricted imaginations which fill their environment with all manner of evil spirits capable of affecting their lives disastrously.

At the time when Cannon wrote these lines, hundreds of thousands of human beings who were neither superstitious nor ignorant had every reason to see themselves as bewildered victims of an unimaginably hostile world. From the haunted, shadowy world of the concentration camps Viktor Frankl [8] reports a phenomenon that corresponds to voodoo death:

> The prisoner who had lost faith in the future—his future—was doomed. With his loss of belief in the future, he also lost his

spiritual hold; he let himself decline and became subject to mental and physical decay. Usually this happened quite suddenly, in the form of a crisis, the symptoms of which were familiar to the experienced camp inmate. We all feared this moment—not for ourselves, which would have been pointless, but for our friends. Usually it began with the prisoner refusing one morning to get dressed and wash or to go out on the parade grounds. No entreaties, no blows, no threats had any effect. He just lay there.

One of Frankl's fellow prisoners lost his will to live when his own prediction, seen in a dream, did not come true and thereby became a negative self-fulfillment. "I would like to tell you something, Doctor," he said to Frankl,

I have had a strange dream. A voice told me that I could wish for something, that I should only say what I wanted to know, and all my questions would be answered. What do you think I asked? That I would like to know when the war would be over for me. You know what I mean, Doctor—for me! I wanted to know when we, when our camp, would be liberated and our sufferings come to an end. . . . Furtively he whispered to me, "March thirtieth."

But when the day of the prophesied liberation was near and the Allied forces were still far from the camp, things took a fateful turn for Frankl's fellow sufferer, the prisoner F.:

On March twenty-ninth, F. suddenly became ill and ran a high temperature. On March thirtieth, the day his prophecy had told him that the war and suffering would be over for him, he became delirious and lost consciousness. On March thirty-first, he was dead. He had died of typhus.

As a physician, Frankl understood that his friend died because

the expected liberation did not come and he was severely disappointed. This suddenly lowered his body's resistance against the latent typhus infection.

We admire human beings who face death calmly. Dying "decently," in a composed manner, without wrangling with the inevitable, was and is considered in most cultures an expression of wisdom and unusual maturity. All the more surprising and sobering therefore are the results of modern cancer research, which suggest that the mortality rate is higher in those patients who prepare themselves for death in a mature, serene way or who, like the concentration camp prisoner F., fall victim to a negative self-fulfilling prophecy. For those patients, however, who cling to life in a seemingly senseless, irrational, and immature way or who are convinced that they simply "cannot" or "must not" die because they have important work to do or family members to take care of, the prognosis is considerably more favorable. To the American oncologist Carl Simonton, whose name is associated, above all, with the appreciation of the impact of emotional factors, now more and more recognized for their importance in the treatment of cancer, three things are of the utmost significance in this connection: the belief system of the patient, that of the patient's family, and, third, that of the attending physician [21]. That each one of these belief systems can become a self-fulfilling prophecy seems credible in the light of what we have discussed so far. Furthermore, the studies and research reports about the susceptibility of the human immune system to mood swings, suggestions, and visual imagery [22,23] are increasing.

How much can and should a physician tell his patients, not only about the gravity of their illnesses, but also about the dangers inherent in the treatment *itself*? At least in certain countries this question is becoming more and more rhetorical. The risk of getting hit with a malpractice suit because a patient has not been informed about his disease and its treatment down to the last technical detail causes many doctors in the United States, for example, to protect themselves in a way that can have serious consequences. The protection consists in asking the patient for a written consent to treatment in which the most catastrophic possible consequences of the illness and of the measures deemed necessary by the doctor are listed in every detail. It is not hard to imagine that this creates a kind of self-fulfilling prophecy that has a paralyzing effect on the confidence and will to recover of even the most sanguine patient. Who has not read the description of even a seemingly harmless medication and then had the feeling of swallowing poison? How does the layman (or, presumably, even the professional) know that he is not going to be the fourth of the three fatalities reported to date that were inexplicably caused by a medication so far used safely by millions? But *fiat justitia, pereat mundus.*

Since in the patient's eye a doctor is a kind of mediator between life and death, his utterances can easily become self-fulfilling prophecies. The astonishing degree to which this is possible is portrayed in a case reported (but unfortunately not sufficiently documented) by the American psychologist Gordon Allport. What is unusual here is that a misunderstanding shifted the prophecy from death to life:

> In a provincial Austrian hospital, a man lay gravely ill—in fact, at death's door. The medical staff had told him frankly that they could not diagnose his disease, but that if they knew the diagnosis they could probably cure him. They told him further that a famous diagnostician was soon to visit the hospital and that perhaps he could spot the trouble.
>
> Within a few days the diagnostician arrived and proceeded to make the rounds. Coming to this man's bed, he merely glanced at the patient, murmured, "Moribundus," and went on.
>
> Some years later, the patient called on the diagnostician and said, "I've been wanting to thank you for your diagnosis. They told me that if you could diagnose me I'd get well, and so the minute you said 'moribundus' I knew I'd recover" [1].

Knowledge of the healing effect of positive predictions is undoubtedly just as ancient as faith in the inescapable consequences of curses and evil spells. Modern knowing use of positive suggestions and autosuggestions ranges from the "I will recover; I feel better every day" of Emile Coué, through numerous forms of hypnotherapeutic interventions [10], to influencing the course of an illness—and not only cancer— by positive imagery. The extent to which such imagery that a (future) event has already taken place can reach into the physical realm is suggested by several studies according to which it is possible to increase a woman's chest measurement by an average of four to five centimeters through the use of certain self-hypnotic techniques [24,31]. I mention these "successes" with all due skepticism and simply as curiosities testifying to the towering importance of the female breast in the North American erotic ethos.

Brief mention should also be made of the modern physiological and endocrinological studies that indicate more and more the possibility of stimulating the functions of the immune system of the human organism by certain experiences and that these functions are by no means completely autonomous (that is, outside conscious control), as was assumed until quite recently. Medical research is likely to make astonishing discoveries in this field in the near future. For instance, it is now known that the organism itself produces a number of morphium-like substances—the so-called endorphins [2]—that are analgesic and whose production is stimulated by certain emotional processes. There is thus a wide-open, unexplored territory in which the phenomenon of self-fulfilling prophecies begins to achieve scientific respectability.

Just as decisive as a doctor's suggestive comments, expectations, and convictions are the measures he takes and the remedies he administers. Of special interest here are *placebos*[3] [3], those chemically inert substances that resemble certain medicines in shape, taste, or color but which have no pharmaceutical effect. We must remember that until about 100 years ago nearly all medications were practically ineffective in the modern sense. They were only slightly more elegant tinctures and powders than the ground toads, the lizard blood, the "sacred oils," or the pulverized horn of the rhinoceros of even earlier times. During my childhood, people in the rural areas of Austria still believed that a necklace of garlic would protect them from the common cold, to say nothing about the well-known success of magic in the treatment of warts. Even in our time, old "tried and true" remedies or sensational new discoveries (as, for example, Laetrile) are always being unmasked as pharmaceutically ineffective.

---

[3]Latin for "I shall please."

But that is not to say that they were or are *functionally* ineffective. "One should treat as many patients as possible with the new remedies, as long as these are still working," reads the maxim of a famous physician, attributed to Trousseau, Osler, or Sydenham. Scientific interest in placebos is rapidly increasing. In his contribution to the history of the placebo effect Shapiro [20] points out that more articles on this topic were published in scientific journals between 1954 and 1957 alone than in the first fifty years of the twentieth century. Most of these reports discuss traditional pharmaceutical effectiveness studies, in which one group of patients receives the new medication while another takes a placebo. The purpose of this well-meaning procedure is to find out whether the course of the illness of the "actually" treated patients is different from that of the placebo group. Only people whose world view is based on classical linear causal thinking (for which there is only an "objective" relationship between cause and effect) react with consternation when they realize that the patients "treated" with placebos often show a quite "inexplicable" improvement in their condition. In other words, the claim of the doctor who administers the placebo that it is an effective, newly developed medicine and the patient's willingness to believe in its effectiveness create a reality in which the assumption actually becomes a fact.

Enough examples. Self-fulfilling prophecies are phenomena that not only shake up our personal conception of reality, but which can also throw doubt on the world view of science. They all share the obviously reality-creating power of a firm belief in the "suchness" of things, a faith that can be a superstition as well as a seemingly strictly scientific theory derived from objective observation. Until recently it has been possible to categorically reject self-fulfilling prophecies as unscientific or to ascribe them to the inadequate reality adaptation of muddle-headed thinkers and romanticists, but we no longer have this convenient escape hatch open to us.

What all this means cannot yet be appraised with any certainty. The discovery that we create our own realities is comparable to the expulsion from the paradise of the presumed suchness of the world, a world in which we can certainly suffer, but for which we need only feel responsible in a very limited way [27].

And here lies the danger. The insights of constructivism may have the highly desirable advantage of allowing for new and more effective forms of therapy [28], but like all remedies, they can also be abused. Advertising and propaganda are two especially repugnant examples: Both try quite deliberately to bring about attitudes, assumptions, prejudices, and the like, whose realization then seems to follow naturally and logically. Thanks to this brainwashing, the world is then seen as "thus" and therefore *is* "thus." In the novel *1984* [16] this reality-creating propaganda language is called *Newspeak*, and Orwell explains that it "makes all other modes of thinking impossible." In a recent review of a volume of essays published in London on censorship in the People's Republic of Poland [25], Daniel Weiss writes about this magic language:

> Compare for example the great number of adjectives, characteristic for Newspeak: Every development is nothing less than "dynamic," every plenary session of the party "historic," the masses always "proletarian workers." A sober communication scientist will find nothing but *redundance* in this inflation of mechanized epithets, drained of meaning. But after listening repeatedly, this automation is felt to have the equality of an incantation: The spoken word is no longer used to carry information, it has become the instrument of magic [30].

And finally the world simply *is thus.* How it was *made* to be this way was well known to Joseph Goebbels, when he lectured the managers of German radio stations on March 25, 1933:

> This is the secret of propaganda: To totally saturate the person, whom the propaganda wants to lay hold of, with the ideas of the propaganda, without him even noticing that he is being saturated. Propaganda has of course a purpose, but this purpose must be disguised with such shrewdness and virtuosity that he who is supposed to be filled with this purpose never even knows what is happening [9].

In the necessity of disguising the purpose, however, lies the possibility of overcoming it. As we have seen, the invented reality will become "actual" reality only if the invention is believed. Where the element of faith, of blind conviction, is absent, there will be no effect. With the better understanding of self-fulfilling prophecies our ability to transcend them grows. A prophecy that we know to be only a prophecy can no longer fulfill itself. The possibility of choosing differently (of being a heretic) and of disobeying always exists; whether we see it and act on it is, of course, another question. An insight from the seemingly far-removed domain of the mathematical theory of games is of interest here. Wittgenstein already pointed out in his *Remarks on the Foundations of Mathematics* [32] that certain games can be won with a simple trick. As soon as someone calls our attention to the existence of this trick, we no longer have to continue playing naively (and continue losing). Building on these reflections, the mathematician Howard formulated his *existential axiom* which maintains that "if a person becomes 'aware' of a theory concerning his behavior, he is no longer bound by it but is free to disobey it" [12]. Elsewhere he also says that

> a conscious decision maker can always choose to disobey any theory predicting his behavior. We may say that he can always "transcend" such a theory. This indeed seems realistic. We suggest that among socio-economic theories, Marxian theory, for example, failed at least partly because certain ruling class members, when they became aware of the theory, saw that it was in their interest to disobey it [13].

And almost a hundred years before Howard, Dostoevski's underground man writes in his *Letters from the Underworld,*

> As a matter of fact, if ever there shall be discovered a formula which shall exactly express our wills and whims; if ever there shall be discovered a formula which shall make it absolutely clear what those wills depend upon, and what laws they are governed by, and what means of diffusion they possess, and what tend-

encies they follow under given circumstances; if ever there shall be discovered a formula which shall be mathematical in its precision, well, gentlemen, whenever such a formula shall be found, man will have ceased to have a will of his own—he will have ceased even to exist. Who would care to exercise his willpower according to a table of logarithms? In such a case man would become, not a human being at all, but an organ-handle, or something of the kind [6].

But even if this kind of mathematical formulization of our lives could ever be achieved, it would in no way comprehend the complexity of our existence. The best theory is powerless in the face of an antitheory; the fulfillment of even the truest prophecy can be thwarted if we know about it beforehand. Dostoevski saw much more in the nature of man:

Moreover, even if man *were* the keyboard of a piano, and could be convinced that the laws of nature and of mathematics had made him so, he would still decline to change. On the contrary, he would once more, out of sheer ingratitude, attempt the perpetration of something which would enable him to insist upon himself. . . . But if you were to tell me that all this could be set down in tables—I mean the chaos, and the confusion, and the curses, and all the rest of it—so that the possibility of computing everything might remain, and reason continue to rule the roost— well, in that case, I believe, man would *purposely* become a lunatic, in order to become devoid of reason, and therefore able to insist upon himself. I believe this, and I am ready to vouch for this, simply for the reason that every human act arises out of the circumstance that man is for ever striving to prove to his own satisfaction that he is a man and not an organ-handle [6].

However, even the evidence of the underground man is likely to be a self-fulfilling prophecy.

REFERENCES

1. Allport, Gordon W. Mental health: A generic attitude. *Journal of Religion and Health* 4, 1964, 7–21.
2. Beers, Roland F. (ed.). *Mechanisms of Pain and Analgesic Compounds.* Raven Press, New York, 1979.

3. Benson, Herbert, and Epstein, Mark D. The placebo effect: A neglected asset in the care of patients. *American Medical Association Journal* 232, 1975, 1225–1227.
4. Cannon, Walter B. Voodoo death. *American Anthropologist* 44, 1942, 169–181.
5. Cordaro, L. and Ison, J. R. Observer bias in classical conditioning of the planaria. *Psychological Reports* 13, 1963, 787–789.
6. Dostoevski, Feodor M. *Letters from the Underworld.* E. P. Dutton, New York, 1913, pp. 32, 37.
7. Feyerabend, Paul K. *Science in a Free Society.* New Left Books, London, 1978.
8. Frankl, Viktor E. *From Death Camp to Existentialism.* Beacon Press, Boston, 1959, pp. 74–75.
9. Goebbels, Joseph. Quoted in Schneider, Wolf, *Wörter machen Leute. Magie und Macht der Sprache.* Piper, Munich, 1976, p. 120.
10. Haley, Jay. *Uncommon Therapy. The Psychiatric Techniques of Milton H. Erickson, MD.* W. W. Norton, New York, 1973.
11. Heisenberg, Werner. *Physics and Philosophy: The Revolution in Modern Science.* Harper, New York, 1958.
12. Howard, Nigel. The theory of metagames. *General Systems* 2, 1967, 167.
13. Howard, Nigel. *Paradoxes of Rationality, Theory of Metagames and Political Behavior.* MIT Press, Cambridge, Massachusetts, 1971.
14. Jones, Russell A. *Self-Fulfilling Prophecies: Social, Psychological and Physiological Effects of Expectancies.* Halsted, New York, 1974.
15. McConnell, James V., Jacobson, Reva, and Humphries, Barbara M. The effects of ingestion of conditioned planaria on the response level of naive planaria: A pilot study. *Worm Runner's Digest* 3, 1961, 41–45.
16. Orwell, George *1984.* Harcourt, Brace, New York, 1949.
17. Popper, Karl R. *Unended Quest.* Open Court, La Salle, Illinois, 1974.
18. Rosenthal, Robert. *Experimenter Effects in Behavioral Research.* Appleton-Century-Crofts, New York, 1966.
19. Rosenthal, Robert, and Jacobson, Leonore. *Pygmalion in the Classroom: Teacher Expectation and Pupils' Intellectual Development.* Holt, Rinehart, and Winston, New York, 1968.
20. Shapiro, Arthur K. A contribution to a history of the placebo effects. *Behavioral Science* 5, 1960, 109–135.
21. Simonton, O. Carl, and Simonton, Stephanie. Belief systems and management of the emotional aspects of malignancy. *Journal of Transpersonal Psychology* 1, 1975, 29–47.
22. Simonton, O. Carl, and Simonton, Stephanie. *Getting Well Again.* J. P. Tarcher, Los Angeles, 1978.
23. Solomon, G. F. Emotions, stress, the nervous system, and immunity. *Annals of the New York Academy of Sciences* 164, 1969, 335–343.
24. Staib, Allan R., and Logan D. R. Hypnotic stimulation of breast growth. *American Journal of Clinical Hypnosis* 19, 1977, 201–208.
25. Strzyzewski, Tomasz. *Czarna ksiega cenzury PRL* (Black Book of Polish Censorship. "Aneks," London, Vol. 1, 1977; Vol. 2, 1978.
26. Szasz, Thomas S. *The Manufacture of Madness: A Comparative Study of the Inquisition and the Mental Health Movement.* Harper and Row, New York, 1970.
27. Watzlawick, Paul. *How Real Is Real?* Random House, New York, 1976, pp. 45–54.

28. Watzlawick, Paul. *The Language of Change: Elements of Therapeutic Communication.* Basic Books, New York, 1978.
29. Watzlawick, Paul, Bavelas, Janet B., and Jackson, Don D. *Pragmatics of Human Communication: A Study of Interactional Patterns, Pathologies and Paradoxes.* W. W. Norton, New York, 1967, pp. 56–58.
30. Weiss, Daniel. Sprache und Propaganda—Der Sonderfall Polen. *Neue Zürcher Zeitung* 39, 1980, 66.
31. Willard, Richard R. Breast enlargement through visual imagery and hypnosis. *American Journal of Clinical Hypnosis* 19, 1977, 195–200.
32. Wittgenstein, Ludwig. *Remarks on the Foundations of Mathematics.* Blackwell, Oxford, 1956, p. 100.

DAVID L. ROSENHAN

On Being Sane
in Insane Places*

I F SANITY AND insanity exist, how shall we know them?
The question is neither capricious nor itself insane. However much we may be personally convinced that we can tell
the normal from the abnormal, the evidence is simply not
compelling. It is commonplace, for example, to read about
murder trials wherein eminent psychiatrists for the defense
are contradicted by equally eminent psychiatrists for the
prosecution on the matter of the defendant's sanity. More
generally, there are a great deal of conflicting data on the
reliability, utility, and meaning of such terms as *sanity,
insanity, mental illness,* and *schizophrenia* [3,5,9,25,26,33,39,41].
Finally, as early as 1934, Benedict [8] suggested that normality and abnormality are not universal. What is viewed as
normal in one culture may be seen as quite aberrant in
another. Thus notions of normality and abnormality may not
be quite as accurate as people believe they are.

To raise questions regarding normality and abnormality is
in no way to question the fact that some behaviors are deviant
or odd. Murder is deviant. So, too, are hallucinations. Nor
does raising such questions deny the existence of the personal anguish that is often associated with "mental illness."

*This article is a slightly expanded version of a paper of the same title
originally published in *Science* 179, 19 January 1973, pp. 250–258. I thank
W. Mischel, E. Orne, and M. S. Rosenhan for comments on an earlier
draft of this manuscript.

Anxiety and depression exist. Psychological suffering exists. But normality and abnormality, sanity and insanity, and the diagnoses that flow from them may be less substantive than many believe them to be.

At its heart, the question of whether the sane can be distinguished from the insane (and whether degrees of insanity can be distinguished from each other) is a simple matter: Do the salient characteristics that lead to diagnoses reside in the patients themselves or in the environments and contexts in which observers find them? From Bleuler, through Kretschmer, through the formulators of the recently revised *Diagnostic and Statistical Manual* of the American Psychiatric Association, the belief has been strong that patients present symptoms, that those symptoms can be categorized, and, implicitly, that the sane are distinguishable from the insane. More recently, however, this belief has been questioned. Based in part on theoretical and anthropological considerations, but also on philosophical, legal, and therapeutic ones, the view has grown that psychological categorization of mental illness is useless at best and downright harmful, misleading, and pejorative at worst. Psychiatric diagnoses, in this view, are in the minds of the observers and are not valid summaries of characteristics displayed by the observed [8, 10,14,19,20,22,27,32,36,38,43,44].

Gains can be made in deciding which of these is more nearly accurate by getting normal people (that is, people who do not have and have never suffered symptoms of serious psychiatric disorders) admitted to psychiatric hospitals and then determining whether they were discovered to be sane and, if so, how. If the sanity of such pseudopatients were always detected, there would be prima facie evidence that a sane individual can be distinguished from the insane context in which he is found. Normality (and presumably abnormality) is distinct enough that it can be recognized wherever it occurs, for it is carried within the person. If, on the other hand, the sanity of the pseudopatients were never discovered, serious difficulties would arise for those who support traditional modes of psychiatric diagnosis. Given that the hospital staff was not incompetent, that the pseudopatient had been behaving as sanely as he had been outside of the hospital, and that it had never been previously suggested that he belonged in a psychiatric hospital, such an unlikely outcome would support the view that psychiatric diagnosis betrays little about the patient, but much about the environment in which an observer finds him.

This article describes such an experiment. Eight sane people gained secret admission to twelve different hospitals.[1] Their diagnostic experiences constitute the data of the first part of this article; the remainder is devoted to a description of their experiences in psychiatric institutions. Too few psychiatrists and psychologists, even those who have worked in such hospitals, know what the experience is like. They rarely talk about it with former patients, perhaps because they distrust information coming from the previously insane. Those who have worked in psychiatric hospitals are likely to have adapted so thoroughly to the settings that they are insensitive to the impact of that experience. And while there have been occasional reports of researchers who submitted themselves to psychiatric hospitalization [4,7,13,21], these researchers have commonly remained in the hospitals for short periods of time, often with the knowledge of the hospital staff. It is difficult to know the extent to which they were treated like patients or like research colleagues. Nevertheless, their reports about the inside of the psychiatric hospital have been valuable. This article extends those efforts.

Pseudopatients and Their Settings

The eight pseudopatients were a varied group. One was a psychology graduate student in his 20s. The remaining seven were older and "established." Among them were three psychologists, a pediatrician, a psychiatrist, a painter, and a housewife. Three pseudopatients were women, five were

---

[1]Data from a ninth pseudopatient are not incorporated in this report because, although his sanity went undetected, he falsified aspects of his personal history, including his marital status and parental relationships. His experimental behaviors therefore were not identical to those of the other pseudopatients.

men. All of them employed pseudonyms, lest their alleged diagnoses embarass them later. Those who were in mental health professions alleged another occupation in order to avoid the special attentions that might be accorded by staff, as a matter of courtesy or caution, to ailing colleagues.[2] With the exception of myself (I was the first pseudopatient and my presence was known to the hospital administrator and chief psychologist and, so far as I can tell, to them alone), the presence of pseudopatients and the nature of the research program was not known to the hospital staffs.[3]

The settings were similarly varied. In order to generalize the findings, admission into a variety of hospitals was sought. The twelve hospitals in the sample were located in five different states on the East and West coasts. Some were old and shabby, some were quite new; some were research oriented, others not; some had good staff–patient ratios, others were quite understaffed. Only one was a strictly private hospital; all of the others were supported by state or federal funds or, in one instance, by university funds.

After calling the hospital for an appointment, the pseudopatient arrived at the admissions office complaining that he had been hearing voices. Asked what the voices said, he replied that they were often unclear, but as far as he could tell they said "empty," "hollow," and "thud." The voices

---

[2]Beyond the personal difficulties that the pseudopatient is likely to experience in the hospital, there are legal and social ones that, combined, require considerable attention before entry. For example, once admitted to a psychiatric institution, it is difficult, if not impossible, to be discharged on short notice, state law to the contrary notwithstanding. I was not sensitive to these difficulties at the outset of the project, nor to the personal and situational emergencies that can arise, but later a writ of habeas corpus was prepared for each of the entering pseudopatients and an attorney was kept "on call" during every hospitalization. I am grateful to John Kaplan and Robert Bartels for legal advice and assistance in these matters.

[3]However distasteful such concealment is, it was a necessary first step to examining these questions. Without concealment, there would have been no way to know how valid these experiences were; nor was there any way of knowing whether whatever detections occurred were a tribute to the diagnostic acumen of the staff or to the hospital's rumor network. Obviously, since my concerns are general ones that cut across individual hospitals and staffs, I have respected their anonymity and have eliminated clues that might lead to their identification.

were unfamiliar and were of the same sex as the pseudopatient. The choice of these symptoms was occasioned by their
apparent similarity to existential symptoms. Such symptoms
are alleged to arise from painful concerns about the perceived meaninglessness of one's life. It is as if the hallucinat-
ing person were saying, "My life is empty and hollow." The
choice of these symptoms was also determined by the *absence*
of a single report of existential psychoses in the literature.

Beyond alleging the symptoms and falsifying name, vocation, and employment, no further alterations of person, history, or circumstances were made. The significant events
of the pseudopatient's life history were presented as they
had actually occurred. Relationships with parents and sib-
lings, with spouse and children, with people at work and in
school, consistent with the aforementioned exceptions, were
described as they were or had been. Frustrations and upsets
were described along with joys and satisfactions. These facts
are important to remember. If anything, they strongly biased
the subsequent results in favor of detecting sanity, since none
of their histories or current behaviors were seriously pathological in any way.

Immediately upon admission to the psychiatric ward, the
pseudopatient ceased simulating *any* symptoms of abnormality. In some cases, there was a brief period of mild nervousness and anxiety, since none of the pseudopatients really
believed that they would be admitted so easily. Indeed, their
shared fear was that they would be immediately exposed as
frauds and greatly embarrassed. Moreover, many of them had
never visited a psychiatric ward; even those who had nevertheless had some genuine fears about what might happen to
them. Their nervousness, then, was quite appropriate to the
novelty of the hospital setting, and it abated rapidly.

Apart from that short-lived nervousness, the pseudopatient behaved on the ward as he "normally" behaved. The
pseudopatient spoke to patients and staff as he might ordinarily. Because there is uncommonly little to do on a psychiatric ward, he attempted to engage others in conversation.
When asked by staff how he was feeling, he indicated that
he was fine, that he no longer experienced symptoms. He

responded to instructions from attendants, to calls for medication (which was not swallowed), and to dining-hall instructions. Beyond such activities as were available to him on the admissions ward, he spent his time writing down his observations about the ward, its patients, and the staff. Initially these notes were written "secretly," but as it soon became clear that no one much cared, they were subsequently written on standard tablets of paper in such public places as the dayroom. No secret was made of these activities.

The pseudopatient, very much as a true psychiatric patient, entered a hospital with no foreknowledge of when he would be discharged. Each was told that he would have to get out by his own devices, especially by convincing the staff that he was sane. The psychological stresses associated with hospitalization were considerable, and all but one of the pseudopatients desired to be discharged almost immediately after being admitted. They were, therefore, motivated not only to behave sanely, but to be paragons of cooperation. That their behavior was in no way disruptive is confirmed by nursing reports, which have been obtained on most of the patients. These reports uniformly indicate that the patients were "friendly," "cooperative," and "exhibited no abnormal indications."

The Normal Are Not Detectably Sane

Despite their public "show" of sanity, the pseudopatients were never detected. Admitted, except in one case, with a diagnosis of schizophrenia,[4] each was discharged with a diagnosis of schizophrenia "in remission." The label *in remission* should in no way be dismissed as a formality, for at no time during any hospitalization had any question been

---

[4]Interestingly, of the twelve admissions, eleven were diagnosed as schizophrenic and one, with the identical symptomatology, as manic-depressive psychosis. This diagnosis has a more favorable prognosis, and it was given by the only private hospital in our sample. On the relations between social class and psychiatric diagnosis, see Hollingshead and Redlich [23].

raised about any pseudopatient's simulation. Nor are there any indications in the hospital records that the pseudopatient's status was suspect. Rather, the evidence is strong that, once labeled schizophrenic, the pseudopatient was struck with that label. If the pseudopatient was to be discharged, he must naturally be "in remission"; but he was not sane, nor, in the institution's view, had he ever been sane. In this way an obvious human "reality" was constructed.

The uniform failure to recognize sanity cannot be attributed to the quality of the hospitals, for, although there were considerable variations among them, several are considered excellent. Nor can it be alleged that there was simply not enough time to observe the pseudopatients. Length of hospitalization ranged from 7 to 52 days, with an average of 19 days. The pseudopatients were not, in fact, carefully observed, but this failure clearly speaks more to traditions within psychiatric hospitals than to lack of opportunity.

Finally, it cannot be said that the failure to recognize the pseudopatients' sanity was due to the fact that they were not behaving sanely. While there was clearly some tension present in all of them, their daily visitors could detect no serious behavioral consequences—nor, indeed, could other patients. It was quite common for the patients to "detect" the pseudopatients' sanity. During the first three hospitalizations, when accurate counts were kept, 35 of a total of 118 patients on the admissions ward voiced their suspicions, some vigorously. "You're not crazy. You're a journalist, or a professor [referring to the continual note-taking]. You're checking up on the hospital." While most of the patients were reassured by the pseudopatient's insistence that he had been sick before he came in but was fine now, some continued to believe that the pseudopatient was sane throughout his hospitalization.[5] The fact that the patients often recognized nor-

---

[5]It is possible, of course, that patients have quite broad latitudes in diagnosis and therefore are inclined to call many people sane, even those whose behavior is patently aberrant. However, although we have no hard data on this matter, it was our distinct impression that this was not the case. In many instances, patients not only singled us out for attention, but came to imitate our behaviors and styles.

mality when staff did not raises important questions.

Failure to detect sanity during the course of hospitalization may be due to the fact that physicians operate with a strong bias toward what statisticians call the type 2 error [38]. This is to say that physicians are more inclined to call a healthy person sick (a false positive, type 2) than a sick person healthy (a false negative, type 1). The reasons for this are not hard to find: It is clearly more dangerous to misdiagnose illness than health. Better to err on the side of caution, to suspect illness even among the healthy.

But what holds for medicine does not hold equally well for psychiatry. Medical illnesses, while unfortunate, are not commonly pejorative. Psychiatric diagnoses, on the contrary, carry with them personal, legal, and social stigmas [15–17,24,28]. It was therefore important to see whether the tendency toward diagnosing the sane insane could be reversed. The following experiment was arranged at a research and teaching hospital whose staff had heard these findings but doubted that such an error could occur in their hospital. The staff was informed that at some time during the following three months, one or more pseudopatients would attempt to be admitted into the psychiatric hospital. Each staff member was asked to rate each patient who presented himself at admissions or on the ward according to the likelihood that the patient was a pseudopatient. A 10-point scale was used, with a 1 and 2 reflecting high confidence that the patient was a pseudopatient.

Judgments were obtained on 193 patients who were admitted for psychiatric treatment. All staff who had had sustained contact with or primary responsibility for the patient—attendants, nurses, psychiatrists, physicians, and psychologists—were asked to make judgments. Forty-one patients were alleged, with high confidence, to be pseudopatients by at least one member of the staff; twenty-three were considered suspect by at least one psychiatrist; nineteen were suspected by one psychiatrist *and* one other staff member. Actually, no genuine pseudopatient (at least from my group) presented himself during this period.

The experiment is instructive. It indicates that the tendency to designate sane people as insane can be reversed when the stakes (in this case, prestige and diagnostic acumen) are high. But what can be said of the nineteen people who were suspected of being "sane" by one psychiatrist and another staff member? Were these people truly "sane" or was it rather the case that in the course of avoiding the type 2 error the staff tended to make more errors of the first sort—calling the crazy "sane"? There is no way of knowing. But one thing is certain: Any diagnostic process that lends itself so readily to massive errors of this sort cannot be a very reliable one.

The Stickiness of Psychodiagnostic Labels

Beyond the tendency to call the healthy sick—a tendency that accounts better for diagnostic behavior on admission than it does for such behavior after a lengthy period of exposure—the data speak to the massive role of labeling in psychiatric assessment. Having once been labeled schizophrenic, there is nothing the pseudopatient can do to overcome the tag. The tag profoundly colors others' perceptions of him and his behavior. Again, in a very real sense, a specific "reality" is thus constructed.

From one viewpoint, these data are hardly surprising, for it has long been known that elements are given meaning by the context in which they occur. Gestalt psychology made this point vigorously, and Asch [1] demonstrated that there are "central" personality traits (such as "warm" versus "cold") which are so powerful that they markedly color the meaning of other information in forming an impression of a given personality [11,12,14,46]. "Insane," "schizophrenic," "manic depressive," and "crazy" are probably among the most powerful of such central traits. Once a person is designated abnormal, all of his other behaviors and characteristics are colored by that label. Indeed, that label is so powerful that many of the pseudopatients' normal behaviors were overlooked entirely or profoundly misinterpreted to make them fit into the assumed reality. Some examples may clarify this issue.

Earlier I indicated that there were no changes in the pseudopatient's personal history and current status beyond those of name, employment, and, where necessary, vocation. Otherwise, a veridical description of personal history and circumstances was offered. Those circumstances were not psychotic. How were they made consonant with the diagnosis of psychosis? Or were those diagnoses modified in such a way as to bring them into accord with the circumstances of the pseudopatient's life, as described by him?

As far as I can determine, diagnoses were in no way affected by the relative health of the circumstances of a pseudopatient's life; rather, the reverse occurred: The perception of his circumstances was shaped entirely by the diagnosis. A clear example of such a mechanism of reality construction is found in the case of a pseudopatiernt who had had a close relationship with his mother but was rather remote from his father during his early childhood. During adolescence and beyond, however, his father became a close friend, while his relationship with his mother cooled. His present relationship with his wife was characteristically close and warm. Apart from occasional angry exchanges, friction was minimal. The children had rarely been spanked. Surely there is nothing especially pathological about such a history. Indeed, many readers may see a similar pattern in their own experiences, with no markedly deleterious consequences. Observe, however, how such a history was translated in the psychopathological context, this from the case summary prepared after the patient was discharged.

> This white 39-year-old male . . . manifests a long history of considerable ambivalence in close relationships, which begins in early childhood. A warm relationship with his mother cools during his adolescence. A distant relationship to his father is described as becoming very intense. Affective stability is absent. His attempts to control emotionality with his wife and children are punctuated by angry outbursts and, in the case of the children, spankings. And while he says that he has several good friends, one senses considerable ambivalence embedded in those relationships also.

The facts of the case were unintentionally distorted by the staff to achieve consistency with a popular theory of the dynamics of a schizophrenic reaction.[6] Nothing of an ambivalent nature had been described in relations with parents, spouse, or friends. To the extent that ambivalence could be inferred, it was probably not greater than is found in all human relationships. It is true the pseudopatient's relationships with his parents changed over time, but in the ordinary context that would hardly be remarkable—indeed, it might very well be expected. Clearly, the meaning ascribed to his verbalizations (that is, ambivalence, affective instability) was determined by the diagnosis: schizophrenia. An entirely different meaning would have been ascribed if it were known that the man was "normal."

All pseudopatients took extensive notes publicly. Under ordinary circumstances, such behavior would have raised questions in the minds of observers, as, in fact, it did among patients. Indeed, it seemed so certain that the notes would elicit suspicion that elaborate precautions were taken to remove them from the ward each day. But the precautions proved needless. The closest any staff member came to questioning these notes occurred when one pseudopatient asked his physician what kind of medication he was receiving and began to write down the response. "You needn't write it," he was told gently. "If you have trouble remembering, just ask me again."

If no questions were asked of the pseudopatients, how was their writing interpreted? Nursing records for three patients indicate that the writing was seen as an aspect of their pathological behavior. "Patient engages in writing behavior" was the daily nursing comment on one of the pseudopatients who was never questioned about his writing. Given that the patient is in the hospital, he must be psychologically disturbed. And given that he is disturbed, continuous writing must be a behavioral manifestation of that disturbance,

---

[6]For an example of a similar self-fulfilling prophecy, in this instance dealing with the "central" trait of intelligence, see Rosenthal and Lenore [34].

perhaps a subset of the compulsive behaviors that are sometimes correlated with schizophrenia.

One tacit characteristic of psychiatric diagnosis is that it
locates the sources of aberration within the individual and
only rarely within the complex of stimuli that surrounds him.
Consequently, behaviors that are stimulated by the environment are commonly misattributed to the patient's disorder.
For example, one kindly nurse found a pseudopatient pacing
the long hospital corridors. "Nervous, Mr. X?" she asked.
"No, bored," he said.

The notes kept by pseudopatients are full of patient behaviors that were misinterpreted by well-intentioned staff. Often
enough, a patient would go "berserk" because he had, wit-
tingly or unwittingly, been mistreated by, say, an attendant.
A nurse coming upon the scene would rarely inquire even
cursorily into the environmental stimuli of the patient's
behavior; rather, she assumed that his upset derived from
his pathology, not from his present interactions with other
staff members. Occasionally, the staff might assume that the
patient's family (especially when they had recently visited)
or other patients had stimulated the outburst. But never were
the staff found to assume that one of themselves or the structure of the hospital had anything to do with a patient's
behavior. One psychiatrist pointed to a group of patients who
were sitting outside the cafeteria entrance half an hour before
lunchtime. To a group of young residents he indicated that
such behavior was characteristic of the oral-acquisitive nature
of the syndrome. It seemed not to occur to him that there
were very few things to anticipate in a psychiatric hospital
besides eating.

A psychiatric label produces its own reality and with it its
own effect. Once the impression has been formed that the
patient is schizophrenic, the expectation is that he will continue to be schizophrenic. When a sufficient amount of time
has passed, during which the patient has done nothing
bizarre, he is considered to be in remission and available for
discharge. But the label endures beyond discharge, with the
unconfirmed expectation that he will behave as a schizophrenic again. Such labels, conferred by mental health pro-

fessionals, are as influential on the patient as they are on his relatives and friends, and it should not surprise anyone that the diagnosis acts on all of them as a self-fulfilling prophecy. Eventually, the patient himself accepts the diagnosis, with all of its surplus meanings and expectations, and behaves accordingly [38]. As soon as he does this, he has adapted himself to this construction of an interpersonal "reality."

The inferences to be made from these matters are quite simple. Much as Zigler and Phillips have demonstrated that there is enormous overlap in the symptoms presented by patients who have been variously diagnosed [18,47], so there is an enormous overlap in the behaviors of the sane and the insane. The sane are not "sane" all of the time. We lose our tempers "for no good reason." We are occasionally depressed or anxious, again for no good reason. And we may find it difficult to get along with one or another person—again for no reason that we can specify. Similarly, the insane are not always insane. Indeed, it was the impression of the pseudo-patients while living with them that they were sane for long periods of time—that the bizarre behaviors upon which their diagnoses were allegedly predicated constituted only a small fraction of their total behavior. If it makes no sense to label ourselves permanently depressed on the basis of an occasional depression, then it takes better evidence than is presently available to label all patients insane or schizophrenic on the basis of bizarre behaviors or cognitions. It seems more useful, as Mischel [30] has pointed out to limit our discussions to *behaviors*, the stimuli that provoke them, and their correlates.

It is not known why powerful impressions of personality traits, such as "crazy" or "insane," arise. Conceivably, when the origins of and stimuli that give rise to a behavior are remote or unknown, or when the behavior strikes us as immutable, trait labels regarding the *behaver* arise. When, on the other hand, the origins and stimuli are known and available, discourse is limited to the behavior itself. Thus I may hallucinate because I am sleeping or I may hallucinate because I have ingested a peculiar drug. These are termed sleep-induced hallucinations, or dreams, and drug-induced hallucinations, respectively. But when the stimuli to my hallucinations are unknown, that is called craziness, or schizophrenia—as if that inference were somehow as illuminating as the others.

The Experience of Psychiatric Hospitalization

The term *mental illness* is of recent origin. It was coined by people who were humane in their inclinations and who wanted very much to raise the station of (and the public's sympathies toward) the psychologically disturbed from that of witches and "crazies" to one that was akin to the physically ill. And they were at least partially successful, for the treatment of the mentally ill *has* improved considerably over the years. But while treatment has improved, it is doubtful that people really regard the mentally ill in the same way that they view the physically ill. A broken leg is something one recovers from, but mental illness allegedly endures forever.[7] A broken leg does not threaten the observer, but a crazy schizophrenic? There is by now a host of evidence that attitudes toward the mentally ill are characterized by fear, hostility, aloofness, suspicion, and dread [36,37]. The mentally ill are society's lepers.

That such attitudes infect the general population is perhaps not surprising, only upsetting. But that they affect the professionals—attendants, nurses, physicians, psychologists, and social workers—who treat and deal with the mentally ill is more disconcerting, both because such attitudes are self-evidently pernicious and because they are unwitting. Most mental health professionals would insist that they are sympathetic toward the mentally ill, that they are neither avoidant nor hostile. But it is more likely that an exquisite ambivalence characterizes their relations with psychiatric patients, such that their avowed impulses are only part of their entire attitude. Negative attitudes are there too and can

---

[7]The most recent and unfortunate instance of this tenet is that of Senator Thomas Eagleton.

easily be detected. Such attitudes should not surprise us. They are the natural offspring of the labels patients wear and the places in which they are found.

Consider the structure of the typical psychiatric hospital. Staff and patients are strictly segregated. Staff have their own living space, including their dining facilities, bathrooms, and assembly places. The glassed quarters that contain the professional staff, which the pseudopatients came to call "the cage," sit out on every dayroom. The staff emerge primarily for caretaking purposes—to give medication, to conduct a therapy or group meeting, to instruct or reprimand a patient. Otherwise, staff keep to themselves, almost as if the disorder that afflicts their charges is somehow catching.

So much is patient–staff segregation the rule that, for four public hospitals in which an attempt was made to measure the degree to which staff and patients mingle, it was necessary to use "time out of the staff cage" as the operational measure. While it was not the case that all time spent out of the cage was spent mingling with patients (attendants, for example, would occasionally emerge to watch television in the dayroom), it was the only way in which one could gather reliable data on time for measuring.

The average amount of time spent by attendants outside of the cage was 11.3 percent (range, 3–52 percent). This figure does not represent only time spent mingling with patients, but also includes time spent on such chores as folding laundry, supervising patients while they shave, directing ward cleanup, and sending patients to off-ward activities. It was the relatively rare attendant who spent time talking with patients or playing games with them. It proved impossible to obtain a "percent mingling time" for nurses, since the amount of time they spent out of the cage was too brief. Rather, we counted instances of emergence from the cage. On the average, daytime nurses emerged from the cage 11.5 times per shift, including instances when they left the ward entirely (range, 4–39 times). Late afternoon and night nurses were even less available, emerging on the average 9.4 times per shift (range, 4–41 times). Data on early morning nurses, who arrived usually after midnight and departed at 8 A.M., are not available because patients were asleep during most of this period.

Physicians, especially psychiatrists, were even less available. They were rarely seen on the wards. Quite commonly, they would be seen only when they arrived and departed, with the remaining time being spent in their offices or in the cage. On the average, physicians emerged on the ward 6.7 times per day (range, 1–17 times). It proved difficult to make an accurate estimate in this regard, since physicians often maintained hours that allowed them to come and go at different times.

The hierarchical organization of the psychiatric hospital has been commented on before [42], but the latent meaning of that kind of organization is worth noting again. Those with the most power have least to do with patients, and those with the least power are most involved with them. Recall, however, that the acquisition of role-appropriate behaviors occurs mainly through the observation of others, with the most powerful having the most influence. Consequently, it is understandable that attendants not only spend more time with patients than do any other members of the staff—that is required by their station in the hierarchy—but also, insofar as they learn from their superiors' behavior, spend as little time with patients as they can. Attendants are seen mainly in the cage, which is where the models, the action, and the power are.

I turn now to a different set of studies, these dealing with staff response to patient-initiated contact. It has long been known that the amount of time a person spends with you can be an index of your significance to him. If he initiates and maintains eye contact, there is reason to believe that he is considering your requests and needs. If he pauses to chat or actually stops and talks, there is added reason to infer that he is individuating you. In four hosopitals, the pseudopatient approached the staff member with a request that took the following form: "Pardon me, Mr. [or Dr. or Mrs.] X, could you tell me when I will be eligible for grounds privileges?" (or "when I will be presented at the staff meeting?" or "when I am likely to be discharged?"). While the content of the question varied according to the appropriateness of the target and the pseudopatient's (apparent) current needs the form was always a courteous and relevant request for information. Care was taken never to approach a particular member of the staff more than once a day, lest the staff member become suspicious or irritated. In examining these data, remember that the behavior of the pseudopatients was neither bizarre nor disruptive. One could indeed engage in good conversation with them.

The data for these experiments are shown in Table 1, separately for physicians (column 1) and for nurses and attendants (column 2). Minor differences between these four institutions were overwhelmed by the degree to which staff avoided continuing contacts that patients had initiated. By far, their most common response consisted of either a brief response to the question, offered while they were "on the move" and with head averted, or no response at all.

The encounter frequently took the following bizarre form: (Pseudopatient) "Pardon me, Dr. X. Could you tell me when I am eligible for grounds privileges?" (Physician) "Good morning, Dave. How are you today?" (Moves off without waiting for a response.)

It is instructive to compare these data with data recently obtained at Stanford University. It has been alleged that large and eminent universities are characterized by faculty who are so busy that they have no time for students. For this comparison, a young lady approached individual faculty members who seemed to be walking purposefully to some meeting or teaching engagement and asked them the following six questions.

1. "Pardon me, could you direct me to Encina Hall?" (at the medical school, ". . . to the Clinical Research Center?").

2. "Do you know where Fish Annex is?" (there is no Fish Annex at Stanford).

3. "Do you teach here?"

4. "How does one apply for admission to the college?" (at the medical school: ". . . to the medical school?").

5. "Is it difficult to get in?"

6. "Is there financial aid?"

Table 1. Self-Initiated Contact by Pseudopatients with Psychiatrists, Nurses, and Attendants, Compared to Contact with Other Groups

Contact	Psychiatric hospitals		University campus (nonmedical)	University medical center physicians		
	(1) Psychiatrists	(2) Nurses and attendants	(3) Faculty	(4) "Looking for a psychiatrist"	(5) "Looking for an internist"	(6) No additional comment
Responses						
Moves on, head averted (%)	71	88	0	0	0	0
Makes eye contact (%)	23	10	0	11	0	0
Pauses and chats (%)	2	2	0	11	0	10
Stops and talks (%)	4	0.5	100	78	100	90
Mean number of questions answered (out of 6)	a	a	6	3.8	4.8	4.5
Respondents (no.)	13	47	14	18	15	10
Attempts (no.)	185	1283	14	18	15	10

aNot applicable.

Without exception, as can be seen in Table 1 (column 3), all of the questions were answered. No matter how rushed they were, all respondents not only maintained eye contact, but stopped to talk. Indeed, many of the respondents went out of their way to direct or take the questioner to the office she was seeking, to try to locate "Fish Annex," or to discuss with her the possibilities of being admitted to the university.

Similar data, also shown in Table 1 (columns 4, 5, and 6), were obtained in the hospital. Here too, the young lady came prepared with six questions. After the first question, however, she remarked to 18 of her respondents (column 4), "I'm looking for a psychiatrist," and to 15 others (column 5), "I'm looking for an internist." Ten other respondents received no inserted comment (column 6). The general degree of cooperative responses is considerably higher for these university groups than it was for pseudopatients in psychiatric hospitals. Even so, differences are apparent within the medical school setting. Once having indicated that she was looking for a psychiatrist, the degree of cooperation elicited was less than when she sought an internist.

Powerlessness and Depersonalization

Eye contact and verbal contact reflect concern and individuation; their absence, avoidance and depersonalization. The data I have presented do not do justice to the rich daily encounters that grew up around matters of depersonalization and avoidance. I have records of patients who were beaten by staff for the sin of having initiated verbal contact. During my own experience, for example, one patient was beaten in the presence of other patients for having approached an attendant and told him, "I like you." Occasionally, punishment meted out to patients for misdemeanors seemed so excessive that it could not be justified by the most radical interpretations of psychiatric canon. Nevertheless, they appeared to go unquestioned. Tempers were often short. A patient who had not heard a call for medication would be roundly excoriated, and the morning attendants would often wake patients with, "Come on, you m—— f——s, out of bed!"

Neither anecdotal nor "hard" data can convey the overwhelming sense of powerlessness which invades the individual as he is continually exposed to the depersonalization of the psychiatric hospital. It hardly matters *which* psychiatric hospital—the excellent public ones and the very plush private hospital were better than the rural and shabby ones in this regard, but, again, the features that psychiatric hospitals had in common overwhelmed by far their apparent differences.

Powerlessness was evident everywhere. The patient is deprived of many of his legal rights by dint of his psychiatric commitment [45]. He is shorn of credibility by virtue of his psychiatric label. His freedom of movement is restricted. He cannot initiate contact with the staff, but may only respond to such overtures as they make. Personal privacy is minimal. Patient quarters and possessions can be entered and examined by any staff member, for whatever reason. His personal history and anguish is available to any staff member (often including the "gray lady" and "candy striper" volunteer) who chooses to read his folder, regardless of their therapeutic relationship to him. His personal hygiene and waste evacuation are often monitored. The water closets may have no doors.

At times, depersonalization reached such proportions that pseudopatients had the sense that they were invisible, or at least unworthy of account. Upon being admitted, I and other pseudopatients took the initial physical examinations in a semipublic room, where staff members went about their own business as if we were not there.

On the ward, attendants delivered verbal and occasionally serious physical abuse to patients in the presence of other observing patients, some of whom (the pseudopatients) were writing it all down. Abusive behavior, on the other hand, terminated quite abruptly when other staff members were known to be coming. Staff are credible witnesses, patients are not.

A nurse unbuttoned her uniform to adjust her brassiere in the presence of an entire ward of viewing men. One did not have the sense that she was being seductive, rather, she didn't notice us. A group of staff persons might point to a patient in the dayroom and discuss him animatedly, as if he were not there.

One illuminating instance of depersonalization and invisibility occurred with regard to medications. All told, the pseudopatients were administered nearly 2,100 pills, including Elavil, Stelazine, Compazine, and Thorazine, to name but a few. (That such a variety of medications should have been administered to patients presenting identical symptoms is itself worthy of note.) Only two were swallowed. The rest were either pocketed or deposited in the toilet. The pseudopatients were not alone in this. Although I have no precise records on how many patients rejected their medications, the pseudopatients frequently found the medications of other patients in the toilet before they deposited their own. As long as they were cooperative, their behavior and the pseudopatients' own in this matter, as in other important matters, went unnoticed throughout.

Reactions to such depersonalization among pseudopatients were intense. Although they had come to the hospital as participant observers and were fully aware that they did not "belong," they nevertheless found themselves caught up in and fighting the process of depersonalization. Some examples: A graduate student in psychology asked his wife to bring his textbooks to the hospital so he could "catch up on his homework"— this despite the elaborate precautions taken to conceal his professional association. The same student, who had trained for quite some time to get into the hospital, and who had looked forward to the experience, "remembered" some drag races that he had wanted to see on the weekend and insisted that he be discharged by that time. Another pseudopatient attempted a romance with a nurse. Subsequently, he informed the staff that he was applying for admission to graduate school in psychology and was very likely to be admitted, since a graduate professor was one of his regular hospital visitors. The same person began to engage in psychotherapy with other patients—all of this as a way of becoming a person in an impersonal reality.

The Sources of Depersonalization

What are the origins of depersonalization? I have already mentioned two. First are attitudes held by all of us toward the mentally ill—including those who treat them—attitudes characterized by fear, distrust, and horrible expectations on the one hand, and benevolent intentions on the other. Our ambivalence leads, in this instance as in others, to avoidance.

Second, and not entirely separate, the hierarchical structure of the psychiatric hospital facilitates depersonalization. Those who are at the top have least to do with patients, and their behavior inspires the rest of the staff. Average daily contact with psychiatrists, psychologists, residents, and physicians combined ranged from 3.9 to 25.1 minutes, with an overall mean of 6.8 (six pseudopatients over a total of 129 days of hospitalization). Included in this average are time spent in the admissions interview, ward meetings in the presence of a senior staff member, group and individual psychotherapy contacts, case presentation conferences, and discharge meetings. Clearly, patients do not spend much time in interpersonal contact with doctoral staff, and doctoral staff serve as models for nurses and attendants.

There are probably other sources. Psychiatric installations are presently in serious financial straits. Staff shortages are pervasive, staff time at a premium. Something has to give, and that something is patient contact. Yet, while financial stresses are realities, too much can be made of them. I have the impression that the psychological forces that result in depersonalization are much stronger than the fiscal ones and that the addition of more staff would not correspondingly improve patient care in this regard. The incidence of staff meetings and the enormous amount of record keeping on patients, for example, have not been as substantially reduced as has patient contact. Priorities exist, even during hard times.

Patient contact is not a significant priority in the traditional psychiatric hospital, and fiscal pressures do not account for this. Avoidance and depersonalization may.

Heavy reliance upon psychotropic medication tacitly contributes to depersonalization by convincing staff that treatment is indeed being conducted and that further patient contact may not be necessary. Even here, however, caution needs to be exercised in understanding the role of psychotropic drugs. If patients were powerful rather than powerless, if they were viewed as interesting individuals rather than diagnostic entities, if they were socially significant rather than social lepers, if their anguish truly and wholly compelled our sympathies and concerns, would we not *seek* contact with them, despite the availability of medications? Perhaps for the pleasure of it all?

The Consequences of Labeling and Depersonalization

Whenever the ratio of what is known to what needs to be known approaches zero, we tend to invent "knowledge" and assume that we understand more than we actually do. We seem unable to acknowledge that we simply don't know. The needs for diagnosis and remediation of behavioral and emotional problems are enormous. But rather than acknowledge that we are just embarking on understanding, we continue to label patients "schizophrenic," "manic depressive," and "insane," as if in those words we had captured the essence of understanding. The facts of the matter are that we have known for a long time that diagnoses are often not useful or reliable, but we have nevertheless continued to use them. We now know that we cannot distinguish insanity from sanity. It is depressing to consider how that information will be used.

Not merely depressing, but frightening. How many people, one wonders, are sane but not recognized as such in our psychiatric institutions? How many have been needlessly stripped of their privileges of citizenship, from the right to vote and drive to that of handling their own accounts? How many have feigned insanity in order to avoid the criminal consequences of their behavior, and, conversely, how many would rather stand trial than live interminably in a psychiatric hospital—but are wrongly thought to be mentally ill? How many have been stigmatized by well-intentioned but nevertheless erroneous, diagnoses? On the last point, recall again that a "type 2 error" in psychiatric diagnosis does not have the same consequences it does in medical diagnosis. A diagnosis of cancer that has been found to be in error is cause for celebration. But psychiatric diagnoses are rarely found to be in error. The label sticks, a mark of inadequacy forever.

Finally, how many patients might be "sane" outside the psychiatric hospital but seem insane in it—not because craziness resides in them, as it were, but because they are responding to a bizarre setting, one that may be unique one to institutions which harbor nether people? Goffman [19] calls the process of socialization to such institutions "mortification"—an apt metaphor that includes the processes of depersonalization which have been described here. And while it is impossible to know whether the pseudopatients' responses to these processes are characteristic of all inmates—they were, after all, not real patients—it is difficult to believe that these processes of socialization to a psychiatric hospital provide useful attitudes or habits of response for living in the "real world."

Summary and Conclusions

It is clear that we cannot distinguish the sane from the insane in psychiatric hospitals. The hospital creates a reality of its own in which the meanings of behavior can then easily be misunderstood. The consequences to patients hospitalized in such an environment—the powerlessness, depersonalization, segregation, mortification, and self-labeling—seem undoubtedly countertherapeutic.

I do not, even now, understand this problem well enough to perceive solutions, but two matters seem to have some promise. The first concerns the proliferation of community mental health facilities, of crisis intervention centers, of the human potential movement, and of behavior therapies that, for all of their own problems, tend to avoid psychiatric labels, to focus on specific problems and behaviors, and to retain the individual in a relatively nonpejorative environment. Clearly, to the extent that we refrain from sending the distressed to insane places, our impressions of them are less likely to be distorted. (The risk of distorted perceptions, it seems to me, is always present, since we are much more sensitive to an individual's behaviors and verbalizations than we are to the subtle contextual stimuli that often promote them. At issue here is a matter of magnitude. And, as I have shown, the magnitude of distortion is exceedingly high in the extreme context that is a psychiatric hospital.)

The second matter that might prove promising speaks to the need to increase the sensitivity of mental health workers and researchers to the *Catch 22* position of psychiatric patients. Simply reading materials in this area will be of help to some such workers and researchers. For others, directly experiencing the impact of psychiatric hospitalization will be of enormous use. Clearly, further research into the social psychology of such total institutions will both facilitate treatment and deepen understanding.

I and the other pseudopatients in the psychiatric setting had distinctly negative reactions. We do not pretend to describe the subjective experiences of true patients. Theirs may be different from ours, particularly with the passage of time and the necessary process of adaptation to one's environment. But we can and do speak to the relatively more objective indices of treatment within the hospital. It could be a mistake, and a very unfortunate one, to consider that what happened to us derived from malice or stupidity on the part of the staff. Quite the contrary, our overwhelming impression of them was of people who really cared, who were committed and who were uncommonly intelligent. Where they failed, as they sometimes did painfully, it would be more accurate to attribute those failures to the environment in which they, too, found themselves than to personal callousness. Their perceptions and behavior were controlled by the situation, rather than being motivated by a malicious disposition. In a more benign environment, one that was less attached to global diagnosis, their behaviors and judgments might have been more benign and effective.

REFERENCES

1. Asch, Solomon E. Forming impressions of personality. *Journal of Abnormal and Social Psychology* 41, 1946, 258.
2. Asch, Solomon E. *Social Psychology.* Prentice Hall, New York, 1952.
3. Ash, P. The reliability of psychiatric diagnoses, *Journal of Abnormal and Social Psychology* 44, 1949, 272.
4. Barry, A. *Bellevue Is a a State of Mind.* Harcourt Brace Jovanovich, New York, 1971.
5. Beck, A. T. Reliability of psychiatric diagnoses: I. A critique of systematic studies. *American Journal of Psychiatry* 119, 1962, 210–216
6. Becker, H. *Outsiders: Studies in the Sociology of Deviance,* Free Press, New York, 1963.
7. Belknap. E. *Human Problems of a State Mental Hospital.* McGraw-Hill, New York, 1956.
8. Benedict, R. Anthropology and the abnormal. *Journal of General Psychology* 10, 1934, 59–82.
9. Boisen, A. T. Types of dementia praecox—A study in psychiatric classification. *Psychiatry* 2, 1938, 233–236.
10. Braginsky, B. M., Braginsky, D. D., and Ring, K. *Methods of Madness: The Mental Hospital as a Last Resort.* Holt, Rinehart, and Winston, New York, 1969.
11. Bruner, J. S., and Tagiuri, R. The perception of people. In *Handbook of Social Psychology* (G. Lindzey, ed.). Addison-Wesley, Cambridge, Massachusetts, 1954, pp. 634–654.
12. Bruner, J. S., Shapiro, D., and Tagiuri, R. The meaning of traits in isolation and in combination. In *Person Perception and Interpersonal Behavior* (R. Tagiuri and L. Petrullo, eds.). Stanford University Press, Stanford, 1958, pp. 277–288.
13. Caudill, William, Redlich, Frederic C., Gilmore, Helen R., and Brody, Eugene. Social structure and interaction processes on a psychiatric ward. *American Journal of Orthopsychiatry* 22, 1952, 314.
14. Crocetti, G. M., and Lemkau, P. V. On rejection of the mentally ill. *American Sociological Review* 30, 1965, 577.
15. Cumming, John and Elaine. On the stigma of mental illness. *Community Mental Health Journal* 1, 1965, 135–143.
16. Farina, A., and Ring, K. The influence of perceived mental illness on interpersonal relations. *Journal of Abnormal Psychology* 70, 1965, 47.
17. Freeman, H. G., and Simmons, O. G. *The Mental Patient Comes Home.* Wiley, New York, 1963.
18. Freudenberg, R. K., and Robertson, J. P. Symptoms in relation to psychiatric diagnosis and treatment. *Archives of Neurology and Psychiatry* 76, 1956, 14–22.
19. Goffman, Erving. *Asylums.* Doubleday, Garden City, New York, 1961.
20. Goffman, Erving. *Behavior in Public Places.* Free Press, New York, 1969.

21. Goldman, A. R., et al. On posing as mental patients: Reminiscences and recommendations. *Professional Psychology* 1, 1970, 427.
22. Gove, W. R. Societal reaction as an explanation of mental illness: An evaluation. *American Sociological Review* 35, 1970, 873.
23. Hollingshead, A., and Redlich, F. C. *Social Class and Mental Illness: A Community Study*, Wiley, New York, 1958.
24. Johannsen, W. J. Attitudes toward mental patients; a review of empirical research. *Mental Hygiene* 53, 1969, 218.
25. Kreitman, N. The reliability of psychiatric assessment: An analysis. *Journal of Mental Science* 107, 1961, 887–908.
26. Kreitman, N., et al. Reliability of psychiatric diagnosis. *Journal of Mental Science* 107, 1961, 876–886.
27. Laing, Ronald D. *The Divided Self*. Quadrangle, Chicago, 1960.
28. Linsky, Arnold S. Who shall be excluded? The influence of personal attributes in community reaction to the mentally ill. *Social Psychiatry* 5, 1970, 166–171.
29. Mensh, I. N., and Wishner, J. Asch on "Forming impressions on personality": Further evidence. *Journal of Personality* 16, 1947, 188.
30. Mischel, Walter. *Personality and Assessment*. Wiley, New York, 1968.
31. Nunnally, J. C. *Popular Conceptions of Mental Health*. Rinehart and Winston, New York, 1961.
32. Phillips, D. L. Rejections: A possible consequence of seeking help for mental disorder. *American Sociological Review* 28, 1963, 963.
33. Phillips, L., and Draguns, J. G. Classification of behavior disorders. *Annual Review of Psychology* 22, 1971, 447–482.
34. Rosenthal, Robert, and Jacobson, Lenore. *Pygmalion in the Classroom*. Holt, Rinehart, and Winston, New York, 1968.
35. Sarbin, Theodore R. On the futility of the proposition that some people should be labelled "mentally ill." *Journal of Consulting and Clinical Psychology* 31, 1967, 447–453.
36. Sarbin, Theodore R. Schizophrenia is a myth, born of metaphor, meaningless. *Psychology Today* 6, 1972, 18.
37. Sarbin, Theodore R. and Mancuso, J. C. Failure of a moral enterprise: Attitudes of the public toward mental illness. *Journal of Consulting and Clinical Psychology* 35, 1970, 159–179.
38. Scheff, T. J. *Being Mentally Ill: A Sociological Theory*. Doubleday, Garden City, New York, 1961.
39. Schmitt, H. O., and Fonda, C. P. The reliability of psychiatric diagnosis: A new look. *Journal of Abnormal and Social Psychology* 52, 1956, 262.
40. Schur, E. Reactions to deviance: A critical assessment. *American Journal of Sociology* 75, 1969, 309.
41. Seeman, W. Psychiatric diagnosis: An investigation of interperson reliability after didactic instruction. *Journal of Nervous and Mental Disease* 118, 1953, 541–544.
42. Stanton, A. H., and Schwartz, M. S. *The Mental Hospital: A Study of Institutional Participation in Psychiatric Illness and Treatment*. Basic Books, New York, 1954.
43. Szasz, Thomas S. *The Myth of Mental Illness: Foundations of a Theory of Mental Illness*. Hoeber-Harper, New York, 1963.
44. Szasz, Thomas S. *Law, Liberty and Psychiatry*. Macmillan, New York, 1963.
45. Wexler, D. B., and Scoville, S. E. The administration of psychiatric jus-

144 DAVID L. ROSENHAN

tice: Theory and practice in Arizona. *Arizona Law Review* 13, 1971, 1.
46. Wishner, J. Reanalysis of "Impressions of personality." *Psychology Review* 67, 1960, 96.
47. Zigler, E., and Phillips, L. Psychiatric diagnosis and symptomatology. *Journal of Abnormal and Social Psychology* 63, 1961, 69.

ROLF BREUER

Self-Reflexivity in Literature:
The Example of Samuel Beckett's
Novel Trilogy*

I

IT WOULD SEEM reasonable, indeed almost self-evident, that
a volume with the title *The Invented Reality* should also
contain a chapter on literature, for literature is certainly a
primary example of what is meant by "fiction," "fictitious"
and by "invention." We have only to examine the word *poet*,
which in Greek means "maker," "inventor," or "creator," to
establish how ancient the awareness of this fact is.

Such a self-evident truth, however, cannot be the basic aim
of constructivism, since the world that is described or presented in a literary work of art is by definition and through
the process of composition fictive. Fictitiousness belongs to
literature in the same way that singing belongs to opera and
is inherent in the logic of this art form, so that it is self-evident
and uninterpretable: Lohengrin is not amazed that Elsa
should "sing" to him; her singing has the same ontological
status as the spoken word in a play. Thus when the constructivists state that the given "objectivity" of the world is only
apparent and that it is incorrect to assume that biologists,
psychologists, anthropologists, or physicists discover reality
and represent it through description or formalism, when they
stress that these scientists and, furthermore, all of us—in and

*An original contribution, translated, under supervision of the author, by
Terence McKay.

by means of our prescientific efforts at description and explanation—rather create reality or, at the very least, structure and modify it, then obviously they mean something beyond the literary theorist's truism that fictional texts represent a fictitious reality.

What, then, is the equivalent in opera of singing, where singing "belongs," to singing in drama, where it is "singing"? We have to go one level higher, and the result would be "metasinging," the singing of singing. Something similar is true of literature. If the world presented in literature is by its very nature fictitious, and if, in addition and according to constructivism, the "real" world is also invented, then the resulting reality presented in literature must be doubly fictive, and the kind of literature that would coincide with the level of constructivist insight would be a literature that made the fact of its having been constructed explicit, in other words, a self-reflexive literature.

In the following, taking as a point of departure the constructivist concept of self-referentiality, I will thus attempt to consider the problem of self-reflexivity, which has become so important in modern literature. In other words, I shall attempt to discuss the phenomenon of metaliterature, a literature that, above all, is concerned with itself, that reflects the conditions which make possible its own composition, that treats in general of the possibility of fictional speech, or that questions the basis of the fictional contract between the work and the reader.

This attempt concurs with a suggestion in an essay by Heinz von Foerster [10], where, from the fact that there can be no objective perception as such, in other words, no objects without observers, the conclusion is drawn that we need, above all, a theory of the observer or the "describer." Von Foerster continues that since only living organisms are possible candidates for observers, the construction of such a theory must be the task of the biologist. Since, however, the latter also is a living creature, he must not only take account of himself in his theory, but must also include the theory-building process itself in the theory. This is, in fact, the situation of many writers in the twentieth century who no longer desire to lustily tell stories but have found, just as scientists and philosophers in other fields have found, that their medium language, together with all the traditional processes of writing, has, after a period of optimism, become problematic. Thus they have found themselves forced to reflect on the process of writing itself.

II

Self-reflexivity in literature has actually existed for a long time and in all genres. As far as poetry is concerned, what springs to mind is above all the so-called "poetological" poem, in other words, the poem whose theme is that of poetry writing or even the process of writing the actual poem itself.[1] Self-reflexivity often appears, however, in a more hidden form, for instance, in the case of poems that on the surface appear to be landscape poetry, but which on closer analysis reveal themselves to be about the process of writing. As an example I could mention S. T. Coleridge's "Kubla Khan."

In drama there are various ways of demonstrating that the apparent reality of the events on the stage is artificial, is an "invented reality."[2] Above all, in comedy, and again and again since classical times, passages can be found in which the level of representation is interrupted by references to the spectators or to the fictive nature of the play. At the same time those logical foundations are undermined on which the—illusionary—assumption is based that a self-contained independent world is presented. One could mention, for example, Aristophanes' *The Clouds* or *The Wasps*, but also the "epic theater" with its emphasis on the fact that the *seriousness* of the play is after all only the seriousness of a *play* ("alienation effect"). One could mention here authors such as Bert Brecht or Thornton Wilder. An independent "state within the state" in many plays is the so-called "play within

---

[1]See here, for example, Alfred Weber [24].
[2]See Dietrich Schwanitz [19], who above all analyzed Elizabethan drama and modern drama in terms of role-theory categories. See also June Schlueter [18], who dedicates Chapter 3 of her book to Beckett's *Waiting for Godot*.

the play,"[3] in other words, scenes such as that in *Hamlet* in which Hamlet makes the actors perform a play that presents, with a few minor differences, exactly those events to which, as Hamlet fears, his father has fallen a victim, or such as that in *A Midsummer Night's Dream*, where the story of Pyramus and Thisby is performed. Such a device is self-reflexive to the extent that it draws attention to the play element that is part of every, even the most serious, play. The play within the play draws attention to the nature of play inherent in the theater and this mirrors the nature of play inherent in the world.[4]

It is modern narrative literature, however, that is the true home of self-reflexivity. Prose fiction is distinguishable from drama by the presence of a narrator, and it is the narrator as organizing consciousness of the text who most freely allows for the introduction and integration of reflexive structures. Miguel de Cervantes, Laurence Sterne, but also many German romantics spring to mind in this connection. Nevertheless, although many more examples could be cited, up to Romanticism it was a question of isolated voices, and the majority of such self-reflexive moments tended to appear in a comical context. It is only from around the year 1900 onward that one can begin to speak of self-reflexive literature as opposed to self-reflexivity in literature. Mentionable in this context would be Marcel Proust's *Remembrance of Things Past*, André Gide's *The Counterfeiters*, a whole series of works by Samuel Beckett, the American so-called "postmodernists,"[5] but also the French *nouveau roman*.[6]

Rather than remaining, however, with simply a list of names and titles, I would like to present more precisely the procedures of the writers and the significance of their activ-

---

[3]See, for example, Joachim Voigt [21] or Wolfgang Iser [14] for comments on this subject.
[4]See, for example, Lionel Abel [1] for contemporary drama. Abel does not accept Martin Esslin's characterization of post-1950 drama as "Theater of the Absurd." The title of his book *Metatheatre* is suggestive of what he believes to be the characteristic feature of this drama.
[5]See Maurice Beebe [5], Steven G. Kellman [16], or Peter Freese [11] for commentary.
[6]See Winfried Wehle [25].

ity on the basis of one example, namely, that of Beckett's novel trilogy *Molloy, Malone Dies,* and *The Unnamable,* written in 1948 and 1949 in French and then translated, mainly by the author himself, into English[7] On the one hand, the aspect of self-reflexivity touches upon a decisive feature of the work itself; on the other hand, the whole artistic tradition can be exemplified on the basis of this work.

However, before discussing Beckett, I would like to glance briefly at that particular work, which like no other stands at the beginning of twentieth century novel writing, above all with regard to the theme of self-reflexivity and its realization as metaliterature. Marcel Proust's *Remembrance of Things Past,* together with James Joyce's *Ulysses,* is certainly the most influential novel of the century and in relation to the problem of self-reflexivity is fundamental in the same way that Luigi Pirandello's play *Six Characters in Search of an Author* is fundamental in the field of drama. The reflexive nature of the 3,000-page mammoth work is characterized by the fact that the first-person narrator is finally ready at the end to write the novel that he has prepared over many years in his head and in all his senses, the novel which the reader has just at this moment finished reading. . . . As Gabriel Josipovici[8] has demonstrated, the first person narrator Marcel, who wants to write a novel, can find no subject matter for his work because the truth—as he himself recognizes—does not reside in objects: These, events as well as people, are always accidental. If Marcel described this reality, it would be as equally arbitrary as if he were to invent persons and stories that he could also invent in a totally different way. In the face of such a situation, an art form that deserves this title must not so much deal with events, with friends, with women, since these can be replaced by others and are in the last analysis of little importance; it must, rather, disclose the *structure* of life. The appropriate subject matter for a work of art of this level of awareness is the discovery of this insight, in other words, a

---

[7]All the following references are based on the edition published by Calder and Boyars in London [3].

[8]See *The World and the Book* [15], p. 19 ff.

metasubject. Marcel Proust thus takes the insight of his first person narrator to its logical conclusion and makes the search for the subject matter of the novel the subject matter of the novel[9]

Beckett, who knew Proust's *Remembrance of Things Past* very well,[10] took this problematic position as his point of departure and then radicalized it, as will be specified in more detail in the following.

III

The works of Samuel Beckett's middle period, which extends from the four *Stories* up to *How It Is* and covers the years from 1945 until 1960, are characterized by two elements: One is the literary motif of the quest[11] and the other, both as theme and as form, the mixing of level and meta-level,[12] in the process of which the two elements are very closely interrelated, as will be demonstrated in the following.[13]

Above all, the three novels *Molloy, Malone Dies*, and *The Unnamable*, which Beckett later published in a single volume, thus identifying them as a trilogy, can be understood, perhaps can *only* be understood, from this double viewpoint. Here we are confronted with the peak—and, given the

---

[9]See Paul Watzlawick et al. [23] for the logical problems that are connected with such novel structures.

[10]He published in the year 1931, at the age of 25, a study of Proust [4] that, however, reveals more about Beckett than about Proust and which has nothing of interest to say about the problem under discussion here.

[11]By "quest" is meant the metaphor of the search, a more specific form of the journey metaphor, whereby an internal development is depicted as an external series of events by means of which it is made visible. An example of this would be the quest for the Holy Grail in the Middle Ages.

[12]In the sense of Bertrand Russell's theory of types, by means of which paradoxes, such as that of the Cretan who says that all Cretans are liars, can be resolved.

[13]See in this connection Rolf Breuer [6], whose fifth chapter is the point of departure for the following analysis. (I would like to thank W. Fink Verlag for permission to reuse certain passages.) There is further information about Beckett research in that work, which, for reasons of space and the different aim of the Beckett interpretation here, is outside the scope of this discussion.

consistency and radical nature of the effort, the final word—
in the field of self-reflexive literature.

Molloy, the first novel of the trilogy, is divided into two
parts. In the first part the first-person narrator Molloy gives
an account of his search for his mother, although, unfortunately, he neither knows exactly where she is living nor is he
particularly concerned about his own specific location. The
possibility of a successful outcome to this search is made more
improbable by his progressive physical deterioration. At the
end we see Molloy, paralyzed in both legs, crawling painfully through the wood until he comes to a halt, lying in a
ditch at the edge of the wood, and in front of the town where
perhaps his mother is living. The second part is the story of
Jacques Moran, a detective, who, via a messenger called
Gaber, is commissioned by a certain Youdi to find Molloy.
Moran, too, does not know where he should really begin to
look for the object of his search and he experiences the same
sort of progressive physical deterioration as Molloy. As he is
lying with a stiff leg in the wood, looking at the town of
Bally, the messenger Gaber appears once again in order to
inform him of Youdi's order to return home immediately.
With difficulty, Moran drags himself home.

A summary of the content is even less useful here than is
usual in literary texts; we shall see that the content of the
story makes way to the writing situation itself. Nevertheless,
the action, rudimentary though it may be, demonstrates
clearly the double quest structure of this novel. Since, however, in both cases the goal of the quest is not reached and
since both "heroes" in the process endure greater and greater
physical deterioration, one could speak here, to a certain
extent, of the inversion or perversion of a novel of education
or a novel of development to which tradition *Molloy*, nevertheless, clearly belongs.

The first part is a kind of parody of the Homeric *Odyssey*.
It is possible to discern the faint outline of a Nausicaa epi-
sode; the goal of the classical journey—home and spouse—is
replaced by the home town and the mother; Circe finds her
counterpart in Madame Lousse, whose attractiveness in
comparison to the mythological ideal is as clearly run down

as is the total sexual and general indifference of the miserable old tramp Molloy in contrast to the kind of active involvement with the world found in the typological Greek hero.

After Molloy has torn himself away from the sour charms of the gaunt, old, masculine Madame Lousse and continues his journey on foot (up to that point he had been using a bicycle, which he must now leave behind), his other leg goes stiff (the first had gone stiff before his departure). His progress through a wood and a swamp toward the town where he suspects his mother might be finally becomes slower and slower. In the end he can only crawl forward on his stomach:

> Flat on my belly, using my crutches like grapnels, I plunged them ahead of me into the undergrowth, and when I felt they had a hold, I pulled myself forward, with an effort of the wrists. . . The advantage of this mode of locomotion compared to others, I mean those I have tried, is this, that when you want to rest you stop and rest, without further ado [p. 89].

With the town in view he remains lying there (presumably it is the same town as that described in the second part of the novel). Later, however, he must have reached his goal, perhaps in an ambulance, since at the very beginning of his narrative, even before he begins to tell the story of his search, he has said in the present tense that he is in his mother's room.[14] Nevertheless, Molloy would not be a true Beckett protagonist if he had really reached the goal of his search. In reality, his mother has died before or at the very least upon his arrival. Notwithstanding, he assumes her place, has almost become identical with her, as he says at the beginning.

Also the second part of the novel, Moran's search for Molloy, is an explicit quest, and, insofar that it is a quest for a questor, it is a quest of the second degree. This quest, too, is circular in its layout; indeed, its progression is, in general, completely parallel to Molloy's journey. The first-person narrator is supposed to find Molloy without knowing where he

---

[14]See Manfred Smuda [20] (p. 62 ff.) for a discussion of the present tense in the modern novel.

is actually staying or what to do with him should he find him. Moran is as little able to find Molloy as Molloy was to find his mother. Moran, just like Molloy, loses his capacity to move in the course of the journey. Like Molloy, he uses a bicycle for part of the journey. Both commit a murder in the wood, well known as a place of adventure and personal trial from untold numbers of fairy tales and quest novels. Finally, like Molloy before him, Moran remains lying with the town in view, before Youdi via Gaber orders him back. The circle of Moran's journey closes as he returns home exactly a year after his departure, exactly at the same time (midnight). Both parts, therefore, of the novel complement each other as a double circle ("bi-cycle"!).

A further kind of parallelism between the two parts of the novel is the situation in which the writing takes place. Each part consists of a report prepared by the respective narrator for someone who has commissioned it. Both begin with a short description of the fictive present, in other words, the situation in which the "I" begins writing down the events of the quest.

The most important parallelism, however, lies in the fusion of both protagonists to a single identity. At first sight such a thesis might seem, perhaps, implausible: Molloy is an isolated, dissolute, forgetful, blaspheming vagabond; Moran, on the other hand, has a house and a profession, lives with his son and a housekeeper, is pedantic about order and propriety, goes to church, and receives the sacrament regularly. For all this, a large number of critics have successfully shown that there are similarities between both narrator-heroes, whereby in general it is assumed that Moran develops in the direction of Molloy. Moran seems to be Molloy at an earlier stage of his development, and his deterioration, which is presented in the novel, discloses the pedantic, petty bourgeois character as a thin veneer over the threatening chaos that is present beneath the surface. If, however, Moran is an earlier version of Molloy, why should his quest appear later in the novel? To begin with, this is certainly because it would otherwise not be possible to represent the extent to which Molloy is already part of Moran. To do this it is necessary to show the later state first. More importantly, however, it would seem that the regressive nature of the personal development of both heroes is shown also in the form of the novel. The chronology of the persons is: (mother →) Moran → Molloy → union with the mother. Insofar that the novel begins with the mother's death (death as a new beginning) and then procedes via Molloy to Moran, it reflects the regression in its inverted structure.

Above all, what must be mentioned in connection with this is the parallelism, which has been commented upon by many critics, between the beginning and the end of the second part. This section of the novel begins with the following sentences:

> It is midnight. The rain is beating on the windows. I am calm. All is sleeping. Nevertheless I get up and go to my desk. I can't sleep. My lamp sheds a soft steady light. I have trimmed it. It will last till morning. I hear the eagle-owl. What a terrible battle-cry! Once I listened to it unmoved. My son is sleeping. Let him sleep. The night will come when he too, unable to sleep, will get up and go to his desk. I shall be forgotten.
> My report will be long. Perhaps I shall not finish it [p. 92].

As the tenses indicate, narration time and narrated time are identical. Then the actual story, "the report," begins. As it is closed with Moran's return home from his unsuccessful search, we find the following:

> I have spoken of a voice telling me things. . . . It told me to write the report [p. 176].

One is reminded of Proust's novel, the actual writing of which also began at that moment when the narration of the prehistory was over. Beckett, however, turns the situation into something negative, emphasizing the fictive nature of the fictional process. Moran thus continues:

> Then I went back into the house and wrote, It is midnight. The rain is beating on the windows. It was not midnight. It was not raining [p. 162].

And that is the end of the novel. The end, however, refers back to the beginning: It *is* the beginning, although at the same time it revokes the beginning and thus discloses the whole for what it is, namely, *invented* reality. The fictitious report contains its own disclosure as a *fictitious* report. The reader, however, has been prepared for this in a number of ways. This begins immediately at the beginning with Molloy's description of the situation in which he himself is writing (see p. 7 ff.).[15] It is reinforced by a whole series of comments by Molloy about his report that suggest that the report is perhaps not always true (see p. 9) or that it is badly written (p. 16), and it ends with the general silliness and incoherence of the story, which was once the pride of earlier authors, indeed the center of their art. The same is true of Moran's description of the situation in which he is writing (see p. 92), of his commentary on his own scribble (see, e.g., pp. 100, 132, and 133), of the "constructed" nature of his own story (see p. 138), which perhaps has only been "dictated" to him by that voice which, after his return from his interrupted search, he hears more and more clearly (see pp. 170 and 176). Just as earlier writers believed that they were "inspired" and thus saw themselves as the mouthpiece of (divine) truth, so Beckett, with the characteristic gesture of the writer of our secularized, late-bourgeois age, exposes the mechanism of inspiration: It is hallucination; any other interpretation is a lie or self-deception.

To this extent, then, Molloy's and Moran's experiences are arbitrary, are merely an artistic device. The spatial quests of both the protagonists are simply images, "material." The actual quest in this double novel is contained in the act of writing, in the attempts by Molloy and Moran to render accountable their futile efforts, to follow the changes in their bodies and in their personalities, and to preserve their identity and, indeed, to understand it in the transmutation.

---

[15]So as not to complicate matters too much, I will refrain from including the author, Beckett, in this play with the levels, although, firstly the autobiographical features are recognizable enough for the specialist and secondly the layout of the novel results in the text pointing, as it were, beyond itself.

In *Malone Dies* the situation is intensified or, rather (since Beckett does not proceed in an arbitrary fashion), it has become more radical; the situation left by *Molloy* is taken to its logical conclusion. The protagonist's external movements have come to a standstill. Malone lies in bed and awaits his death. Until this comes he will pass the time by telling stories. To begin with, however, he talks about his present condition, incapable of any action other than to push the food bowl and the chamber pot backward and forward with his arms, with the help of a stick, and to rummage through his belongings. The first story is about a man called Saposcat, later called Macman. Nevertheless, it is constantly interrupted by sections in which the narrator talks about himself. When Malone is about to deliver the promised inventory of his belongings, he finds to his astonishment that he has lost his stick. Then we hear once again of Macman, who is now living in an asylum. His nurse is Moll, later, after her death, Lemuel. Lemuel and Macman, together with some other inmates, go on a boat trip, the course of which becomes more and more fantastic until finally the disintegration of the narrator's speech signals his death (and the death of his characters).

The association of death and a journey by boat is a motif that reminds the reader once more, at the end of *Malone Dies,* of the quest character of this work, since for centuries it has been precisely the authors of adventure, travel, and *peregrinatio* novels that have had their characters reach the realm of the dead by crossing a river, lake, or sea.

The radicalization on the thematic level in *Malone Dies* in contrast to *Molloy* may best be seen in the fact that the movement toward the mother has become the journey toward death. Like many other Beckett protagonists, Molloy, a run-down, aging man, tries, in his return to the mother—to his mother's room (and the word "room" rhymes with "womb")—to take back, as it were, his own birth, to wipe out the sin of being born (a concept of Calderón often quoted by Beckett). Malone, who as many details indicate, is a further stage in Molloy's decay, imagines his own death, which he immediately mentions in the first sentence of the novel

("I shall soon be quite dead at last in spite of all"; p. 179), as a process of birth. When, toward the end of the novel—in other words, shortly before the notes in his notebook break off—he actually, "finally" lies in the throes of death, he describes this as a birth, whereby the room becomes a womb:

> I am swelling. What if I should burst? The ceiling rises and falls, rises and falls, rhythmically, as when I was a foetus. . . . I am being given, if I may venture the expression, birth to into death, such is my impression. The feet are clear already, of the great cunt of existence. Favourable presentation I trust. My head will be the last to die. . . . That is the end of me. I shall say I no more [p. 285].

Malone Dies also goes further than *Molloy* in the mixture of narrative and account of the narrative; in other words, in the mixture of text and metatext. Whereas in *Molloy* the account of the act of writing is limited mainly to the beginning and end of the novel, here it occupies much more space and the story is essentially composed of different (and only partly realized) stories, the fictive character of which is clearly emphasized. The constant interruption of the narrative process by reflections upon it is so obvious—recognizable by the constant switch from the "narrative" past tense to the present tense representing the present in which Malone is a narrator—that a detailed explanation can be dispensed with. Two passages are quoted here as representative, the first because the refinement is taken to its limit here, insofar that the process of writing is described in the most literal sense possible, and the second because of the extent to which it makes the two levels of the text explicit:

> My little finger glides before my pencil across the page and gives warning, falling over the edge, that the end of the line is near [p. 227]. . . .
> I fear I must have fallen asleep again. In vain I grope, I cannot find my exercise-book. But I still have the pencil in my hand. I shall have to wait for day to break. God knows what I am going to do till then.
> I have just written, I fear I must have fallen, etc. [p. 209].

In addition to these self-reflexive passages one could quote dozens of comments in which Malone denigrates the stories he is telling (himself) as boring (see pp. 187, 189, 216, and 218) or awful (see p. 191) or suddenly interrupts the flow of the narrative: "no, that won't do" (p. 190), "no, I can't do it" (p. 196), "I pause to record that I feel in extraordinary form. Delirium perhaps" (p. 258).

Of course, nowadays a novel such as this, in which text and metatext are mixed, in which the fictional character is not only emphasized but where this emphasis becomes itself an integral part of the artistic aim, can no longer be considered exceptional. On the contrary; this self-reflexivity, the paradoxes of the mixing of levels have actually become a fashion and a gag that is available whenever needed. In this connection one only needs to think of the so-called "postmodernists" above all in the U.S.A. [11,12,17]. Authors such as John Barth, Donald Barthelme, Robert Coover, or Ronald Sukenik appear to me, in contrast to the earlier Samuel Beckett, only to have added certain nuances, whereas it seems to me justifiable to see Beckett's trilogy as the logical conclusion to metaliterature, even though the work belongs, rather, to the very earliest that represented not simply self-reflexivity in literature but self-reflexive literature. In the meantime this procedure has become so ubiquitous that not only have exceptional authors such as Tom Stoppard been seduced by this theme,[16] but self-reflexivity has actually permeated through to the daily round of German television[17] and to sophisticated children's literature (see Ende [8]). In the face of such an inflated proliferation of metaliterature, the involved enthusiast might well become impatient, just as Hegel in his time saw "romantic irony" as, in the last analysis, frivolous. Just as irony turns into constraint and masquerade when it becomes a fixed gesture, so the novel of self-reflexivity is subject, more than other literature, to a process of erosion. However, Beckett's method, thirty-five years ago, was not

---

[16]In this connection see Ulrich Broich [7].

[17]See the cartoon mannequins, the so-called "Mainzelmännchen" on the second channel of German television, where reality and the image of reality are frequently confused; for example, a reality mannequin drawing the picture of another mannequin who then comes alive, and so forth.

only original: This is true of an artist like Maurits Cornelius Escher, too, and yet one would hardly want to compare him with Beckett. It appears to me that the reason for this is the fact that games of this sort do not exhaust a novel such as *Malone Dies:* It is much richer. Above all, Beckett's method is the result of a process of derivation: What for later authors has become a readily available device, which can be used for the fun of it, at any time and without difficulty, was something Beckett had to work out, invent, something bound up with the very essence of his existence as an artist. I will return to this in the following.

Malone Dies is thus a novel in which the traditional fable firstly is only present in fragments, secondly, is made explicitly recognizable at every point as invented, and, thirdly, is constantly being interrupted by the first-person narrator's commentary about the writing situation. This commentary, however, is authentic: In it and in the underlying living situation of Malone Beckett demonstrates the seriousness and the tenacity of his art. One only need consider the end, as Malone's prose disintegrates, obviously as a result of the onset of the process of dying. When he feels his end approaching, Malone has the nurse, Lemuel, use his axe to kill the protagonists, whereupon the apparent story is, as it were, "suspended." Then finally

> Lemuel is in charge, he raises his hatchet on which the blood will never dry, but not to hit anyone, he will not hit anyone, he will not hit anyone any more, he will not touch anyone any more, either with it or with it or with it or with or
> or with it or with his hammer or with his stick or with his fist or in thought in dream I mean never he will never
> or with his pencil or with his stick or
> or light light I mean
> never there he will never
> never anything
> there
> any more [p. 289]

It is clear from the association of the axe with the stick and pencil that Malone identifies himself to a certain degree with Lemuel. *He* kills his inventions after he has brought them

into being. The presumption of the writers who as "mak-
ers," "creators," in other words, as "poets" have often compared themselves with God is retracted; at the very least it is
unmasked.

However, is it not the case that Beckett has perpetuated the
lie insofar that he has actually written yet another novel? Has
Beckett's unmasking in his own work been radical enough?
Has he not, regardless of the thoroughness with which he
discloses the fictional-fictive procedures of all art, nevertheless comfortably kept himself out of it? Beckett decides to
write a continuation: It still was not enough; the self-invest-
ment was still not total, since the attempt to resolve the problem of the search, the attempt to abolish the invented reality
had resulted once more in a search, had produced a new
novel.

These paradoxes are the points of departure for *The
Unnamable*. The first-person narrator, nameless, outside of
time and place, speaks, mainly in the present tense, about
himself, rejecting any fictional procedure. Nevertheless,
occasionally he relapses into storytelling. The protagonist
who crops up sporadically is called Basilius, later renamed
Mahood. From what can be made out, it seems that, after
years of wandering, Mahood, now reduced to a trunk, is on
display in a large earthenware jar in the street, opposite a
restaurant. The proprietress of the latter looks after him and
covers him with a tarpaulin when it snows. Another figure
appears, called Worm, who is almost without any real substance and not always unambiguously distinguishable from
the narrator's voice. In the second half of the novel the
Unnamable, a further development of Malone, speaks more
and more about his "quest," his attempt to be silent, to
achieve silence. The storytelling is over: "Ah yes, all lies,
God and man, . . . all invented. . . . There will be no more
about them" (p. 306). The language is without paragraphs,
toward the end almost without sentences (full stops occur
only every other page), and I will not conceal the fact that the
structure becomes opaque, that the whole contains little
"human interest," does without the black comedy, and the—
for Beckett—grim and acid humor that is usually character-

istic. The author pursues his point with logical consistency, but perhaps with a certain barrenness and pedantry. However, perhaps it must look like this, the novel of necessity, the novel of having to talk in order finally to be able to be silent and to be allowed to be silent:

> I think I'll soon be dead, I hope I find it a change. I should have liked to go silent first, there were moments I thought that would be my reward for having spoken so long and so valiantly, to enter living into silence, so as to be able to enjoy it, no, I won't know why [p. 400].

Moran wrote a report because he was ordered to do so by his employer. Molloy began a report because he was to be paid for it, but he did so of his own free will. Malone "invented" only for himself. The Unnamable writes (from the style of the language, rather *speaks*) simply in order to be freed from the visions that afflict him, from the voices that he hears (see, e.g., p. 311 or 397). The Unnamable must speak, and the structure of his monologue betrays the nature of the torrent of words as a kind of logorrhea. The novel as genre has come to an end: fable, plot, place, time, characters, structure, imagery, the whole inventory of the narrative art has disappeared, or in any case has been reduced to the point of unrecognizability. Beckett the artist seeks to free himself from the compulsion to express himself (a motif that plays a role in many of Beckett's works) and every effort is made to establish the identity of the first person narrator as the author. In no other work are so many references made to earlier protagonists of other Beckett novels—and in the last analysis these are *Beckett's* creations and not the Unnamable's. The novel has become a discourse on the novel, and, more precisely, since it is a negative goal, the novel is a discourse on the termination of novel writing, a logical conclusion, no doubt, to the principle of self-reflexivity in literature.

IV

Finally, an attempt will be made to establish Beckett's position in literary history and at the same time his relationship to the topic of this collection of essays. It is true that literature has always been very much concerned with itself—the theater, for example, with the stage and acting situation; poetry with the process of inspiration; the novel, for example, with the conditions and the meaning of storytelling. Literature has done this more than, for example, leading articles have concerned themselves with leading articles, quiz programs with quiz programs, biological studies with biological studies, or legal texts with legal texts. The reason for this is the fact that in the case of literature—as with art in general—vision is at least as important as the object viewed, the representation at least as important as what is represented. Since fictional texts are concerned with an invented reality, with "constructions," and not with factual descriptions or texts relating to a reality outside of themselves, the "structure" must necessarily be as interesting as the reality that is seemingly described. Whole literary genres, for instance, parody or travesty, draw their strength from this situation. *Don Quixote* by Miguel de Cervantes, for example, is just as much a novel about other novels as a story about an anachronistic knight. In particular, it ridicules those romances in which sixteenth century knight-errants still travel the land, liberating virgins from the claws of dragons and fighting with giants and lions, although the real and spiritual background that had given the romances of the medieval courts their meaning had long since disappeared, Spain being subject to emigration and inflation and early bourgeois capitalism producing its first successes.

There are three recognizable peaks in the history of self-reflexive literature: The first is about 1600, the second about 1800, and the third since the end of the First World War. As even a mere sketch of the historical development is beyond the scope of this discussion, I will confine myself to a few comments on the literature of the twentieth century.

The theory of self-reflexive literature must be developed within the framework of the more comprehensive history and theory of the modern ego, of bourgeois subjectivity. René Descartes is surely one of the first to be named here: The subject derives his reality from the general certainty of his thinking (or doubting) (*"cogito ergo sum"*). After English philosophers such as John Locke and George Berkeley, German idealism took Descartes' thesis a stage further: The subject, certain of himself, secures the foundation of thought and reality; reflexion is essentially self-reflexion. Later the problematic tendencies inherent in these theses by J. G. Fichte and G. W. F. Hegel became radicalized as so-called solipsism: What began as the inclusion by Kant of the subject in the process of cognition became the exclusion of the world from the cognitive process. The unbearable rift between the ego and the world is overcome insofar that the subject is declared to be the sole object of the subject. In this way the old unity of life is restored, though at the expense of excluding the world from cognition.

Of course, the theory of cognition is to a large degree a reflex of material and social changes, of an individualism that on the whole can be seen to have been growing continually since the Renaissance. This can only be suggested here. Without doubt, literary developments must also be seen within this framework. To give a brief synopsis, Beckett's three novels are, from a formal viewpoint, several giant monologues (more precisely, "monographs," since the narrators are supposed to *write* rather than *speak*) and stand at the end of the tradition of the stream-of-consciousness novel as developed by James Joyce and Virginia Woolf and where the subject with his inner life is made the main object. However, Beckett goes further. Consider the following sentence from Fichte:

> Knowledge has now been found and stands in front of us as an eye resting on itself and closed. It sees nothing outside of itself, but it sees itself [9].

Beckett's trilogy can be seen as an attempt to exhaust the inherent problems and the impasse involved in this approach. In *The Unnamable* the writing moves in the direction of Fichte's point of departure, but this time as an end point. The narrator, presumably echoing the eye metaphor just quoted, says, [my body,] whose very eyes can no longer close . . . to rest me from seeing, to rest me from waking, to darken me to sleep, and no longer look away, or down, or up open to heaven, but must remain forever fixed and staring on the narrow space before them where there is nothing to be seen, ninety-nine per cent of the time. They must be as red as live coals. I sometimes wonder if the two retinae are not facing each other [p. 303].

Here the two eyes a human being has serve as a metaphor for the split into subject and object, which nevertheless must both be identical insofar that the object is also the subject. Complete and perfect self-knowledge is, however, impossible, since knowing more about oneself extends what it is that one wants to know more about and indeed to exactly the same extent that the ego discovers more about itself. To this extent the solipsistic position is not only fruitless, but also bound to fail as a strategy. Beckett recognizes this at the end of the trilogy: The final words are

you must go on, I can't go on, I'll go on [p. 418].

Beckett has continued writing—even if it seemed to him for a time as if he had written himself into an impasse. He has abandoned quests and metaliterature, and in the last fifteen years has found his way to a new form of literature. This is a highly concentrated form of short plays and short novels in which he represents very seriously and with great sympathy the solitude, loss of ego, and the fears of modern man.

The phase of self-reflexivity—apparently over and done with for Beckett personally—is correlated to the loss, which had long since taken place in other disciplines, of the belief that there is an objective reality and one that is objectively accessible to us. After a period of naive optimism it is now understood in physics that the mathematical formulas with which the researcher works so successfully represent much less reality itself than our *understanding* of reality. (For other areas see the contributions in this collection of essays.) Something similar must be the case with many writers in our century: After a period of interest in storytelling (one can think of Sir Walter Scott, Charles Dickens, and the mass production of three-volume novels toward the end of the nine-teenth century, not to speak of Eugène Sue, Karl May, and similar phenomena) they no longer trusted the justification for or the possibility of a naive storytelling, in other words, of the description of an apparently unproblematic, positive, and given reality. This can perhaps, among other things, help to explain why Beckett's texts are so difficult to read, why in fact they must be like this if they are not to remain behind their time. That is not to say that after Beckett one can only write in an ever more complicated fashion, that art in our time and in the future, like atomic physics or set theory, can only be accessible to a small elite. It is enough to bear in mind that with Beckett a particular kind of art reached a peak that seems hardly possible to surpass. (Beckett himself has become thematically more naive in his works since about the middle of the sixties.)

What, however, are the *artistic* reasons for self-reflexive literature as represented in Beckett?[18] One reason is surely sheer satiation with the well-made play, the well-told story. When Cervantes, as early as in the sixteenth century, produced an antiromance in reaction to the hack writers of his time, when Laurence Sterne in reaction to the self-complacent eigh-teenth-century novel produced an antinovel, how much more must a writer in our times suffer from the inflation of fiction, detective stories, comics, science fiction, soap operas on tele-vision, and so on. If all the stories have been told, why should yet another one be invented? And if it is a question of inven-tions anyway, why should it have to be precisely *this* story? (Compare the paragraph above on Proust.)

In addition to this, there is also the general state of doubt about language, not only from a philosophical viewpoint, as expressed in the oft-quoted formulation of Ludwig Wittgen-stein, when he said, "Philosophy is the fight against the bewitchment of our understanding through our language" [26], but also from a literary viewpoint, for example, in the sense in which Hugo von Hofmannsthal's Lord Chandos

---

[18]For conclusions similar to those reached here but arrived at from a dif-ferent standpoint, see Theodor W. Adorno [2].

speaks of it in an equally well-known passage in *Ein Brief* when he says that the words decay in his mouth "like mouldy fungus" [13]. Thus it is simply a matter of consistency on the part of writers when in their writings they should be even more concerned with the conditions, potentialities, and limits of their work than would be required of them anyway by a form of communication in which form is as important as content. Watzlawick et al. [22] have described how, in the case of whatever kind of human interaction one cares to examine, the importance of the definition of the relationship, in other words, the communication about the communication, increases in proportion to the extent of conflict between two partners in a communication (see p. 52). The position is familiar from problematic personal relationships, which can often be characterized by the fact that those involved scarcely communicate real content but, rather, spend most of their time, or at least their energy, explaining to each other (and probably no less to themselves) what they think about the way they communicate with each other. Communication is suffocated by metacommunication (and even when they are quarreling about real content, for example, about money or the washing up, these are only pretexts for conflicts in the relationship—in the last analysis they are *not* quarreling about money, etc.). Literature is unlikely to behave any differently. In a time when naive storytelling, when the construction of well-made plays, when trust in the instrument of language altogether had become problematic for the more sensitive artists, when trust in the old forms, trust in the relationship with the public had vanished, when the understanding with the reading public—alternatively, theater audience—that was known to the writer and easy to keep in perspective was lost (this was the result of a complete regrouping of this public, loss of confidence on the part of the artist, and the advent of the new media film and television): In a time such as this, the author of fictional texts who found himself in the midst of such disintegration could—at least so it seemed for some time—only write about writing or, more precisely, could only write about the impossibility of writing and thus hope in this paradoxical manner to continue his profession. Beckett was also theoretically aware of this position. In the three dialogues that he had in 1949 (in the period when he was working on the novel-trilogy) with Georges Duthuit, he said, with reference to the painters of the "Informel," but without doubt also referring to himself,

> I speak of an art turning from it [the plane of the feasible] in disgust, weary of puny exploits, weary of pretending to be able, of being able, of doing a little better the same old thing, of going a little further along the dreary road.

And in answer to Duthuit's question of what the artist should prefer, he continued [4],

> The expression that there is nothing to express, nothing with which to express, nothing from which to express, no power to express, no desire to express, together with the obligation to express [p. 103].[19]

REFERENCES

1. Abel, Lionel. *Metatheatre. A New View of Dramatic Form.* Hill and Wang, New York, 1963.
2. Adorno, Theodor W. Standort des Erzahlers im zeitgenossischen Roman. In *Noten zur Literatur I.* Suhrkamp, Frankfurt am Main, 1973, p. 61 ff.
3. Beckett, Samuel. *Molloy—Malone Dies—The Unnamable.* Calder and Boyars, London, 1959.
4. Beckett, Samuel. *Proust. Three Dialogues* (with Georges Duthuit). Calder, London, 1965.
5. Beebe, Maurice. Reflective and reflexive trends in modern fiction. *Bucknell Review* 22, 1976, 13–26.
6. Breuer, Rolf. *Die Kunst der Paradoxie. Sinnsuche und Scheitern bei Samuel Beckett.* Fink, Munich, 1976.
7. Broich, Ulrich. Dramatische Spiegelkabinette—Zum Motiv des Spiels im Spiel in den Dramen Tom Stoppards. In *Anglistentag 1980.* Hoffmann-Verlag, Grossen-Linden, 1981, pp. 139–158.
8. Ende, Michael. *Die unendliche Geschichte.* Thienemann, Stuttgart, 1979.
9. Fichte, Johann Gottlieb. *Werke,* Vol. 2 (I. H. Fichte, ed.). de Gruyter, Berlin, 1971, p. 38.
10. Foerster, Heinz von. Notes on an epistemology for living things. In *Biological Computer Laboratory,* Report No. 9.3. Urbana, Illinois, 1972, p. 1 ff.

---

[19]For useful suggestions and helpful criticism I wish to thank Horst Breuer (Marburg) and Wolfram K. Köck (Paderborn).

11. Freese, Peter. Die Story ist tot, es lebe die Story: Von der Short Story über die Anti-Story zur Meta-Story der Gegenwart. In *Die amerikanische Literatur der Gegenwart: Aspekte und Tendenzen* (H. Bungert, ed.). Reclam, Stuttgart, 1977, p. 228 ff.
12. Hansen, Arlene J. The celebration of solipsism: A new trend in American fiction. *Modern Fiction Studies* 19, 1973, 5–15.
13. Hofmannsthal, Hugo von. Ein Brief. In *Ausgewählte Werke*, Vol. 2. Fischer, Frankfurt am Main, 1966, p. 342.
14. Iser, Wolfgang. Das Spiel im Spiel: Formen dramatischer Ironie bei Shakespeare. *Archiv für das Studium der neueren Sprachen und Literaturen* 198, 1962, 209–226.
15. Josipovici, Gabriel. *The World and the Book. A Study of Modern Fiction.* Macmillan, London, 1979.
16. Kellman, Steven G. *The Self-Begetting Novel.* Columbia University Press, New York, 1980.
17. Russell, Charles. The vault of language: Self-reflective artifice in contemporary American fiction. *Modern Fiction Studies* 8, 1974, 349–359.
18. Schlueter, June. *Metafictional Characters in Modern Drama.* Columbia University Press, New York, 1979.
19. Schwanitz, Dietrich. *Die Wirklichkeit der Inszenierung und die Inszenierung der Wirklichkeit.* Hain, Meisenheim am Glan, 1977.
20. Smuda, Manfred. *Der Gegenstand in der Kunst und Literatur.* Fink, Munich, 1979.
21. Voigt, Joachim. *Das Spiel im Spiel. Versuch einer Formbestimmung,* Ph.D. thesis, Gottingen University, Gottingen, 1954.
22. Watzlawick, Paul, Beavin, Janet H., and Jackson, Don D. *Pragmatics of Human Communication. A Study of Interactional Patterns, Pathologies, and Paradoxes.* W. W. Norton, New York, 1967.
23. Watzlawick, Paul, Weakland, John H., and Fisch, Richard. *Change: Principles of Problem Formation and Problem Resolution.* W. W. Norton, New York, 1974.
24. Weber, Alfred. Poetologische Gedichte und Kunstlererzahlungen als Dokumente der Poetik. In *Anglistentag 1979* (K. Schumann, ed.). Universitätsbibliothek der Technischen Universität, Berlin, 1980, pp. 67–97.
25. Wehle, Winfried (ed.). *Nouveau roman.* Wissenschaftliche Buchgesellschaft, Darmstadt, 1980.
26. Wittgenstein, Ludwig. *Philosophische Untersuchungen.* In *Schriften,* Vol. 1. Suhrkamp, Frankfurt am Main, 1963, p. 342.

PART 3

The Imperfect Perfection

PAUL WATZLAWICK

> *To think*
> *that I will no longer think of you*
> *is still thinking of you.*
> *Let me then try*
> *not to think*
> *that I will no longer think of you.*

*T*hese words, attributed to a Zen master, summarize the essence
of the third part of this book.

In a world based on classical linear causality, two properties
emerge with seeming logic and necessity: the split between
observer (subject) and observed (object) and the all-inclusive
ordering of that world into pairs of opposites, an order for which
common sense manages to find confirmation everywhere—cause–
effect, inside–outside, day–night, life–death, good–evil, body–soul,
past–future, health–illness; the list could go on for pages.

The reality thus constructed reverberates from the violent clash
of these opposites. No matter how long and how furiously the
struggle has been raging, neither side seems capable of gaining
the upper hand. This, of course, does not exclude the possibility
that the losses and the suffering may at times reach horrifying
proportions.

Does the power of one's own attack lend special force to the
attacked, and is there something in the nature of defense, rejection, and negation that increases the strength of the opponent?
The question is rhetorical. Heraclitus already knew: To exist,
everything needs its opposite. Long before the constructions of
the Manichaeans and the Gnostics, Lao Tsu lucidly traced the
course of this development in his Tao Te Ching, especially in
Chapters 2 and 18:

Under heaven all can see beauty as beauty only because there is ugliness,
All can know good only because there is evil.

and

> *When the great Tao is forgotten,*
> *Kindness and morality arise.*
> *When wisdom and intelligence are born,*
> *The great pretense begins.*
>
> *When there is no peace in the family,*
> *Filial pity and devotion arise.*
> *When the country is confused and in chaos,*
> *Loyal ministers appear* [4].

In Taoism the decisive event leading to the splitting of the world into pairs of opposites is thus the loss of Tao; for the ancient Greeks it was man's falling out of the state of pleroma; *in the Kabbalah it is the "breaking of the vessels"; for Christianity, the eating of the forbidden fruit. In modern science it is the strict separation of the observing subject and the observed object; a separation whose hopeless absurdity was noted by Heisenberg, who stated that a truly objective world, totally devoid of all subjectivity, would* for this very reason *be unobservable.*

Modern man has increasing reason to suspect that there is something in the nature of attempted perfection that leads to imperfection. This realization, however, typically does not lead to a radical reexamination of this quest for perfection, but only to the conclusion that the attempted perfection is not yet the perfect one and that it is therefore necessary to do more of the same striving for perfection [6]. *Hence our bewildered amazement when we discover that both scientific and social constructions produce realities that are the very opposite of the intended ideal: Medicine begins to contribute to illness* [2]; *ever more highly specialized schools produce increasing mediocrity; "communication training" makes people mentally deaf and dumb; ever more rapid means of transportation and other time-saving devices leave us with less and less leisure* [1]; *increasingly comprehensive welfare pro-*

grams contribute to the mounting incompetence of the average citizen [5]; justice and the penal system seem to supply us with additional criminals; and every further social progress appears to precipitate further erosion of individual liberties [7].

In our inner, private world, the situation is not much different, as the Zen quotation points out. He who wants to forget remembers even more painfully; he who tries to force himself to fall asleep stays awake; he who wants to be specially witty is boring; and he who tells himself to have neither right nor reason to be sad sinks into depression.

A state of perfection presupposes the eradication of everything imperfect. But in attempting this, the striving for perfection entangles itself in the strange snares and paradoxes of negation.

What is involved here is essentially the following: One may reject an idea (or assumption, ideology, belief, etc.) either because one holds the opposite view or because one adheres neither to the idea nor to its negation (opposite). In the latter case one is not caught in the conflict between assertion and negation; in other words, one is neither for nor against, one stands outside this pair of opposites, one is autonomous.[1]

However, in taking this autonomous position, one still runs afoul of the apparently all-embracing, definitive Manichaean separation of the world into pairs of opposites. For since one is not for, one is (by this horrible simplification) still against. Tertium non datur—a third possibility exists neither in Mani's nor in Aristotle's worlds.

But there is an escape; it becomes possible as soon as we understand that the negation of the opposite (which, after all, requires its recognition) and the standing outside that pair of opposites are two fundamentally different forms of negation. We begin to see that only by a sort of sleight of hand and inside the frame of a world constructed out of the primitive yes–no thinking did the two forms of negation appear to be identical. We then also become

---

[1]This autonomy must not be confused with the Hegelian concept of the synthesis that brings together and resolves thesis and antithesis.

aware of the inhumanity of this construction that reaches far into our everyday lives, and, finally, we wonder how we managed to keep ourselves blind to this and accepted it as an apparent given of the real world.

This world is the subject of the first contribution to part 3. In it the Norwegian philosopher Jon Elster shows the need for a strict separation of the concepts of active and passive negation, and describes the consequences of their uncritical confusion. The reader who is unfamiliar with symbolic logic should not allow himself to be deterred by the very few paragraphs dealing with formal logic: He will be richly rewarded, for not only does Elster's essay provide an analysis of unusual clarity, but its raw material, so to speak, is the novels of the Soviet dissident Alexander Zinoviev, which speak for themselves and presuppose no professional specialization. To quote Elster, in his books "Zinoviev has created a literary genre for which he is himself the only example." In grasping the essence of the "Ivanian regime," the reader experiences what Kuhn [3] has called a paradigmatic change.

The second contribution to this part attempts to show the stereotypical characteristics of the reality that emerges as the result of the conviction that the final, true explanation of the world has been found. In its claim to perfection, any such utopian construction plunges into the paradoxes of self-reflexivity; no system can prove its own truth from within itself. But since the primitive, Manichaean thinking of ideologies cannot afford to see its unavoidable, innate imperfection as the direct, self-reflexive consequence of its claim to perfection, this paradox becomes the concrete (and not only metaphorical) stumbling block to all ideologies.

REFERENCES

1. Dupuy, Jean-Pierre, and Robert, Jean. *La Trahison de l'opulence.* Presses Universitaires de France, Paris, 1976.
2. Illich, Ivan D. *Medical Nemesis.* Pantheon Books, New York, 1976.
3. Kuhn, Thomas. *The Structure of Scientific Revolutions.* University of Chicago Press, Chicago, 1970.
4. Lao Tsu. *Tao Te Ching* (translated by Gia-Fu Feng and Jane English). Vintage Books, New York, 1972.

5. Thayer, Lee. The functions of incompetence. In *Vistas in Physical Reality: Festschrift for Henry Margenau* (Ervin Laszlo and Emily B. Sellow, eds.). Plenum Press, New York, 1976, pp. 171–187.
6. Watzlawick, Paul, Weakland, John H., and Fisch, Richard. *Change.* W. W. Norton, New York, 1974, pp. 31–39.
7. Watzlawick, Paul. Games without end. In *Surviving Failures* (Bo Persson, ed.). Almqvist and Wiksell International, Stockholm, and Humanities Press, Atlantic Highlands, New Jersey, 1979, pp. 225–231.

JON ELSTER

Active and Passive Negation
An Essay
in Ibanskian Sociology*

LOGICIAN BY PROFESSION, novelist and sociologist by vocation, Alexander Zinoviev[1] has created a literary genre
whose only example is his own. In order to have an idea of
the specificity of his approach, one has to imagine the feroc-
ity of Swift, the burlesque of Rabelais, the paradoxes of Lewis
Carroll (like Zinoviev, a logician), the moral height of Sol-

*Originally presented at the Ninth World Congress of Political Science,
Moscow, 12–18 August 1979, and translated from the French by Ronald
Garwood.
[1]This essay is based on the two works published as of this date by Zinoviev outside the field of logic: *Les Hauteurs béantes* (L'Age d'homme, Lausanne, 1977; *The Yawning Heights*, translated from Russian by Gordon
Clough, New York, 1979; in the following abbreviated *YH*), and *L'Avenir
radieux* (L'Age d'homme, Lausanne, 1978; *The Radiant Future*, translated
from Russian by Gordon Clough, New York, 1980; in the following
abbreviated *RF*). It deals solely with the sociological method of the works,
setting aside both any literary judgment and any evaluation of the merit
of the analysis. Undoubtedly, Zinoviev's account has the ring of truth,
even in its obvious exaggerations, to an extent that we cannot *not* accept
it fully, especially since it corresponds to the general impressions that
can be gathered from various sources. It must be said, however, that for
the present, Zinoviev's work remains a (privileged) source of hypotheses,
rather than an ensemble of established conclusions. Just by chance, my
reading of Zinoviev coincided with that of the great work of Paul Veyne,
Le Pain et le cirque (Seuil, Paris, 1976) and with the re-reading of Tocqueville's *Democracy in America*. From time to time I will have the opportunity to point out several areas where these three works converge. I hope
to be able to devote a separate study to them. I would like to thank Cle-
mens Heller for encouraging me to read Zinoviev and to take a serious
look at this aspect of social irrationality.

zhenitsyn, and the sociological intuition of Simmel. But a description by juxtaposition is perforce inadequate. In order to summarize the work of Zinoviev, I would use, rather, a comparison that would perhaps not be to the author's liking (but who knows?): He does for Soviet communism what Marx did for the capitalism of his time. Like Marx, who strove to demonstrate the mechanisms of capitalistic irrationality, Zinoviev has us enter an hallucinatory world that is, however, not a chaotic one, but one ruled by principles as irrational as they are intelligible. *Understanding the irrational:* such is the task that Zinoviev proposes. The irrational object is Soviet society; the method used to study it derives in great part from formal logic. It will be seen that Zinoviev takes a place not only in the tradition of formal logic, but also, perhaps without realizing it,[2] in the lineage that includes Hegel, Marx, and Sartre. In his analysis, Soviet irrationality is not produced, as under capitalism, by the shock of incompatible and uncoordinated intentions; we are reminded, rather, of the snake that bites its own tail, of the right hand that steals from the left, of the dog that chases its shadow, or of the man who verifies the news in a newspaper by buying a second copy of the same newspaper.

From the very first page of *YH*, the reader understands what it is all about: "The objective of the measure was to discover those elements which did not approve of putting it into practice" (*YH*, p. 9). On the one hand, this idea suggests a political system stripped of content, or whose content would be its form itself; on the other hand, it is characteristic of the logical paradoxes that have upset formal logic in our cen-

---

[2]Of course, dialectics is an integral part of the Soviet system; therefore it is derided time and time again. But Zinoviev also seems to recognize a dialectics less stagnant than the *diamat*: "That's how I can get rid of Anton. I'm irresistibly attracted to him. I can't pass one single day without thinking of him. And at the same time, I have no more urgent desire than that of fleeing him. People put down dialectics, but we can't make one step without its help" (*RF*, p. 124). This thought belongs to the very ambiguous protagonist of the book, and nothing would justify attributing it to Zinoviev. We will see, however, that Zinoviev is describing here his own method behind the "dialectics."

tury.[3] In its theoretical version, the paradigm of such a paradox is the proposition, "This proposition is false." Zinoviev suggests a more practical version: "One has to obey this order, under penalty of death." Which order? The self-reference and the infinite regression bring about a feeling of vertigo, no doubt analogous to the vague feelings of guilt that hover permanently over every citizen of Ibansk, mythic locale of *YH*. We could quote other examples of the same type,[4] but the essence of Zinoviev's idea is not there. Central to his analysis is a logical distinction between what I will call *active negation* and *passive negation*, a distinction going back as far as Kant, and that later assumed an importance crucial to modern psychiatry and psychology. Zinoviev makes a double usage of it. On the one hand, he sees in the confusion of the two forms a fundamental aspect of the irrationality of the régime; on the other hand, he uses the distinction as a conceptual tool important for the analysis of Soviet institutions. As for the first usage, we could put forth the definition that the negligence of this distinction characterizes the *primitive mentality*, by resolutely making abstraction of all other connotations that this discredited term has had in the past.[5] Whatever the fecundity of this notion might be, we shall see that, starting with the tendency to confuse the two negations, the analysis of the irrational is called for in several cases.

---

[3]For some amusing and informative insights, see R. Smullyan, *What Is the Name of This Book?* (Prentice-Hall, Englewood Cliffs, New Jersey, 1978) and D. R. Hofstadter, *Gödel, Escher, Bach: An Eternal Golden Braid* (Basic Books, New York, 1979).

[4]For example, on p. 81 of *YH*, where it is a question of an Ibanskian delegation returning to Ibansk bringing "pairs of tight pants trimmed in leather and with the bizarre label 'Fabriqué abroad' "; or better, the motto of Ibanskian democracy, "Everything obsolete and out of date has to be nipped in the bud" (*YH*, p. 161); or on p. 237 of *RF*, which points out "one more paradox of our life: one of the fundamental tendencies of the communist way of life is the attempt to escape from the rules of that very way of life"; or, finally, p. 819 of *YH*, which humorously depicts a character called Collaborateur who "could be seen . . . in the shortest line, the one where people had the right to not wait to cash their paychecks."

[5]For another attempt at reviving this notion, see R. Shweder, Likeliness and likelihood in everyday thought: Magical thinking in judgments about personality, *Current Anthropology* 18, 1977, 637–658.

Starting with logical analysis, we will trace the history of the thought and arrive finally at Zinoviev. Consider the following propositions:

I. Person A believes statement p to be true [abbreviated: A believes p].

II. It is not the case that A believes p [abbreviated: Not (A believes p)].

III. A believes the contrary of p [abbreviated: A believes not−p].

Proposition II is the passive negation of I; proposition III is its active negation. In general, the negation of formal logic is passive negation. For example, the laws of thought always invoke that form of negation. Thus the principle of contradiction "Not(I and not−I)" is to be understood as "Not (I and II)"; the principle of the excluded middle "I or not−I" understood as "I or II." The first characteristic of a primitive mentality would be, then, to accept these principles for both active negation and passive negation. Therefore one would be faced with the impossibility of simultaneously having two contradictory opinions or, in a more general sense, having an ensemble of opinions from which one can deduce a contradiction.

This conclusion—as attractive as it is fallacious—is found in several recent books[6] and even in Aristotle.[7] In an analogous manner, the primitive mentality would deny the distinction between atheism, active negation of God, and agnosticism, the passive negation.[8] Who wouldn't recognize

---

[6]See references in my *Logic and Society* (Cambridge University Press, Cambridge 1979), pp. 81 and 94.

[7]In *Metaphysics*, §1005b.

[8]For this problem, see P. W. Pruyser, *Between Belief and Unbelief* (New York, 1974), as well as Tocqueville: "In the periods just covered, people abandoned beliefs out of indifference, rather than out of hate; one doesn't reject them, they leave" (*Democracy in America*, Paris, 1961). But following William James, Pruyser (*op. cit.*, p. 126) points out that one can also be agnostic out of a passionate conviction, and not only out of indifference; this is the case of the desired indifference discussed below. In this context, we can also quote Paul Veyne (*Le Pain et le cirque*, p. 589) where he writes of Roman emperors: "The godliness of the ruler had no believ-

here the, "Either you're for me or against me!" of everyday Manichaeism?

The example just given is a specific case of a larger group of problems studied in modal logic.[9] In the classic paradigm of this theory, Np represents the necessity of proposition p, and Mp its possibility. The passive negation of Np is therefore Not(Np), which is the equivalent of M(Not$-p$); the active negation is N(Not$-p$). Now the operatives N and M lend themselves to other interpretations, namely, the following. In *deontological logic Np* is read as, "It is mandatory to do p," and Mp as, "It is permitted to do p"; the distinction between active and passive shown here is important and will be taken up later on. Then there are several versions of *epistemological logic:* In the *logic of knowledge* we read Np as "A knows p," in the *logic of opinion* as "A believes p," Mp being understood as Not[N(not$-p$)] in both cases. Notice that the logic of opinion is an axiomatization of the *rational* opinion, which implies a principle of contradiction even for the active negation. On the other hand, there is no principle of the excluded middle for active negation. Among the modal systems, we can mention *temporal logic* and *logic of intention*. In this last instance, then, we have to make the distinction between the desire to not do x and the absence of desire to do x. We will come back to this.

We can point out two other distinctions closely linked to those in the preceding paragraph. Firstly, there is the distinction between the negation of a conjunction and the conjunction of negations. In the primitive mentality,[10] to deny the conjunction of the propositions $p,q, \ldots ,r$ is the equivalent of denying each of them; consequently a system of thoughts or a political platform is to be abandoned or taken

ers, but they did have their non-believers—Christians!" The emperors' godliness existed only as an object of negation in the mind of Christians; no one attached a positive belief in them, despite appearances. It would be difficult not to think of the Marxist–Leninist cult.

[9]See the fine introduction in D. P. Snyder, *Modal Logic and Its Applications* (New York, 1971); see also *Logic and Society*, Chapter 1 for a general discussion.

[10]On this topic, see B. Inhelder and J. Piaget, *La Genèse des structures élémentaires* (Neuchâtel, 1976), Chapter V.4.

as a whole. In a Norwegian fairy tale,[11] we can see this style
of primitive thinking in its purest form. Two girls, one nice
and angelic, the other bad and wicked, have to go through a
series of obstacles arranged in such a manner that the final
outcome depends on success with each and every obstacle.
The good girl, of course, overcomes all the obstacles, and *the
bad girl fails in them all*, even though one failure alone would
have sufficed to assure a final failure. In traditional societies,
it is difficult to imagine that excellence can come in degrees,
that it can be ranked, that there can be multiple scales of
superiority.[12] In general, the recourse to stereotypes simpli-
fies life and provides an inner peace.[13] Undoubtedly the units
of a denied conjunction are often linked to each other in a
cause–effect relation, justifying their treatment as a whole,
but it is in the nature of the primitive mentality to go beyond
experience and fall into preconception.

The second distinction comes under the heading of an esoteric problem of logic: how to render in formal language *definite description*, that is to say, expressions beginning with
the definite article *the*. In a new famous article[14] Bertrand
Russell demonstrated that these expressions are only subject
to analysis when in the context of a proposition. Thus, "The
King of France is bald" asserts (1) there exists an object x,
such that x possesses the quality "to be King of France"; (2)
that while possessing this quality, $y = x$; and (3) that the object
x is bald. Read in 1982, this proposition is simply false, since
the first of the three constituents of the proposition is false.

---

[11]P. C. Asbjørnsen and J. Moe, Manndatteren og Kjerringdatteren, *Samlede
Eventyr*, Vol. 2, Oslo, 1957.

[12]P. Veyne, *op. cit.*, pp. 114 and 773. This phenonemon can no doubt be
linked to the fact that "every solution tends to oversolve its problem"
(*ibid.*, p. 708). In fact, the example suggested by Veyne in the following
quote is very reminiscent of the distinction between active and passive
negation: "Christian ascetic theology teaches that is is not enough to
renounce evil pleasures, not even enough to sacrifice dangerous pleasures; one also has to deprive oneself of permitted pleasures" (*ibid.*, p.
790). A passion can never be supplanted, except by another passion; see
A. Hirschman, *The Passions and the Interests* (Princeton University Press,
Princeton, 1977), p. 20ff.

[13]See, for example, R. A. Jones, *Self-fulfilling Prophecies* (Halsted, New York,
1974), chapters 2 and 3.

[14]Bertrand Russell, "On denoting," *Mind* 14, 1905, 479–493.

Now, how do we evaluate its negation, "The King of France is not bald"? The passive negation is the true proposition that denies the conjunction (1), (2), and (3); the active negation is the false proposition which asserts (1) and (2) while denying (3). Faced with the question, Is the King of France bald? we sense that both yes and no are equally inadequate responses, since each presupposes the inadmissible fact of a King of France whose baldness alone is in question. And what about the trap question, Do you still beat your wife?[15] Ibansk joins the universe of *Catch 22* on the list of places where all questions are similarly rigged. The primitive mentality is not only the one that falls into the trap; it can set them, also, while all the time not knowing that the dilemma posed is not really a dilemma at all. We can even say that the primitive mentality does a good job of setting traps, deliberate manipulations being in general less efficacious than complicity in the absurd. We will return to this point below.

In his short precritical treatise "Versuch, den Begriff der negativen Grössen in die Weltweisheit einzuführen," Kant introduces the distinction between active and passive negation. The text is obscure, being part of a physicophilosophical controversy that no longer concerns us[16]; nevertheless, we can profitably consider the examples Kant puts forth in order to explain the distinction. (1) The passive negation of movement is repose, the active negation being movement in the opposite direction. (2) The passive negation of wealth is poverty, the active negation indebtedness. (3) The passive negation of pleasure is either indifference or equilibrium, corresponding to the absence of causes of pleasure and of displeasure and to the presence of causes that are suppressed in their effect; the active negation is displeasure. (4) The pas-

---

[15]See P. Watzlawick, *The Language of Change* (Basic Books, New York, 1978), p. 108ff, for other examples of this dilemma, whose general form is to pose as contradictory two ideas not at all opposed; thus a child is asked if he prefers to go to bed at eight o'clock or at a quarter to eight. Among these dilemmas, the real trap questions are those that only have yes or no as choices, two contradictory responses masking two ideas in opposition to each other.

[16]See my *Leibniz et la formation de l'esprit capitaliste* (Aubier, Paris, 1975, p. 224 ff.

sive negation of virtue is not the sin of omission that, no less than the sin of commission, constitutes an active negation of virtue; only the deficiency in a saint or the mistake of a noble person would represent passive negation. (5) The passive negation of attention is indifference, the active negation is abstraction; in other words, the absence of consciousness of x is something other than the consciousness of the absence of x. (6) The passive negation of obligation is nonobligation, and the active negation is interdiction. (7) The passive negation of desire is, again, indifference, the active negation disgust; we could say that the absence of desire in x is something other than the desire for the absence of x.

As we can see, these examples fall into two categories: In one are cases (5)–(7), which correspond to the modal distinction between Not(Np) and N(not $-p$); in the other are the examples (1)–(4), which cannot be classified using that distinction. In other words, strictly speaking, negation is an operation attaching itself only to propositions: To speak of the negation of a movement, of a pleasure, or of a virtue makes no sense. Kant obviously had in mind the idea of a movement, action, or sensation that in some way would nullify an initial disposition, a notion that is understood for movement in space, but which loses all meaning in the domain of morality. One could be pardoned for a wrong action; one would not know how to act as though it had never happened. We can add that one can be pardoned in more than one way, so that it is difficult to speak of *the* negation that reestablishes equilibrium. Having said this, we can see that Kant's idea remains stimulating even in these less rigorous cases. We will see that Zinoviev himself uses it in the strict sense and, at the same time, in the larger sense.[17]

---

[17]It is still no less true that even in this less rigorous sense, the confusion of the passive negation and the (or an) active negation remains possible. There is a classic example of this in Leibniz: *"regredimur nisi progredia-mur, quia stari non potest"* (*Textes inédits,* Paris, 1948, p. 94), and in a related example, the idea that love either grows or disappears (if it hasn't already). The novelist is familiar with the danger of painting his characters too vividly, having experienced the problem of bringing a less colorful character to the forefront; how, then, can we speak of a nonentity? See also P. Veyne's example in footnote 12.

In the desire for the absence of *x*, or in the consciousness of the absence of *x*, *x* is at the same time absent and present, present as intentional object of the desire of absence. In Hegel this observation, made by Kant only in passing, is the object of a systematic development. We note, in particular, Chapter IV of *Phenomenology of Mind*, where the consciousness is initially presented as *desire* whose fundamental goal is to dominate the exterior world (and to assert itself) by *consuming* it. Now the resultant satisfaction turns out to be fragile:

> In this state of satisfaction, however, the consciousness of oneself has experience of the independence of its object. Desire and the certainty of its self obtained in the gratification of desire are conditioned by the object; for the certainty exists in cancelling this other. *In order that this cancelling may be effected, there must be this other.* Self-consciousness is thus unable by its negative relation to the object to abolish it; because of that relation it rather produces it again, as well as the desire.[18]

In the sentence I have italicized, Hegel explains in the clearest possible terms the paradox of active negation. This paradox, whose independence requires the destruction of an exterior object, actually depends on it in its very being and could never, without contradiction, desire the destruction of that exterior object. Two hundred years earlier John Donne had already written the following in *The Prohibition:*

> Take heed of hating me,
> Or too much triumph in the victory
> Not that I shall be mine own officer,
> And hate with hate again retaliate:
> But thou wilt lose the style of conqueror,
> If I, thy conquest, perish by thy hate.
> Then, lest my being nothing lessen thee,
> If thou hate me, take heed of hating me.

On reflection, it is a question of an omnipresent phenomenon. Thus militant atheism would never be able to exist

---

[18]G. W. F. Hegel, *Phenomenology of Mind*, Vol. 1, 1807.

without the believers it opposes, just as a certain form of communism lives in symbiotic union with private property[19]: We can also mention the anticommunist whose world would collapse if one day he succeeded in destroying "the God that failed." In the case of atheism two distinct paradoxes arise: On the one hand, there is the already mentioned difficulty of accepting the distinction between atheism and agnosticism, a distinction too sophisticated for the primitive mentality; on the other hand, there is the negative belief of the atheist who is as bound to God as is the believer (or even more so).[20] In fact, the two paradoxes are linked, for the inefficacy of atheism comes about precisely because it wants to achieve the impossible: to establish, by active negation, a state of passive negation.

Rather than stop here to discuss the prolongation of these ideas in Sartre, by way of Koyré and Kojève, we will conclude this historical glimpse with remarks on their importance in contemporary psychiatry. According to the so-called Palo Alto group,[21] an important element of the etiology of certain pathological family situations is the *contradictory injunction,* an order whose overt content contradicts its pragmatic presuppositions. Hence the order, "Don't be so obedient"—corresponding to the Sartrian idea of love—places its recipient in an impossible situation: In order to obey, he has to not obey. In a like manner, the injunction, "Be spontaneous," asks for a deliberate effort to achieve a state whose essence is nondeliberation. Bad emperors of classical antiquity commanded, "Adore me"[22]; American slave traders demanded recognition from their slaves,[23] propositions as incoherent as they are impossible. A last example, the most

---

[19]"Just as atheism ceases to be significant when the affirmation of man is no longer dependent on the negation of God, in the same way socialism in the full sense is the direct affirmation of humanity independent of the negation of private property": (L. Kolakowski, *Main Currents of Marxism,* Vol. 1, Oxford, 1978, p. 140).

[20]See the observation of Paul Veyne quoted in footnote 8.

[21]See P. Watzlawick, et al., *Change* (W. W. Norton, New York, 1974).

[22]P. Veyne, *op. cit.,* pp. 488, 569, 701, 721.

[23]See my *Logic and Society,* Wiley, London, 1978. p. 71 ff, for this Hegelian idea taken up in the works of Eugene Genovese on American slavery (*The Political Economy of Slavery,* Pantheon, New York, 1974).

important for this context, concerns a mother who commands her daughter, "Remember that you must not even think of that forbidden thing," which is the same as telling her to give it much thought so that she won't think about it. Consider this passage of Emily Dickinson (*Complete Poems*, Thomas H. Johnson, ed., Faber and Faber, London, 1970):

> The Heart cannot forget
> Unless it contemplate
> What it declines

The will to forget is an example of what has been called "to want what couldn't be wanted,"[24] an impossibility, since it relies on the confusion of active and passive negation. Forgetfulness, or indifference, is a passive negation—simply the absence of consciousness of x—while the will to forget requires the consciousness of the absence of x. Wanting to forget is like deciding to create obscurity from light. Just like forgetfulness, or indifference, states of mind like sincerity, spontaneity, innocence, or faith could never be created by an act of intentional will.

In order to get at the importance of these distinctions in Zinoviev's works, we will first look at his analysis of the Ibanskian regime, then at the relations of the regime to its opposition (interior and exterior), and finally at the internal structure of the interior opposition. Out of this will come an initial conclusion as to the profound impotence of the regime, permitting us ultimately to distinguish two meanings for the notion "negation of the negation" as a form of historical evaluation.

The tragiburlesque air of YH comes about because Zinoviev submits to sociological analysis phenomena such as denunciation and "arrivism" (ladder climbing, ambition), both burlesque in the particular, tragic on the whole. Indeed, "a farce which is regularly repeated is actually a tragedy" (*YH*, p. 468), for "trivialities come and go, but the system of trivia stays in place" (*YH*, p. 374), to which it can be added

---

[24]See L. Farber, *Lying, Despair, Jealousy, Envy, Sex, Suicide, Drugs and the Good Life* (Basic Books, New York, 1976).

that history repeats itself "the first time as tragedy, the second as catastrophe" (YH, p. 710). As for denunciation, a constituent phenomenon of every social group in Ibansk, it tends to be the substitute for information: "Information is a mass of lies, in that it is a public and official phenomenon, and it is quickly transformed into denunciation, in that it is a secret phenomenon" (YH, p. 107). One could naïvely surmise that in every totalitarian regime there must be a branch within the Interior Minister's office that would have complete and reliable information at its disposal, if only to make oppression more efficient, but, according to Zinoviev, this is hardly the case, since it is in no one's interest to tell the truth.

We have to consider Zinoviev as the founder of the sociology of arrivism, a fundamental and universal trait in Ibansk. In RF the author-protagonist shares with us his reflections on this phenomenon, beginning with its most intelligible form, one characterized by cynicism, the total absence of moral consciousness, and skill in the game of personal interactions. But there is more:

> But Agafonov has confused all my ideas about Soviet careerism. He is a handsome enough lad, although not exactly a film star. You can't say that he is particularly bright, but neither is he stupid. He won't say no to a drink. He's not malicious. He is good natured. Idle. A bit sleepy. And he has no family connections. No one to protect him in the way than Kanareikin has protected me. He's published a couple of down-market pamphlets on philosophy (philosophy for housewives and mental deficients, as they were described by such outstanding degenerates as Kanareikin and Petin). And yet he took off like a rocket for no particular reason. He was suddenly included in the editorial board of a leading journal, given a professorship, appointed editor and elected a corresponding member all before my very eyes [p. 143].

Equally mysteriously is the awarding of a literary prize to an author who not only lacks any trace of talent, which goes without saying, but who has not rendered service either to the state or to the party (RF, p. 235 ff). It is in YH that we find the key to this second type of arrivism, in the observation that Stalin was not an arrivist of great talent but, rather, someone extraordinarily mediocre (*YH*, p. 398). To be a talented arrivist implies the possession of outstanding negative qualities; to be extraordinarily mediocre implies an outstanding lack of qualities. In Ibanskian society, the greatest success belongs to the latter: "The most able careerist (arrivist) is the one with the least talent as a careerist" (*YH*, p. 398); or better,

> the most successful method of making a career in Ibanskian conditions, and this is certainly the method chosen by that undoubtedly talented careerist Claimant, gives enormous advantage to the *un*-talented careerist. Even the Boss himself [i.e., Stalin] seized power and established his own system of power not because he was a genius at his own filthy business, but exclusively because even in that very business he was a total nonentity. He was completely fitted to that business as a person. The leader of rats cannot be a lion [p. 214].

From this we get the "impression . . . of being up against an extraordinarily insignificant force which, by virtue of this very fact, is invincible" (*YH* p. 399). It would be out of the question to oppose an absence; it is much more preferable to have the presence of a negative that would serve as an object of opposition. Here Zinoviev takes up the theme of the triviality of evil, transposing it from the individual to the societal level. According to Yeats, the most dreaded situation is that one where "the best have lost all conviction and the worst are full of passionate intensity"; for Tocqueville the crisis in religion would be to have only "lukewarm friends and ardent adversaries"[25]; and according to the early Marx, the danger for freedom of the press in Germany resided in having platonic friends and fervent enemies.[26] In a sense, they are right, but to exist as an object of negation is still a form of existence more preferable to the total absence of consciousness in men. Evil triumphs only when it has become the passive and banal negation of Good.

In order to explain the success of mediocrity, we can invoke

---

[25]*Democracy in America*, Vol. 1; see also the observation of Paul Veyne in footnote 8.

[26]*Rheinische Zeitung*, May 5, 1842.

the following general principle: Certain conducts are efficacious only when they don't have efficiency as an end.[27]
Intention always does a poor job of hiding itself; "man merkt
die Absicht und wird verstimmt." One could neither shock
the bourgeois in wanting to shock the bourgeois,[28] nor always
profit from a love that one inspires,[29] nor engender in a systematic manner random numbers.[30] We all know of the difficulties a talented writer experiences when he sets out to
write a best seller in order to earn a living. The result will
invariably be either too good or too bad; to find the right
tone, he would have to share, and not exploit, the narrow
vision and prejudices of the general public; "The better you
do your work, the more trouble it gets you into. And if you
do it poorly, you'll only be ruined that much more because,
when it comes to botched up work, they know much more
about it than you do" (RF, p. 102).

But this analysis of the Ibanskian man would seem to contradict the view revealed in the following passage:

> An outstanding intelligence is regarded here as an abnormality,
> and outstanding stupidity as outstanding intelligence. Highly
> moral people are regarded as amoral villains, and the most abject
> nonentities as models of virtue. What is in question here is not
> the absence of one quality, but the presence of another. As a
> result a strangely negative type of personality is formed which
> reacts to the positive in the same way as the electron to the posi-
> tron (or vice versa). Just as the presence of a negative charge is
> not the absence of a positive, and of a positive charge is not the
> absence of a negative, so in the given case, I repeat, a negative
> type of personality is a personality which has certain specific
> attributes [YH, p. 102].

Is the Ibanskian man the active negation of the moral and
rational man, as the preceding passage seems to suggest, or

---

[27]Paul Veyne, op. cit., p. 679, treats this in incomparable style.
[28]Ibid., p. 98.
[29]We think of the love of Stendhal's character Lucien Leuwen for Mme. de
Chasteller.
[30]According to John von Neumann, "anyone who considers arithmetical
methods of producing random digits is, of course, in a state of sin" (quoted
in H. H. Goldstine, The Computer from Pascal to Neumann, Princeton University Press, Princeton, 1972, p. 297).

the passive negation of the Agafanov type? We have to think that passive negation is the most highly developed form of the Ibanskian personality, even if the active negation of it is the most striking by virtue of its specific attributes. This interpretation is supported by Zinoviev's insistence on the *normality* of the universe he describes: There is no question of trying to effect a cure, for it is perfectly normal and healthy (*RF*, p. 191). The universe is not inhabited by evil and immoral people; at the very most, we can speak of amorality. It is true that "moral consciousness has declined, just like the classical types predicted" (*RF*, p. 134), but the result is on this side of morality, rather than beyond it.[31] If moral behavior is the negation of blindly reckless behavior, then Ibansk represents the negation of negation—but in the logical sense rather than in the dialectical sense.

Contradiction dominates every aspect of Ibanskian life, be it economic planning, education, or the struggle against criminality. The following general principle can be posited: instead of looking for efficient solutions for real problems, it is necessary to look for a problem which corresponds to possible or desired solutions. (Note the procedure in mathematical economics that looks for those conditions permitting the demonstration of a theorem judged to be important—for example, the existence of general economic equilibrium—rather than the theorems which follow from conditions judged to be plausible.) A grotesque example: To reduce the percentage of unpunished crimes, the number of ficticious crimes can be raised. Setting n as the number of real crimes, m as the number of real crimes punished, and a as the number of ficticious crimes attributed to innocent people punished, authorities have an interest in making a as large as possible since the percentage $(m + a) / (n + a)$ is an increasing function of a, the only problem being that "they need to reconcile objectives that are in dialectical contradiction: there should

---

[31]See my *Ulysses and the Sirens* (Cambridge University Press, Cambridge, 1979), p. 107 ff. for this distinction between the two ways of not or no longer living morally, corresponding on the whole to the distinction between the id and the ego in Freudian theory, respectively, on this side and on that side of the superego.

be no crimes committed in any unit; it has to be demonstrated to higher authorities that any crimes committed are
successfully uncovered" (YH, p. 72). The synthesis that sup-
presses the contradiction would be to "destroy the criminals
before they manage to commit their crime" (YH, p. 819), a
ludicrous idea that finds, however, an important analogy in
the struggle against speculators and other crooks who "try to
overhaul the monetary system": To suppress them, it would
suffice to stop the "production of goods which are the object
of speculation" (YH, p. 804).

On the subject of education, we can quote the brilliant
passage where Zinoviev explains the necessity for being relatively hypocritical in order to escape the frankly hypocritical
practices in Ibansk:

> "I become more and more convinced that the critical literature of
> the recent past has done a great deal of harm by attacking wordly
> hypocrisy. It's been based on a very banal principle, that a man
> who behaves decently towards others (smiles, says he's pleased
> to see you, sympathises when things go wrong, and so on) thinks
> something else privately—(that he looks down on you, envies
> you, is pleased with your failures, upset by your successes, and
> so on). This was seen as hypocrisy. It was considered that people
> who were of little worth were passing themselves off as decent
> and good. But that isn't only (or always) hypocrisy. It can also be
> the result of good education, which is one of the social means of
> self-defence that people use against their own selves. It's the
> ability to control oneself, without which no normal relationships
> are possible. Without this good education life becomes a night-
> mare. Without it, it's virtually impossible to meet anyone. We
> cannot talk of man as if he possessed something secret and gen-
> uine which developed a mask to suit any given situation. A man's
> character includes what he is at home and what he is at work,
> and what he is among his friends and acquaintances, and what
> he thinks and what he says." "Yes, but there's more than a lack
> of wordly education here," said Chatterer. "You'd have to talk
> more about anti-wordly education. To ignore and trample
> underfoot everything that is outstanding and to hold up me-
> diocrity for praise is a particular kind of education, not a void.
> Hypocrisy that takes the form of a negation of hypocrisy is
> hypocrisy squared" [YH, pp. 350–351].

Therefore, the Ibanskian citizen is inwardly the passive negation of the moral and rational man, but he is the product of an education that is the active negation of a rational and moral education. Antieducation does not produce the anti-man. Surprising at first, on reflection this conclusion is affirmed, because the systematic absence of outstanding traits—be they positive or negative—could never be realized in the absence of a systematic education. The mere lack of education would produce all sorts of men, which would be incompatible with the Ibanskian standard of mediocrity. Even if I had no way of producing a state of negation within myself, by an act of active negation,[32] nothing prevents me from achieving this result in another. Even if I couldn't make up my mind to forget, I could induce a state of forgetfulness in others.

I now take up the relation of the regime to the opposition by beginning with the question of Ibanskian law, whose fundamental given is the confusion of nonobligation and interdiction. In a rational society "a distinction must be drawn between the absence of a standard and the existence of a negation-standard" (*YH*, p. 618), but in Ibansk the absence of an obligation implies the presence of an interdiction, except where the contrary is expressly stated. "And there are cases, too, when it is not enough to have no ban on an action, but official permission has to be sought as well. Sometimes even that it not enough, and a rule is needed to prevent the obstruction of acts which are permitted or at any rate not prohibited" (*YH*, pp. 78 and 179).

We will see below how this confusion even looms over the attempts to dispel it. We can, however, first point out two other contrasts between rational law and Ibanskian law. The right to emigrate is a fundamental principle of human rights, as is the absence of a governmental right to exile,[33] but in

---

[32]Except, of course, by means of indirect strategies of the kind Pascal used: to become a true believer by pretending to believe. For this idea see my *Ulysses and the Sirens*, Chapter III.

[33]Using terms of S. Kanger and H. Kanger (Rights and parliamentarism, in *Contemporary Philosophy in Scandinavia*, R. Olson and A. Paul, eds., Johns Hopkins Press, Baltimore, 1972), the individual possesses vis-à-vis the

Ibansk people live in an upside-down world[34]: The government reserves for itself the right to exile whomever they
choose, denies the right of emigration, considers the desire
to emigrate a crime whose seriousness can lead to expulsion,
but nevertheless refuses requests to emigrate. We have only
to consider the stunning passage where Zinoviev sums up
the Ibanskian mechanism and its specific irrationality: "And
a free people cannot allow that. They even want to fulfill their
own will as regards me despite my own will" (YH, p. 541).
The world of Catch 22 comes immediately to mind[35]; this
association is reinforced by the following passage:

> [The Patriot] had been sentenced to ten days for requesting to be
> sent to the front, but that he could see no logic in this, since fifty
> cadets were being dispatched to the front without the slightest
> desire to go. Deviationist observed that this merely demon-
> strated the iron logic of the social laws since, according to these
> laws, Patriot's destiny was at the whim of his superiors and not
> under his own control, and by putting in a request for transfer
> to the front, he had offended against the social laws by evincing
> a wish to control his own fate by his own will—so he had got
> everything he deserved [YH, p. 64].

Another crucial problem concerns the rapport between the
letter and the spirit of the law. It is generally known that the
Chinese wanted to avoid an elaborate code of laws, fearing
that corrupt people would invoke the letter of the law against
its spirit.[36] On the other hand, the Western notion of law

---

state both a *power* and a *counterimmunity* with regard to the act of leaving
his country.

[34] Without insisting on this term, it is nonetheless curious to re-read the
section in *Phenomenology of Mind* that deals with this concept of the
upside-down world.

[35] In the novel of Joseph Heller this paradox takes the following form:
Whoever accepts to fly combat missions is by definition insane and, being
insane, has the right to be exempted for psychiatric reasons. He only has
to ask to be relieved. But the very fact of asking, the very desire to no
longer fly combat missions, is proof of sanity and prevents one from
being grounded.

[36] See J. Needham, *Science and Civilisation in China*, Vol. 2 (Cambridge University Press, Cambridge, 1956, p. 522); see also Paul Veyne, *op. cit.*, p.
625 ff.

permits the possibility—and even the inevitability[37]—of unwanted interpretations of the law and prescribes that in such cases one must change the letter of the law rather than invoke its spirit. In the Western world, people are not found guilty of libel for having said, "If I told my opinion, I would be found guilty"; in Ibansk the letter of the law is ignored, and they go directly to its spirit:

> What matters above all is not whether a law is bad or good. What matters is whether or not the law exists. A bad law is nevertheless a law. Good illegality is nevertheless illegal. I shall take it upon myself to prove the mathematical theorem that any society with a rule of law, no matter how bad that law may be, allows the existence of an opposition. The very existence of an opposition is a sign that the society lives by the law. And the absence of an opposition is an indication that a society is lawless. But let us look more closely at the question. Let us take a certain text A. Let there be a legal system B, according to which this text is assessed to be hostile to the given society (as an "anti" text). Consequently the author of A is prosecuted. And if, for example, I say "N asserts that A," I am not asserting A, I am asserting that N asserts A. What then, from the point of view of society B, is the nature of a text of the type "N asserts that A"? Is that an "anti" text? Fine, but how will the prosecutor look, when in court he accuses me of asserting the text "N asserts that A"? Will he

---

[37]The law always says too much; it is in its unwanted consequences that it is unjust. It always says too little; it is silent regarding unforeseen cases. As Tocqueville said (*op. cit.*, Vol. 1), Americans "believe that the courts are powerless to control the press, and since the flexibility of human languages always eludes judicial scrutiny, crimes of this nature remain, in a sense, hidden from the hand [of the law] that reaches out to seize them". More generally, only a very naïve lawmaker would think that, after the passage of a certain law, men will continue to act as they did before its passage, which doesn't prevent naïveté from being widespread: Take, for example, a law that forbids employers to lay off workers with more than x years of seniority. The same law greatly increases the layoffs of those with x years minus six months of seniority, thereby reducing rather than assuring stability of employment. (On this problem see F. Kydland and E. Prescott, Rules rather than discretion: The inconsistency of optimal plans, *Journal of Political Economy*, 1977.) I do not think that Zinoviev took up this sociological tradition; as a logician, he only had to translate into legal terms the theorem of Löwenheim-Skolem on the nonstandard interpretations of logical systems (see especially in the text quoted the reference to "mathematical theorem").

be seen as a man pronouncing an "anti" text? No? But why? Where is the formal criterion which lets us make this distinction? Admittedly I have used the word "asserts" once, and the prosecutor has used it twice. But if such a law is adopted, all I have to do is pronounce in advance the following text: "M asserts that N asserts A." I have only cited one logical progression. But there are many more. Construct for me a code B of laws which permit texts to be assessed as "anti", and I will undertake, for any text which is so assessed, to construct a text which can not be assessed according to code B, but which all the same will be understood as an opposition text. Every rigorous law is 'a priori' a possibility of opposition [YH, p. 306].

The relation of the regime to the opposition can be defined in the mode of either passive or active negation: silence or condemnation. This choice poses the following dilemma: "It was time, it was necessary to make a high-level response to that individual. But on the other hand, that would attract attention to his filthy little books. However, if we keep silent, people will think that they are right" (RF, p. 230). In other words, to condemn is to recognize and to make known, even if it also means to point out a threat. Therefore, from a certain point of view, the opposition sees the movement from silence to condemnation as a step forward; accordingly, in criticizing modernist painters, their works have to be reproduced and consequently made known (RF, p. 134), from which we get the stronghold of the opposition: "Condemn me."

Actually the silence of the regime is not an active negation in the complete sense; it is a desired silence that differs from simple indifference. It is an effort toward active negation hidden behind the appearance of passive negation. Now the distinction between desired and true indifference can be easily made, by virtue of the exclusively systematic form of the former. Here, again, attention is too lightly veiled; never speaking of a person whose existence one can hardly ignore can be just as good evidence of an obsession as can be nonstop discussion of that person: Any husband knowing that his wife cheats on him knows this; the Ibanskian dissidents don't ignore it either:

It's not only the attacks that are frightening, said Chatterer. Persecution amounts to official recognition. It's the deliberate indifference to everything you do. And the more important your work is, and the better its results, the greater the indifference becomes. I'm not talking about indifference as a mere lack of interest, but an active indifference. That's something positive [*YH*, p. 745].

As one would expect from an expert in many-valued logic,[38] Zinoviev makes here a distinction between *three* types of negation; it seems possible, however, to reduce them to two basic forms. Active indifference is, as stated previously, active negation hiding behind passive appearance. One could undoubtedly imagine an endless stream of such appearances, each more complex than the preceding one and capable of deceiving a great number of people; nevertheless, they would never be able to ignore their origin in active negation. By affecting indifference—from the first to the nth degree—one will never *become* indifferent, like Pascal's believer who would become a believer by pretending to be one.

Aside from interior opposition, there is exterior opposition—the West. In Zinoviev's works there are constant references to trips abroad, notably to scientific meetings. For the Ibanskian, the foreigner is fascinating, provided that he rejects Ibanskian ways:

Ibanskians adore foreigners and are prepared to give them their last shirt. If the foreigner doesn't take the shirt, he's called a swine. And quite rightly. Take what you're given, without wanting to get yourself thumped. So take it, damn you, if you don't want a thick ear. There's no need to play hard-to-get. They're being good-hearted, showing good feelings. So go on, make the most of it, they're not like this every day, and if you don't. . . . But if the foreigner accepts the shirt and goes on behaving as he feels like doing, he's still called a swine. And that's only right. He could've refused it. But if he accepts, he ought to abide by the rules. We've acted with the best intentions, with open generosity. But as for

---

[38]See A. Zinoviev, *Philosophical Problems of Many-Valued Logic*, D. Reidel, Dordrecht, 1963.

him. . . . It's no use looking for gratitude. They're swine, and that's all there is to it. But if the foreigner takes the shirt and behaves like a proper Ibanskian, then he's an even bigger swine, because then he's clearly one of our own people, and with our own people there's no need to stand on ceremony [YH, p. 460].

As Groucho Marx said, "I'd never belong to a club that would accept me as a member." This is a case of the effect of contamination: If the foreigner were really stupid enough to recognize us, we would be even more stupid to recognize him.[39] It is also an ironic variation on the "Timeo Danaos" theme: Ibanskians are to be feared, even when they are bearing gifts.[40]

Khrushchev occupies a special place in the Ibanskian world. He symbolizes the inability of the regime to effect change or to change itself:

Even if they suddenly were to wish to stop being oppressors they could not desist from oppression, since their lack of will to oppress could only be realised in the form of oppression, which would entail nothing more than a change in the aspect and sphere of application of oppression [YH, p. 582].

We have to recall the deceptively liberating command: Don't be so obedient. Khrushchev's failure can be summed up in his project of de-Stalinization. There was too rapid a passage from the permission to no longer quote Stalin to the recommendation to not quote him (RF, p. 58), as if the for-

---

[39]The same effect of contamination, but in the opposite sense, is at work in the dialectic between the master and the slave: The individual who seeks recognition from a slave whom he does not recognize shows by this very fact that he is unworthy of recognition. For a brilliant analysis of bad emperors, corrupted and corrupting, see again Paul Veyne, op. cit.

[40]Concerning an analogous case in classical antiquity, Paul Veyne (op. cit., p. 229) observes that
    to refuse a gift is to refuse a friendship which can be intrusive; Phocion refused gifts from Alexander, who had him told angrily that he did not consider those who refused to receive gifts from him to be true "friends"; indeed Phocion did not want to be taken as anyone's unqualified friend; to accept a gift and to not obey in every way was the equivalent of not keeping one's word.

mer state of passive negation were too fragile to last. Therefore Stalin triumphed, even in defeat. The method used to
renounce him was based on the same confusion that exists
between nonobligation and interdiction; this is, inciden-
tally, Stalin's area of expertise. The distinction between active
and passive negation serves also to explain why Khrushchev's plan could never be successful:

> Half-measures in such situations always end in defeat. You say
> that he wouldn't have been allowed to? That he would have been
> toppled? They would have had no chance! Before they could have
> got themselves together, he could have done so much that it would
> have been far too late to have taken any steps against him. The
> further he had gone, the stronger his position. It is true that he
> could not deal a really heavy blow. But not because he under-
> stood the objective impossibility of a heavy blow, but because
> he did not understand the subjective possibilities before him [*YH*,
> p. 188].

"He was not able to" is a key expression that can be looked
at further. Khrushchev was in his way powerless, as one can
be in the two other ways explained in the following passage:

> "How do you know what's senseless and what's not?" asked
> Panicker. "Maybe they have no option." "What do you mean by
> that?" asked Humorist. "Do you mean that they acted the best
> way they could in conditions over which they had no control?
> Or that they acted as they did because that was in their nature?
> That's very far from being the same thing. The former example
> presupposes intelligence and a rational approach. The latter, not"
> [*YH*, p. 417].

If every action is conceived as the final result of two suc-
cessive filters, the first of which is made up of the structural
constraints of the situation and the second by the mode of
choosing an action in the ensemble of actions that simultaneously satisfies all constraints, it is indeed possible to deny
the rational choice in two different ways[41]: Either the structural constraints are so strong and the ensemble of possible

---

[41]For this distinction, see my *Ulysses and the Sirens*, p. 113 ff.

actions so confined that there is no place for choice, rational
or not, or the mode of choice is something besides rational,
dictated by tradition, chance, an obsessive idea. This is
approximately the distinction Zinoviev makes in the last text
quoted; it is also the distinction Joel Feinberg makes between
the *exterior constraints* (positive or negative) and the *positive
interior constraints.*[42] On the other hand, the distinction
between understanding the impossibility and not understanding the possibility—between active and passive negation—amounts to a distinction between exterior constraints
and *negative interior constraints.* As Sartre would put it, *nothing* prevented Khrushchev from waging a victorious struggle
against Stalinism, this nothing being passive negation or lack
of knowledge. His blindness was undoubtedly not fortui-
tous, but there is no reason to think that it was desired. But
acting with an undesired lack of knowledge is less irrational
than acting with an obsessive desire.

Opposition is itself affected by the confusion of active with
passive negation. Thus a dissident

> said previously that he didn't want to submit himself to the bal-
> lot, but he was proposed, and he signed the papers. And he was
> accused of inconsistency. Now was he inconsistent? When I came
> here today, I didn't want a drink. You offered me one, and I took
> it. Inconsistent? No. We merely have to distinguish between the
> absence of desire to do something, and the presence of a positive
> inclination to do it [*YH*, p. 104[.

If other dissidents did not recognize this now familiar distinction, it is because they bear the stamp of the society in
which—and not only against which—they struggle: "It is
impossible to live in a society and remain free from it" (*YH*,
p. 561), or better,

---

[42]Quoted in Steven Lukes, Power and structure, in his *Essays in Social Theory* (MacMillan, London, 1977, p. 11 ff. The analysis with which Lukes
proposes to explain the failure of Bucharin to resist the rise of Stalin is
very near to that Zinoviev proposes in order to explain Khrushchev's
failure to realize the ruin of Stalin: "It wasn't possible" (in one way or
another).

"as a man overcomes these resistances he gradually assumes an ever closer resemblance to that society's Mr. Average. If he fails to do so, he will not be able to penetrate the fissures in the obstacles he faces. It may seem to him that he has preserved his creative individuality and is bringing his ideas to fruition; but in fact he is increasingly conforming to the standard" [*YH*, p. 761].

This remark is particularly applicable to the sculptor Dauber, an ambiguous main character in *The Yawning Heights* who is transformed before our eyes from a born dissident into an opportunist who doesn't know himself. When he mentions that the tombstone he sculpted for Khruschev is an uncompromising work, a friend remarks, "That's true, if the lack of any demand for compromise can be regarded as uncompromising" [*YH*, p. 467]. It is possible to arrive at a compromise without seeking it; we have only to recall the distinction made between the two types of arrivists.

We now come to the question of *power*:

Ibanskian power is both omnipotent and impotent. It is omnipotent in the negative sense that it can do any evil it likes and remain unpunished. It is impotent in the positive sense that any good it may do remains unrewarded. It has a huge destructive force, and a wholly insignificant power of creation [*YH*, p. 483].

Indeed, the notion of power is doubly fraudulent; it implies that we can attain goals *whatever they might be* and *whatever the goals of others might be.*[43] Ibanskian authorities fit the second part of this definition, but not the first. For Tocqueville, centralized power "excels in preventing, not in doing"[44]; "it

---

[43]The first of these fraudulent hypotheses is the essence of a study by A. Goldman, Towards a theory of social power, in *Philosophical Studies* 23, 1972, 221–268; the other is important in the theory of collective choice, where the concept of a *dictator* is defined as an individual capable of dictating social preferences, regardless of the preferences of other individuals. This shows the absurdity of any attempt to demonstrate the existence of a dictator, even where preferences do not differ: Such an individual would only be an *average man*, in the sense that he would have the same preferences as society as a whole. This demonstration was nevertheless attempted by A. Parks, in An impossibility theorem for fixed preferences: A dictatorial Bergson–Samuelson welfare function, *Review of Economic Studies*, 43, 1976, 447–450.
[44]Tocqueville, *op. cit.*, Vol 1.

rarely forces to act, but it is always opposed to action; it destroys nothing; it prevents birth".[45] We see that Zinoviev goes much further, by attributing to the regime an immense destructive power; perhaps we should see in that a difference between an authoritarian regime and a totalitarian one. Whatever the case might be, the asymmetry of doing and undoing does not come about simply because "it is easier to destroy than to construct" (YH, p. 484). Above and beyond that universal obstacle that the second law of thermodynamics poses for any plan creating order, certain specifically Ibanskian obstacles arise. Let us list them: (1) the already mentioned tendency of information to deteriorate into denunciation; (2) the tendency to evaluate solutions according to their ideological rather than their technical efficiency, looking for "a correct social solution for an insoluble economic problem (YH, p. 683); (3) the omnipresence of contradictory plans, such as the attitude toward crime or the directive to "enhance the leadership role of the leadership cadres and to activate an initiative from below" (YH, p. 179); (4) the systematic creation of mediocre personalities that are at the most capable of hindering others' plans; (5) "the effect of social relationships is such that any important problem is regarded as being gnostically difficult" (YH, p. 572), which presents obstacles for every simple and efficient solution; and (6) "an amoral society wastes a huge amount of energy because of its very lack of a high enough level of morality" (YH, p. 800), since men "expect the worst" (RF, p. 187) and take their precautions, thereby contributing to the realization of the worst that they fear.

We can now state the first fundamental law of Ibanskian life, "the well-known rule whereby people who want to make a change never change anything, while changes are only effected by people who had no intention of doing so" (YH, p. 198). In other words, in Ibansk the ensemble of political possibilities is a void.[46] Not that there can never be changes

---

[45]Ibid., Vol. 2.
[46]See my Logic and Society, Chapter 3, for this idea.

and even profound transformations; it is only that they could never be brought about in a desired and intended manner. A distinction has to be made between a solution and a result of the search for a solution (*YH*, p. 749), just as it is necessary "to make a distinction between what is the product of time and what is the product of the new social system (*YH*, p. 530). Since "any decisions taken by the leadership about a particular problem have one and the same result" (*YH*, p. 154), it can be seen that "directives are a result, not a cause" (*YH*, p. 338). In Ibansk, it is understood in advance that all attempts to undertake whatever action sets off a counteraction that will nullify it:

> I was in no way surprised to learn that two diametrically opposed meetings had been held virtually simultaneously, and that each had adopted measures which paralysed measures adopted by the other. That's in the normal run of things, and I have been used to that for a long time. For example, Stupak's father in one and the same day received the Order of Lenin and was expelled from the party (he was arrested later that night) [*RF*, p. 58].

In Ibansk guilt takes the place of causality. A second fundamental law states that "successes achieved under any leadership must be successes achieved by that leadership" (*YH*, p. 156). "The leadership attributes for itself everything positive and calculates its actions so as to never be held responsible for failures and any negative phenomena" (*YH*, p. 410). Expressing this differently,

> from the scientific point of view . . . one must talk of the causes of certain manifestations. But from the official point of view, such a statement of the problem is unacceptable. In any situation, the official consciousness always poses the question: "Where does the fault lie?" And as for the official consciousness, guilt must be personified, since only conscious beings can be accused, and not inanimate nature or dumb beasts, the problem is posed even more sharply: "Who is responsible for this?" From the official point of view, even natural disasters like earthquakes, droughts and floods, must be the responsibility of specific people [*YH*, pp. 99–100].

Thus we arrive at the third fundamental law: For every disaster one can find a guilty person outside the leadership. In a sense, this attitude has existed for ages: The ruler is "the source of good but not responsible for the bad",[47] even though a leader is sometimes overthrown if it rains too much during his administration. But in Ibansk, no one really believes that: The second and third laws do not reflect the spontaneous attitude of the people but, rather, principles of bureaucratic promotion. The regime, therefore, takes credit for the good it is incapable of doing and washes its hands of the bad that it alone can do.

We finally arrive at the theory of the negation of the negation, presented and better developed in *The Radiant Future* than in *The Yawning Heights*. Actually, it is only in a short sentence (*RF*, p. 71), penned in passing, that we learn of Zinoviev's logical acceptation of the notion, according to which the negation of the negation merely reestablishes the point of departure. Both Marx and Zinoviev see the Communist Revolution as negation of the negation, the former in the dialectical sense, the latter in the logical sense.[48] The dialectical is, of course, poorly defined; it has even been said that it doesn't exist and that the negation of the negation forms part of those conceptual tools that are too powerful, since they exclude nothing.[49] But it is possible to encompass—in a fairly rigorous definition—the essence of classical examples. I put forth that a method $p-q-r$ follows the outline of the negation of the negation when (1) any pair of elements among (p,q,r) are mutually incompatible, (2) the passage $p-r$ is impossible, (3) the passage $q-p$ is impossible, and (4) there is no q' ($q \neq q'$) making the passage $p-q'-r$ possible. Therefore one could never pass directly from feudalism to communism; one could never go back from capitalism to feudalism—only

---

[47]Paul Veyne, *op. cit.*, p. 558 ff.

[48]Since a principal thesis of this essay is the great compatibility of dialectics and formal logic, it is understood that this opposition is the exception and not the rule.

[49]See also H. B. Acton, Dialectical materialism, in *The Encyclopedia of Philosophy* Vol. 2 (Paul Edwards, ed., Macmillan, New York, 1967), pp. 389–397.

capitalism can constitute the indispensable intermediate step. For Zinoviev the negation of the negation can only be understood in its logical acceptation, which implies the rejection of the third condition:

> 'In Russia,' said Rebrov, 'a traditional way of life has been preserved despite everything. Just as in China. In the last century Russia instituted a movement towards the Western way of life. But nothing came of it. The Revolution threw us back into a state of serfdom, back to the squalid, gory origins of our imperial history. How many victims will there have to be, and what quagmires will we have to plunge into before the abolition of serfdom becomes a real issue again?' [*RF*, p. 157]

In general, the notions of revolution and counter-revolution are asymmetrical, despite their verbal likeness. The revolution against the revolution against x gives something other than x, and for good reasons, well expressed by Giscard d'Estaing: "There is certainly no question of returning to a pre-1968 situation, first and foremost because that pre-1968 situation includes the very elements that caused 1968."[50] The goal of counter-revolutionists is most assuredly not to create a situation where revolution would again be possible; Eduard Frei should have realized that he could never have assumed power after Allende. Now the preceding remarks reflect the supposition that revolutionary and counter-revolutionary methods are intentional and intelligent actions. Given the Soviet regime's inability to transform society in a deliberate and desired manner, it is only left with purely causal transformations, whose end products no one desires or, if desired, they come about by an unwanted or misdirected process.[51] It is only by this route that one could conceive of the reestablishment of a precommunist order, but, still, the active negation[52] of communism is not a struggle to establish what preceded it:

---

[50]See his interview in *Le Monde*, January 8, 1975.

[51]See my *Logic and Society*, pp. 49 and 144, for this last condition. Power is not just the causal production of a desired result; one has also to make sure that the result is reached in the desired manner.

[52]Can we see here an analogy between the "active negation–passive negation" distinction and the two senses of negation of the negation? The

I don't want to put the clock back. I want to go on going forward, accepting what has happened in the past as an indisputable fact. Criticism of communism on communism's home ground is not a battle against communism. It cannot in principle lead to the restoration of the pre-communist order. It's rather the opposite; it is precisely the suppression of the criticism of communism which tends towards such a restoration, or in the extreme case it tends to a metamorphosis of communism within the spirit of such a restoration [RF, p. 273].

Thanks to an unrelenting process of indifferent degradation, one can set in place a *third servitude* impossible to create deliberately. In a like manner, only a causal process capable of wiping out its own memory could engender states like faith, innocence, sincerity, and forgetfulness.[53] "History leaves no traces. It only leaves consequences which have nothing in common with the circumstances that gave rise to them" (YH, pp. 31 and 632). In a more general way, the past survives into the present either in the form of a memory of the past or in an objectified form where its origin is hidden.[54] Only a society keeping alive the memory of the past is capable of controlling the processes that form the future. Zinoviev has demonstrated in a most striking manner that formal logic and dialectical analysis are not only not incompatible, but that the latter is understood only through the former.[55] This is not to say that this methodological demonstration is his most important feature. In the field of political science

----

answer is only partially in the affirmative. The passive negation of passive negation reestablishes the point of departure; but the active negation of the active negation—in the strict sense where the active negation of Np is $N(\text{Not}-p)$—also reestablishes the point of departure. It is only in the larger and vaguer sense of the notion of active negation that one can say that its repeated application takes us beyond the point of departure, as in the example "revolution against the revolution against x." Thus the denial of the denial of x is something other than the simple affirmation of x, the denial being conceived as a political action and not simply as a logical operation.

[53]*Ulysses and the Sirens*, p. 50.

[54]See my "Notes on hysteresis in the social sciences," *Synthese* 33, 1976, 371–391.

[55]Such is also one of the main conclusions of Chapters 4 and 5 in *Logic and Society*; it was, therefore, a source of great satisfaction to see it confirmed by Zinoviev.

Zinoviev's work opens entirely new perspectives, by treating a previously neglected phenomenon—*political irrationality*. But Zinoviev's undeniable accomplishment is especially
the creation of a fictitious, hallucinatory, detailed, and convincing world where even false teeth go bad (*YH*, p. 771) and
even artificial flowers fade (*YH*, p. 780), a world similar to
nothing—except to reality.

PAUL WATZLAWICK

Components of Ideological "Realities"*

THE TERM *ideology* permits a multitude of definitions, but two elements are common to most of them: the basic supposition that the thought system (the "doctrine") explains the world in its suchness, and, second, the fundamental, all-encompassing (and therefore generally binding) character of ideology.

This study will examine what kind of a "reality" is constructed when one assumes one has found such an ultimate way of viewing the world. Furthermore, the various components of this construction will be defined abstractly (the passages in italics) and then substantiated with reference to their manifestations and with examples of their characteristic symptoms. These references are not intended as proof but, rather, as anecdotal, metaphorical, or anthological illustrations of the given effects; thus they are compiled from the most varied disciplines and sources without any claim to completeness.

Let us set out the thesis itself: *The actual content of the given ideology is of no consequence in regard to the reality created by acceptance of that ideology. It may completely contradict the content of another ideology. The results, however, are of a terrifying stereotypy.*

For the ideologue—as we will laconically, but not alto-

---

*An original contribution, translated by J. Donovan Penrose.

gether correctly, call the founder or champion of an ideology—this thesis is absurd. And he appears to be right. According to content, there are hardly more irreconcilable differences than between the faith of a Torquemada, the *Myth of the 20th Century*, the ultimate, "scientific" interpretation of social reality by Marx and Engels, and the convictions of the Baader-Meinhof gang. Yet the praxis of the Inquisition, the concentration camps, the Gulag Archipelago, or the terrorist scene is of an undeniable, terrible isomorphy. Whether the victim is murdered by Pinochet's henchmen or the Irish Republican Army, the act does not permit a claim to eternal worth for either ideology. The British historian Norman Cohn mentions this phenomenon in his book *The Pursuit of the Millenium:*

> In the history of social behavior there certainly are some patterns which in their main outlines recur again and again, revealing as they do so similarities which become ever more recognisable. And this is nowhere more evident than in the case of highly emotional mass movements such as form the subject-matter of this book. It has happened countless times that people have grouped themselves in millennial movements of one kind or another. It has happened at many different periods of history, in many different parts of the world and in societies which have differed greatly in their technologies and institutions, values and beliefs. These movements have varied in tone from the most violent aggressiveness to the mildest pacifism and in aim from the most ethereal spirituality to the most earth-bound materialism [. . .] but similarities can present themselves as well as differences; and the more carefully one compares the outbreaks of militant social chiliasm during the later Middle Ages with modern totalitarian movements, the more remarkable the similarities appear. The old symbols and the old slogans have indeed disappeared, to be replaced by new ones; but the structure of the basic phantasies seems to have changed scarcely at all [12].

The Pseudo-Divine Origins of Ideologies

Because the cosmic order is incomprehensibel to the average man, an ideology is all the more convincing the more it relies upon an unusual, superhuman, or at least brilliant originator.

The highest authority, and therefore the authority that has been appealed to most frequently, is the word of the creator of the world. If He exists, one can rightfully assume that He knows the origin, meaning, course, and end of the world. But at the same time the question arises as to how He makes His knowledge and His will known. Then the idea of a mediator is necessary. As the history of mankind demonstrates, this mediator must be of divine *and* human origin; demons, demiurges, interpreters of oracles, seers—often physically blind prophets, and divine messengers, born from human mothers, appear and reveal His wisdom.

But nontheological sources have also appeared, presenting ultimate interpretations of the world: philosophical systems, the genius or clairvoyance of certain individuals, the supreme axiomatic significance of reason, of "common sense," or of some simplistic chauvinism, each defined in a very specific way. These are portrayed as the highest authority. Then again, in our day we attribute particularly radical infallibility and finality to an allegedly scientific world view. Furthermore, there are uncritically accepted prejudices, the whole domain of tradition, superstition, and the phenomenon of rumors. "When a whole city says the same thing, there must be something to it," was the answer a team of sociologists received while researching the origin and wild spreading of a rumor in Orleans [43]. "Pure" truth is indeed axiomatic, not probabilistic. Doubts are not desirable. Answering the question why Cuba does not allow the International Red Cross to visit its prisons, Fidel Castro told the American television reporter Barbara Walters simply,

> We fulfill our norms, our principles. What we say is always the truth. If someone wants to doubt this truth, he should do so, but we will never allow someone to try to test our realities or to refute our truths [11].

Another possibility for avoiding refutation or even discussion lies in representing the truth so cryptically or replacing it with a formalism void of meaning so that—in nebulous brilliance, as it were—it appears both bombastic and profound simultaneously. Exemplary in this context is Michael Alexandrovitch Bakunin's definition of freedom. This prophet of terrorism, one of freedom's gravediggers, states in his *Revolutionary Catechism,*

> It is not true that the freedom of one man is limited by that of other men. Man is really free to the extent that his freedom, fully acknowledged and mirrored by the free consent of his fellow-men, finds confirmation and expansion in their liberty [3].

(Pseudo-profound babble, nowadays known under the unkind rubric "Party Chinese.")

The Assumed Psychological Necessity of Ideology

It is perhaps a waste of time to say anything at all about why an ultimate world view is so crucially important to us. We human beings and—as the modern study of primates demonstrates—the other higher mammals appear to be psychologically unable to survive in a universe without meaning and order. Thus it follows that there is a need to fill the vacuum, for this vacuum in its more diluted form can drive us to boredom, and in its most concentrated form to psychosis or suicide. But when so much is at stake, the interpretation of the world must be invulnerable and must not leave any questions unanswered.

Gabriel Marcel sees life as a fight against nothingness. Viktor Frankl's life work gives a wealth of examples about how human beings can fall ill because of a lack of meaning and, on the other hand, how the person who has a reason for living can bear almost any conditions (Nietzsche).

Does it then follow that being threatened personally by hunger, illness, or general insecurity makes an individual particularly susceptible to ideologies? In a similar way, do times of political or social upheaval bring about collective susceptibility? Not necessarily. Orwell writes in his *Essays,*

> The leading writers of the twenties were predominantly pessi-mistic. Was it not because after all these people were writing in

an exceptionally comfortable epoch? It is just in such times that "cosmic despair" can flourish. People with empty bellies never despair of the universe, nor even think about it, for that matter [45].

As we shall later show, the compulsive search for burning questions appears to be a symptom of affluent society. It cannot be denied that resignation can cause a life-endangering situation. Moreover, one can hardly dispute that real misery is a breeding ground for desperate attempts to change the existing injustices by means of violence. But, as Lenin recognized, these spontaneous outbursts are not an expression of an already extant revolutionary awareness but, rather, "much more an expression of desperation and revenge than a battle" [34]. The urge for utopia seems to feed itself much more from sources that have little or nothing to do with material misery. For instance, the American hippies' protest, according to the sociologist Walter Holstein, was a movement that

> was lived out by young people who were able to take advantage of all the privileges and benefits of the system. It was not jealousy and ambition which led to the flower children's revolt, but rather abundance and the desire for something different [23].

The Paradoxes of Eternal Values

Every ideology's claim to finality unavoidably leads to a paradox that has been known in formal logic for millennia. This paradox, however, enables the conceptual system to resolve even the greatest contradictions with no apparent effort. It concerns the introduction of zero or infinity into mathematical equations and its results.

The problems of the negligent use of these two values are traditionally portrayed by means of Zeno's descriptions, which, although almost 2,500 years old, illuminate the paradoxes. For example, there is the story of fleet-foot Achilles, who—contrary to all human quotidian experience—"must" lose a race with the tortoise. Since those days long ago the paradoxes of the infinite (the term goes back to Bernhard Bolzano [8]) have not ceased moving the human spirit to ever new and fascinating variations, such as the one Arthur Schnitzler describes in his story *Flight into Darkness:*

> He remembered an idea that Leinbach once, years ago, had expounded to a large gathering, quite seriously, in fact with a certain impressiveness. Leinbach had discovered a proof that there really is no death. It is beyond question, he had declared, that not only the drowning, but all the dying, live over again their whole past lives in the last moment, with a rapidity inconceivable to the rest of us. This remembered life must also have a last moment, and this last moment its own last moment, and so on; hence dying was itself Eternity: in accordance with the theory of limits one approached death but never got there [54].

In 1940 Arthur Koestler published his famous novel *Darkness at Noon* [27]. The book's French version appeared under the title *Le Zéro et l'infini* [28], a title that surpasses the original by far. The book deals with the political results of introducing zero and infinity into—as Koestler formulates it so suitably elsewhere—the "social equation":

> I remembered a phrase of Malraux's from *Les Conquérants:* "Une vie ne vaut rien, mais rien ne vaut une vie." In the social equation, the value of a single life is nil; in the cosmic equation it is infinite. Now every schoolboy knows that if you smuggle either a nought or the infinite into a finite caculation, the equation will be disrupted and you will be able to prove that three equals five, or five hundred. Not only Communism, but any political movement which implicitly relies on purely utilitarian ethics, must become a victim to the same fatal error. It is a fallacy as naive as a mathematical teaser, and yet its consequences lead straight to Goya's Disasters, to the rein of the guillotine, the torture-chambers of the Inquisition, or the cellars of the Lubianka. Whether the road is paved with quotations from Rousseaux, Marx, Christ or Mohammed, makes little difference [30].

From what has been said, it also follows—almost of necessity—that the final goals of every ideology will have to be utopian, and therefore inhuman.

Here Rosseau's thesis, pulled out the attic and dusted off,

which speaks of the goodness of man in nature and of society that depraves him, makes a glorious comeback. However, it remains unclear, just as in Rousseau's time, why the totality of all the good, natural human beings has degenerated into this dark evil force that is responsible for oppression, mental illness, suicide, divorce, alcoholism, and crime. In 1945, Karl Popper, in his work *The Open Society and Its Enemies* [47], made a comment that sounds almost prophetic now: that the paradise of the happy, primitive society (which, by the way, never existed) is lost for all those who have eaten of the fruit of the tree of knowledge. The more we try to return to the heroic age of tribalism, Popper warns, the more certainly we will reach the inquisition, the secret police, and a romanticized gangsterism. But once the existential problems of the individual, who is good by nature, can be blamed on the "evil" society, nothing stands in the way of sheer imagination. The definition of the benevolent society free of all power is only a question of fantasy. Thus Marx and Engels, for example, see one of the manifestations of bourgeois power in the unavoidable division of labor among individuals and then quickly imagine the solution to the problem:

> For as soon as labour is distributed, each man has a particular, exclusive sphere of activity, which is forced upon him and from which he cannot escape. He is a hunter, a fisherman, a shepherd, or a critical critic, and must remain so if he does not want to lose his means of livelihood; while in communist society, where nobody has one exclusive sphere of activity but each can become accomplished in any branch he wishes, society regulates the general production and thus makes it possible for me to do one thing to-day and another to-morrow, to hunt in the morning, fish in the afternoon, rear cattle in the evening, criticize after dinner, just as I have a mind, without ever becoming hunter, fisherman, shepherd or critic [40].

"I want to see all oppressed people throughout the world free. And the only way we can do this is by moving toward a revolutionary society where the needs and wishes of all people can be respected." With these words the radical philosophy professor Angela Davis paraphrases Isaiah's ancient messianic dream of the lion that will peacefully lie down with the lamb in a completely good world. But what the Biblical prophet perhaps could not know is contained with a clarity that leaves nothing to be desired in the opening sentence of an address of the French Senate to Napoleon I: "Sire, the desire for perfection is one of the worst maladies that can affect the human mind." The authors of this sentence could, of course, take advantage of the dubious benefit of having directly experienced and survived the consequences of the attempted introduction of *liberté, fraternité,* and *égalité.*

The utopian expectations receive further impulses from the assumption that the noble oppressed will change into champions of the most ideal human values after their liberation—precisely because they have experienced injustice and oppression themselves. George Bernard Shaw has pointed out that this is not quite the case in his preface to *The Revolutionist's Handbook:* "Revolutions have never lightened the burden of tyranny; they have only shifted it to another shoulder." How it comes about that the most wonderful utopias turn into the most gruesome oppression is the subject of speculation later in this essay. That the utopias do this is confirmed by history consistently, from Plato's day to the most recent past. And one must bear in mind that most of the classical utopias existed only in the minds of their originators and on the pages of their treatises. Nevertheless, these utopias bear the characteristics of inhumane oppression, even if their models that have never been put into practice. Wolfgang Kraus speaks of this in *Die verratene Anbetung* ("Betrayed Adoration"):

> If one examines the classical social utopias for the values appearing most important to their authors, one comes to amazing results. From Plato's *Republic* and *Laws,* to Plutarch's chapter on Lycurgus, to Thomas More's *Utopia* and Campanella's *State of the Sun,* to Francis Bacon's *Atlantis* and many other works a terrifying disposition to violently established orders manifests itself. The political dictatorships known to us today look like bastions of freedom in comparison to these so-called ideal states [32].

And yet the world still runs after the utopian pied piper until
the bitter end. What remains is disbelief and disappointment, as if this end had not been foreseeable from the start.
Max Frisch expresses this with enviable terseness in *The Fire
Raisers:*

> What all have foreseen
> From the outset,
> And yet in the end it takes place,
> This idiocy,
> The fire its too late to extinguish,
> Called fate.

Different people come to terms with the pain of disillusion-
ment in different ways. In the newspaper *das konzept* of March
1979 Niklaus Meienberg writes,

> For years we have ignored things that could have darkened our
> pretty image of socialism, or then things that we have fought in
> Switzerland we have excused because of the unique politico-
> historical context; not until after our Vietnam had marched into
> Cambodia in a very classical way, with American-like bombs
> and tanks, with authentic Blitzkrieg tactics [. . .] did it become
> instantly clear to some people that the Khmer Rouge had com-
> mitted genocide. But not before [41].

And the Zurich *Zeitdienst* complains,

> There are now, after Prague, Ethiopia and Cambodia, no longer
> any progressive camps that settle differences of opinion or con-
> flicting interests in principle without armed confrontation. There
> are—and this may be the central experience of the next genera-
> tion—no more good, political examples. The time of political
> models is over [65].

The Paradoxes of Perfection and Infinity

*As audacious and powerful as the most sublime philosophical
edifice may be, as much as it may appear to be an iron-clad system, it nevertheless has a fatal flaw: It cannot prove its own logic
and freedom from contradiction from within itself. This funda-*

mental condition for the logical construction of every reality we create has been most thoroughly researched by the mathematicians—above all by Kurt Gödel [19]—and their results are valid for all thought systems having a complexity that corresponds at least to that of arithmetic. In order to establish its freedom from contradiction, it is unavoidable that the given system step out of its own conceptual framework to demonstrate its consistency from without by using interpretive principles that it cannot generate from within. The logical consistency of these new additional principles—that is, of the conceptual metaframe—can in turn only be proven within a metametaframe of another more comprehensive system, and so on *ad infinitum*. We know since Whitehead and Russell [62] that whatever refers to a whole cannot be a part of that whole, that is, cannot refer back to itself without falling into the paradoxes of self-reflexivity. The famous liar who says of himself, "I am lying," illustrates the simplest form of such a paradox. If he actually is lying, then his statement is true. But if it is true, it is false that he is lying, and he therefore lied when he claimed to be lying. Therefore he lied . . . and so on. In other words, the statement, "I am lying," refers at the same time to both the whole (mathematically expressed, the class) of his statements *and* a part (a member) of this whole, namely, this one statement. Where the class and its members are not strictly distinguished, the well-known paradoxes of self-reflexivity [60], demonstrated in formal logic, appear. The map is not the territory; the name is not what it names; an interpretation of reality is only an interpretation and not reality itself. Only a schizophrenic eats the menu instead of the foods listed on the menu.[1]

Kant already recognized that every error of this kind consists in our taking the way we determine, divide, or deduce concepts for qualities of the things in and of themselves.

Thus when an interpretation of the world, an ideology, for example, claims to explain everything, one thing remains inexplicable, namely, the interpretive system itself. And with

---

[1]Compare Varela's contribution to this volume (p. 315 ff.) in which he presents completely new methods of dealing with the problems of self-reflexivity.

that, every claim to completeness and finality falls. Popper points to this issue in his *Conjectures and Refutations* [46] in which he ascertains that no theory can be proven positively. We only learn from its failures; we can never know with certainty. Therefore there is no authority that can raise a claim to authority. All we can achieve are approximations to a never completely comprehensible truth.

The British logician Lucas speaks in greater detail on this subject:

> It is a fair criticism of many philosophies, and not only determinism, that they are hoist with their own petard. The Marxist who says that all ideologies have no independent validity and merely reflect the class interests of those who hold them can be told that in that case his Marxist views merely express the economic interests of his class, and have no more claim to be adjudged true or valid than any other views. So too the Freudian, if he makes out that everybody else's philosophy is merely the consequence of childhood experience, is, by parity of reasoning, revealing merely his delayed response to what happened to him when he was a child. So too the determinist. If what he says is true, he says it merely as the result of his heredity and environment, and of nothing else. He does not hold his determinist views because they are true, but because he has such-and-such stimuli; that is, not because of the *structure* of the universe is such-and-such but only because the configuration of only part of the universe, together with the structure of the determinist's brain, is such as to produce that result [38].

But this incompleteness, which can never be overcome, is unacceptable to the ideologue. His interpretation of the world has to be absolute truth; it has to prove everything and therefore must also contain its own veracity. In the attempt to achieve the impossible, the political ideologue fares worse than his theological *confrères*. The reason why Christianity, for instance, has been able to maintain, in this respect, a consoling consistency for the believer lies in its postponing the realization of Isaiah's dream of the vegetarian lion to the end of time. Thus it escapes the dilemma by introducing the concept of infinity. Thereby the existence of evil, while it is not excused, is at least relativized, although other problems, like the idea of the eternal damnation of the impenitent sinner, original sin, the question whether God is subject to the laws of His own creation or whether He can do the impossible, remain unanswered. Such questions drove Basilides, for example, in the second century A.D., to the heretical position that the cosmos was the frivolous and malicious improvisation of imperfect demiurges. The political ideologue cannot afford to put things off until the end of time; for him the harmony has to start here and now, or at least in the lifetime of the next generation. On this issue Popper argues,

> our fellow men have a claim to our help. No generation must be sacrificed for the sake of future generations, for the sake of an ideal of happiness that may never be realized. In brief, it is my thesis that human misery is the most urgent problem of a rational public policy and that happiness is not such a problem. The attainment of happiness should be left to our private endeavors [48].

With the demand for perfection the ideologue puts on himself, he gets caught between the binary Aristotelian logic of true and false with its excluded *tertium* and the unpredictable tricks of a logic that tries to prove itself recursively and fails. For no ideology can afford to come to terms with the wise, human imperfection, as it is expressed in Ernst-Wolfgang Böckenförde's thesis, according to which "the modern free state lives on the basis of suppositions which it cannot guarantee without putting into question its own freedom" [7]. This thesis poignantly reflects the principle of incompleteness of all interpretations of the world and thus also of all "social equations."

The radical left in particular entangles itself in the inextricable contradiction of its "equation": On the one hand, man is only a wheel in the brazen, once and for all determined, regular course of history; on the other hand he fancies that he is called and obliged to turn the rudder of history as a messianic renewer by acting freely out of his own initiative. So does he act or react? Does the initiative come from within, thus spontaneously, or is it dictated from outside of him— perhaps by the iron-clad logic of historical progress? Lenin had already dealt with this problem. In his famous essay published in 1902, *What Is to Be Done?*, he throws out the question of the spontaneity of the revolution and concludes categorically,

> We said that *there could not yet be* Social-Democratic consciousness among the workers. This consciousness could only be brought to them from without. The history of all countries shows that the working class, exclusively by its own effort, is able to develop only trade union consciousness.

And what is this outside entity that gives the decisive impetus? Surprisingly it is the enemy camp, for Lenin continues,

> The theory of socialism, however, grew out of the philosophic, historical and economic theories that were elaborated by the educated representatives of the propertied classes, the intellectuals. According to their social status, the founders of modern scientific socialism, Marx and Engels, themselves belonged to the bourgeois intelligentsia [35].

Accordingly, then, the metaframe would be the bourgeoisie, and one would have to ask oneself in which metametaframe it is embedded. Instead of forging ahead to the anticipated, final answer, in this way one sinks into the infinite regress we have already spoken of, which contradicts the ideology's claim to prove itself from within its own system. Roger Garaudy, who until 1970 was one of the chief ideologues of the French communists, attempts to approach this problem in a more elegant fashion, but nevertheless entangles himself in the snares of self-reflexivity—which in his case has no serious consequences because the suggested solution leads to castles in the air anyway. In his book *L'Alternative* [17] he grapples with the question of how workers could forge ahead of themselves to self-determination (*autogestion*) and precisely thereby arrive at their own understanding of the whole situation, an understanding that has so far been handed down to them from without. As was amplified elsewhere, the following question then arises:

How does the working class free itself from this tutelage and reach self-determination? Garaudy's answer is of great interest for our topic, for he smoothly concludes that "the step to self-determination must itself be 'self-determined.' " It thus presupposes itself [. . . .] Self-determination becomes an *ouroborus*[2] or, to quote Garaudy again: "Self-management becomes a school for self-management." Practically, this is to be reached by the workers' choosing the engineers and other specialists and being able to dismiss them at any time. These specialists must inform, explain and convince, but the final decision lies with the workers. But this means no more and no less than that on the one hand the workers are aware of their insufficient expertise and thus call on the experts, but that on the other hand they are, so to speak, metaspecialists, passing judgement on specialists. And while Garaudy has critical words for the omniscience of the *leadership* in Stalinist, bureaucratic centralism, in his model the *basis* fortuitously exercises the omniscient function. In this way the *déjà vu* of the Platonic idea of a republic ruled by the wisest comes about in the reader's mind, an idea with all sorts of paradoxes and contradictory consequences which Karl Popper has described in his work *The Open Society and Its Enemies* [61].

The man of action who has not been "sicklied o'er with the pale cast of thought" tends toward Gordian solutions to the paradox. Martin Gregor-Dellin provides a fascinating example of that in a study of socialist semantics in the German Democratic Republic. He analyzes a speech by Erich Honecker and comes across the sentence, "It is a regular process which our party plans and leads with a view to the future." Gregor-Dellin responds,

> Here the vocabulary betrays the deceiver. It unmasks the alleged administrator as mere manipulator. Thus laws are not, as claimed by Marx, determined by the economic and social realities, but rather by the party, which itself "plans and leads these regular processes." It is not my task to prove that Honecker is betraying Marxism. The example only shows how for one fleeting moment a language which has become almost independent of the intellect lets down its visor: What comes to the fore is the cynicism of the

---

[2]The symbol of the snake biting its own tail.

central committee, in which one has for a long time agreed that regularities do not need to be adhered to, but rather must be prescribed [21].

Yet for the believer the appearances are preserved.

Heresy and Paranoia

> . . . weil, so schliesst er messerscharf,
> nicht sein kann was nicht sein darf.
>
> Christian Morgenstern

It follows from the assumption of a universally valid ideology, just as night follows day, that other positions are heresy. The word hairesis *originally did not mean heresy at all but, rather, choice, that is, a condition in which one can choose.* The so-called heretic thus has the freedom to make choices and to live as he sees fit. But in this way he comes into conflict with the ideology, the true faith, the party line. Here it is important to keep in mind that without the true doctrine there would be no heresy at all.

One can distinguish a few typical stops on the road to oppression and liquidation of the heretic.

The idea of possessing the ultimate truth first leads to a messianic attitude that clutches the belief that the truth *qua* truth will prevail in and of itself. At this point the champion of an ideology may still believe in the teachability of or in the possibility of convincing the heretic. But because the world soon proves to be obdurate, unwilling, or unable to open up to the truth, the next inevitable step results in what Hermann Lübbe calls the self-authorization to use violence. In its own deepest interests, the world must have its eyes opened. Lübbe traces this idea back to the August 18, 1919, issue of the Tscheka mouthpiece *Red Sword*, in which the famous principle "for us everything is permitted" is announced and then justified with the baffling explanation "our humanity is absolute."

Lübbe explains how that can be reconciled:

The historicist philosophy of history which above has been
referred to [. . .] as the theoretical precondition of unlimited self-
authorization to use violence, achieves that. Through a critical,
ideological examination it enables one to identify the mystification that holds captive the consciousness of the people, such that
when the people hate where they are supposed to love, the love
for the people on the part of those who see clearly remains free
of disappointment even in the face of absence of acute counter-
love. It is this love for the people which justifies everything [37].

Thus the world's benefactor has no choice; he is the surgeon
who wields the healing scalpel. He does not want the violence, but the reality (which he has invented) drives him to
use violence, in a way, against his will. Throwing a bomb
into a crowded department store thus becomes an act of revolutionary love for mankind (and, in general, to quote Lübbe
again, "his primary intention is not to throw bombs into
department stores or police stations, but rather into public
consciousness"). In the heart of the terrorist mass murderer
Felix Dsershinkski there lived a "soul of deep poetic sensitivity, always driven by pity for the weak and the suffering
[. . .] always living in the tension between his sublime idealism and the slaughter, which was his daily business" [13].
Günther Grass is supposed to have said of the terrorist Gud-
run Ensslin, "She was idealistic, with an innate disgust of
any kind of compromise. She longed for the absolute, for the
perfect solution" [5]. Whoever can certainly tries not to get
his hands dirty. Himmler, watching a mass execution in
Smolensk, became ill after the second volley and had to leave.
But from the aseptic distance of his headquarters, he rendered thanks in a letter to his men for the selfless way in
which they performed their difficult duty.[3] The Nazis' final
solution was admittedly not very ambitious; their ideology
was made for use at home, not throughout the world. They
were satisfied with annihilating their enemies, thus practic-
ing what Elster, in his contribution to this book (p. 177), calls

---

[3] Of course there are those for whom the "difficult duty" is an open pleasure: "Our slogan: terror without limits makes for unlimited fun"; this
motto supposedly originated from the terrorist Michael Baumann.

active negation. The true ideologue, however, who wants to make his pure doctrine absolute and everlasting, feels the necessity of totally exterminating, liquidating, and obliterating every fact or opinion that contradicts that doctrine—in Elster's sense this is a battle against passive negation. But to achieve this, disdain, repudiation, and banishment do not suffice. For, again *sensu* Elster, all ideologues have to recognize what they are fighting. Having introduced the concept of infinity into the social equation, the ideologue is now concerned with introducing zero. "You are a flaw in the pattern," explains the torturer in *1984* to his victim,

> You are a stain that must be wiped out[. . . .] It is intolerable to us that an erroneous thought should exist anywhere in the world, however secret and powerless it may be [44].

One can physically liquidate dissidents and heretics and even—so to speak, *ad majorem gloriam ideologiae*—degrade them psychologically beforehand so much that they not only admit the most absurd charges in a kangaroo court, but also beg to be destroyed. But it is not as simple with the laws of logic; one does not face an enemy of flesh and blood but, rather, the *fata morgana* of a mental construct that withholds its proof from its own architect. As we have already mentioned, the concept of an ultimate, generally valid interpretation of the world implies that no other interpretations can exist beside the one; or, to be more precise, no others are permitted to exist. For otherwise, we would find ourselves in a universe in which finally everything would be true, including its opposite. Where the ideology tries to refer back to itself in order to establish its validity and truth from within itself, a blind spot arises corresponding precisely to what Heinz von Foerster says in this volume on p. 43:

> Note that this localized blindness is not perceived as a dark blotch in our visual field (seeing a dark blotch would imply "seeing"), but this blindness is not perceived at all, that is, neither as something present, nor as something absent: Whatever is perceived is perceived "blotchless."

This localized blindness, which makes itself blind of itself, enables the believer of an ideology to believe in the ultimate truth and completeness of the doctrine. When, however, social equality does not come about, it is obviously not a defect of the pure doctrine but, rather, there must be an undiscovered, insidious enemy lying in wait outside, hoping to sabotage the dawning of the millennium; or perhaps it is a parasite who betrays himself sometimes only by his choice of words, these words deviating from a language that has become obligatory. "The domination of language was not to be changed," writes Schneider about the Nazi period, "the real crime was rebelling against it. At the end of Klemperer's book[4] there is a simple woman's answer to the question why her husband was sent to a concentration camp: 'because of expressions,' she said" [52]. The Polish satirist Wieslav Brudziński knows better; one of his punch lines goes, "He used to begin his speeches pretentiously: 'If I may express my opinion, already Engels said that. . . .' "

As did many other philosophers, Leibniz struggled with the irreconcilability of our imperfect world and the perfection of God. In his famous concluding precept, he postulates that if the existing world were not the best, then God either would not have known how, or would not have been able or would not have desired, to create the best world. But all three assumptions are incompatible with God's character. Therefore the existing world is the best of all possible worlds.

The ideologue reasons in another manner. If our idea were not the only true one, we would either be unable to know the best world, or we would not be able to shape it completely, or would not want to shape it completely. But all three assumptions are incompatible with the essence of our idea; therefore the (undeniable) evil of the world lies with yet undiscovered enemies.

It appears that at this point paranoia enters the ideologue's thought process. It is inherent to the concept of paranoia that it rests on a fundamental assumption that is held to be absolutely true. Because this fundamental assumption is axiomatic, it cannot and need not demonstrate its own veracity.

---

[4]Victor Klemperer, *Die unbewältigte Sprache* ("The Unconquered Language") [26].

Strict logical deductions are then made from this fundamental premise and create a reality in which any failures and inconsistencies of the system are attributed to the deductions, but never to the original premise itself.

In the ivory tower of formal logic, this technical error leads to the *enfant terrible* of paradox over which more practical spirits are able to move nonchalantly onto the daily agenda. For there are no earthshaking practical consequences in the fact that there can be no barber who only shaves those men in his village who do not shave themselves, which leaves unanswered the question as to what happens to his own beard. It only demonstrates that the premise is somehow defective. The ideological premise, however, "can" not be defective; it is sacrosanct. Whoever attacks it thereby proves his depravity and malice. This is the reason, for example, why the January 13, 1974, *Pravda* condemned Solzhenitsyn: Other authors before Solzhenitsyn had criticized the insufficiencies and errors of the past; he, however, sought to prove that the violations of legality had not been violations of the norms of socialist society but, rather, that they were a direct result of the *nature of socialism* (that is, of the ideology). Thus Solzhenitsyn became a traitor, and every upright human being, not just those in the Soviet Union, was supposed to turn away from him in anger and disgust. Whatever does not seem right, whatever does not fit, must be explained by something wrong outside of the ideology; for its perfection is beyond all doubt. In this way the ideology immunizes itself by offering more and more hair-splitting accusations. Betrayal and the dark powers of inner and outer enemies lie in wait everywhere. Theories about conspiracies develop and they conveniently hide the absurdity of the premise, necessitating and justifying bloody purges. As Elster states in his contribution (p. 201), causality is replaced by guilt. Furthermore, one should compare Elster's quotation of Zinoviev's *Yawning Heights:*

> From the official point of view particular individuals can be held responsible even for natural catastrophes (earthquakes, droughts, floods).

This does not apply simply to official catastrophes. Maurice Duverger places the following report at the beginning of his book *Les Orangers du Lac Balaton* [14]:

> At the time while the Stalinist Rákosi was ruling, the Hungarian leaders decided to cultivate oranges on the banks of Lake Balaton. The lake freezes every winter, although the mass of water mitigates the harshness of the continental climate, giving those banks which are protected from the north wind a bit of a Mediterranean appearance. The agricultural expert in charge of the project had the courage to point out that the project was purely a dream. All was in vain. As the interpreter of historical materialism, which proclaims the scientific truth, the party can not err. Thousands of orange trees were planted, having been imported at a very high price in hard currency. They died. As a result, the agricultural expert was charged with sabotage. Hadn't he demonstrated his ill will from the very start by criticizing the Politburo's decision?

Countless examples of this paradoxical, recursive logic go from the ridiculous to the gruesome. We find an example of the first category in the way prophets rationalize their own prophecies' not being fulfilled. According to newspaper reports, during a drought in California that lasted a number of years, 400 San Jose State University students gathered on February 17, 1977, in the main auditorium under the leadership of several instructors to recite Indian rain chants in order to produce rain by means of these "combined energies." One of the organizers explained to a reporter that "negative attitudes could be the only reason why the rain ceremony would not be successful" [58]. Rain did not come. This form of proof is what Popper calls self-sealing; or, as Elster puts it, it corresponds to the primitive Manichaean logic, "Whoever is not for me, is against me." In the sense of what we have said so far, it is an ouroboric logic that is typical for ideology. "A convinced Communist cannot become an anti-Communist; Solzhenitsyn never was a Communist" [42]. In this manner Stalin Prize winner Sergei Michalkov disposes of the phenomenon of Solzhenitsyn. Somehow it is reminiscent of the joke about the wonder rabbi:

"No one can compare with my rabbi. He not only speaks with God directly, but, imagine, God speaks directly with him."

"I don't believe it. Do you have witnesses? If your rabbi says that, he's not only exaggerating, no, he's simply lying."

"Really? Here's the best proof: would God speak with someone who lies?" [10]

How long this logic can be maintained seems to depend on a number of factors, whereby large, rigid, powerful systems appear to have a much longer life-span than individuals. Manès Sperber writes,

> For a while terrorists can win ambitious victories, which temporarily give them the illusion they are masters of their own fate, the same feeling that a kidnapper has when he makes a family, or an entire town, tremble for the child whom he can kill any moment. In as much as politics is the struggle for power, at such a time terrorists may think that they, these wanderers into nothingness, are making head-way on the shortest path to power [57].

When the exalted ideology suffers shipwreck, one can still point to the powers of darkness as the final explanation. Naturally this fit particularly well into Hitlerism's mythology of the twilight of the gods. In his study of *The Myth of the 20th Century*, Kurt Sontheimer writes the following of Rosenberg:

> In Nuremberg, when the myth of the Reich had vanished, he unflinchingly advocated the position that the National Socialist idea had in its essence been right and worthwhile and had failed only because of its corrupt use by others. 'The instinct for the upwelling of profound historical events," an instinct for which the Nazi philosopher Alfred Bäumler had praised him in 1943, had obviously remained so strong that Rosenberg remained unable to recognize the terrible reality even in the hour of reckoning and reflection brought about by the victors [56].

On a recording of Reverend Jim Jones' last speech to his followers on November 18, 1978, shortly before the mass suicide of approximately 900 people in the People's Temple in the Guyana tropical forest, a recording first kept secret by the governments of the United States and Guyana but finally made accessible to the press, one hears the identical excuse and projection of guilt:

> I've tried my best to give you a good life. In spite of all that I've tried, a handful of our people, with their lies, have made our life impossible[. . . .] Not only are we in a compound situation: not only are there those who have left and committed the betrayal of the century; some have stolen children from others and they are in pursuit right now to kill them, because they stole their children[. . . .] We've been so betrayed. We have been so terribly betrayed [24].

The basic theme of a hostile environment that seeks to destroy the ideology has many variations. Hitler fought his life and death struggle against a coalition (constructed by him alone) of "Jewish, plutocratic and Bolshevik powers supported by the Vatican"; Ulrike Meinhof's indignation was directed against "the German parliamentary coalition, the American government, the police, the state and university authorities, the bourgeois, the Shah of Iran, the multinational corporations, the capitalist system" [5]; the opponents of nuclear energy imagine themselves up against a powerful, monolithic alliance of irresponsible corporations, the powers of high finance and all the institutions that are slaves to it: courts, authorities, universities, as well as other research institutions, and political parties.

The transition from at worst eccentric, other-worldly, impractical utopianism to cold, paranoid inhumanity often appears to take place from one day to another, baffling psychiatry. As contradictory as results of research and attempts to interpret the phenomena have been up to now—this research has by no means been limited to historical personalities, but has also considered modern radicals, revolutionaries, terrorists, and, above all, the many sects and cults sprouting up everywhere—they seem to have one thing in common: the fact that the psychological and intellectual consequences of believing in an ideology can be of a demonic pitilessness, in comparison with which the deeds of a hardened criminal only look like regrettable impertinence. The Russian emigrant

Naum Korshavin, one who should know, reflects on this subject in his autobiography written while he was still in Moscow in 1968:

> I hate the paid revolutionaries [. . . .] They embody the most extreme, most expensive (for others), and most merciless form of egoism; they have found the simplest and cheapest means of satisfying their own ambition and of hiding their intellectual void, as well as of arriving at something like the kingdom of heaven without any particular cost of their own (and accordingly all the more at the expense of the lives and fates of others) [31].

In the ideologue's eyes things are admittedly just the opposite. We have already spoken of the assumption of the dissident's malice and depravity. Those who will not have anything to do with the ideology-produced reality and its beneficial consequences can, of course, also be psychologically (and not just morally) abnormal. Desire to emigrate, for example, can be interpreted not only as a refusal to adapt to reality but, rather, also as an individual difficulty in adapting. The Nazi's social parasite was a subject unworthy of life—his unworthiness usually being defined genetically. When in October 1973 Dr. Alfred Freedman, at that time president of the American Psychiatric Association, took part in a psychiatric symposium in the Soviet Union, he and his colleagues came to the conclusion that certain behavior, for instance, demonstrations on Red Square, is seen as a sign of mental disturbance:

> Although it was stated that criticism itself is not a sign of psychopathology, one does get the impression that dissent, criticism or opposition are considered to be bizarre behaviors and important manifestations of disease[. . . .] Tied in with this is the impression that deviance appears tolerable until it is involved with political dissent [16].

The ideological modification and reeducation of opponents are of central importance. With its insistence not only on passive subjugation, but also on active, voluntary acceptance, the ideology falls into a further paradox.

The Paradox of Demanded Spontaneity

The pressing, essentially unanswered question of how the weakness and sinfulness of man can be brought into harmony with the demands of a pure faith crosses all major religions, but especially Christian ethics.

How perfect must one's surrender to the will of God be? Catholic moral theology distinguishes between following God's commandments out of fear of the punishment resulting from disobedience (which is considered a good but less valuable form of faith) and following God's will out of love for Him—thus in voluntary submission. The believer's sorrowful dilemma between his fallible humanity and the pure life of *Imitatio Christi* finds its most poignant portrayal in Dostoevski's Grand Inquisitor. Next to Dostoevski, Pascal comes to mind above all others, for he, more than other thinkers, struggled with the question of how an unbeliever can of himself—that is, spontaneously—come into the state of faith. In Pensée 223, he develops the famous argument in which he maintains that one can summon forth one's own faith by behaving as if one already believes[5]—for instance, by praying, using holy water, going to mass, and carrying out similar tasks of devotion. Considering the potential gain (faith and salvation of the soul), says Pascal, the investment is small. "What do you have to lose?" he asks rhetorically. The paradox of the decision to believe in order to reach a state of faith has been thoroughly analyzed by Elster [15]. Here, too, the problem of self-reflexivity arises. Elster points out that even if it were possible to decide to believe in p, one could not both believe in p and also believe that one's faith in p stems from one's decision to believe in p. In other words, the decision to believe in p (the cause of the faith) cannot at the same time be its own cause (that is, the reason for deciding to believe in p). Therefore Pascal's argument provides no proof of God's existence but, rather, at best offers a proof of the benefits of believing in God—unless one could willingly

---

[5]Ovid, in his *Art of Love*, says the same thing about love: "Convince yourself that you love where you desire only fleetingly. Then believe it. . . . He loves rightly who has succeeded in talking himself into a passion."

forget one's decision to believe. Apart from that, Pascal's argument deals with the demands of a given person on himself and with the paradoxical consequences he has to struggle with.

At the moment, however, the demand is imposed from without, the fallacy cannot be disguised any longer. What results is known in the theory of human communication as the "be spontaneous" paradox. What is meant is the untenable position that comes about when person *B* is in a relation of dependence on *A*, with *A* demanding a certain behavior from *B*, but a behavior which by its very nature must be spontaneous. But precisely because it is demanded, it cannot possibly be spontaneous any more. The demand for spontaneity produces a Russellian paradox, as has already been mentioned in the section The Paradoxes of Perfection and Infinity. An example of this "be spontaneous" paradox is a wife's wish disguised as a question to her husband: "Why don't you ever bring me flowers any more?" There are only two actions open to him: Either he doesn't bring her flowers any more, which indubitably will disappoint her, or he brings her some—an action that is bound to disappoint her, for he was supposed to do spontaneously what was desired, and not merely because she had asked him to do so. In other words, he does the right thing for the wrong reasons.

The dilemma of demanded spontaneity is a component of all ideological realities. Koestler speaks of this in his book *Darkness at Noon*:

> The Party denied the free will of the individual—and at the same time it exacted its willing self-sacrifice. It denied his capacity to choose between two alternatives—and at the same time it demanded that he should always choose the right one. It denied his power to choose between good and evil—and at the same time it spoke accusingly of guilt and treachery. The individual stood under the sign of economic fatality, a wheel in a clockwork which had been wound up for all eternity and could not be stopped or influenced—and the Party demanded that the wheel should revolt against the clockwork and change its course. There was somewhere an error in the calculation; the equation did not work out [27].

And the victim in Orwell's *1984* must be made spontaneous as well:

> We are not content with negative obedience, nor even with the most abject submission. When finally you surrender to us it must be of your own free will. We do not destroy the heretic; as long as he resists us we never destroy him[. . . .] We convert him, we capture his inner mind, we reshape him. We burn all the evil and all illusion out of him; we bring him over to our side, not in appearance, but genuinely, heart and soul. We make him one of ourselves before we kill him [44].

Once again in Elster's sense one could speculate that there are not only two forms of negation, the passive and the active, but also a passive and an active form of acceptance or obedience. An example of the former would perhaps be the "inner emigration" practiced by many people under Hitler. This inner emigration usually went with an external *pro forma* "act as if," and the Nazi ideologues foamed with rage at these inner emigrants wherever they could find them. The spirit of the good soldier Schwejk came back from the days of the imperial Austrian army, and, during the Second World War, fraternized with the insidiousness (the Nazis had a special "insidiousness law" that was supposed to combat this mental state) of Corporal Hirnschal of Radio London.

Both forms of obedience were well-known to the Reichsminister for (armed) Enlightenment and Propaganda. In a speech on September 16, 1935, Goebbels exclaimed, obviously playing on Talleyrand's sentence about the bayonets: "It may be nice to have command over the bayonets, but it is nicer to command the hearts! . . . We must make the heart's coercion into the commandment for action in the German people" [20]. The "be spontaneous" paradox was familiar to him, as Schneider writes,

> What was most baffling was his technique for making the voluntary, the future and the unpredictable into objects of command: 'The command to put up flags is obeyed within half an hour in the cities and in the country in an overwhelming way," he announces on January 15, 1935, after the Saar vote [. . . .] "The

population gathered for giant rallies of a spontaneous character" [53].

Within the frame of any ideology only active obedience is acceptable, because "whoever is not for us, is against us." In this way ideology becomes pseudo-religious. Roger Bernheim, the Moscow correspondent of the *Neue Zürcher Zeitung*, describes the "ecclesiastical" aspects of the Soviet Communist party:

> The Party has its god. The sentence "Lenin lived, lives and will live forever" belongs to the creed of a Soviet Communist, indeed must belong to the creed of every Soviet citizen. The Party has its priests, pastors, its holy scriptures and its scribes. It has its liturgy. It's announcements consist of liturgical formulae. The adjective "great" belongs to the concept October Revolution, the word "glorious" to the Soviet Communist Party, to Lenin the noun "genius". . . . [. . .] If something is said about the Soviet People's support for the Party, then this support must be characterized as unanimous, passionate and unconditional. The workers, the peasants and the intellectuals of the country are "rallied monolithically around the Party" [6].

In the irrational universe of demanded spontaneity the power of state reaches beyond the prohibition of acts contrary to society, assigning itself the task of prescribing the citizen's thoughts and convictions. To quote Revel's concise conclusion, "c'est dans les sociétés totalitaires que l'Etat se charge de 'donner un sens' à la vie des êtres" [51].[6] Thus original thought becomes treason, and life becomes a hell of a particular kind. According to a publication of the literary underground, *Samisdat*, this hell consists of

> a complete surrender of the soul beyond all physical and economic constraints: it demands the constant, active participation in the common lie, which all can see [55].

---

[6]"In totalitarian societies the state assumes the task of giving life a meaning." And Revel adds, "On the other hand the liberal state tends to bring about the conditions in which the collectivity does not impose any kind of life-style or way of feeling on the individual."

The lie creates its own luscious flora. From the alleged Aryan sobs of joy upon seeing the face of the worshipped Führer (one man, Reck-Malleczewen [50], who recklessly referred to it as excrement face, did not come back from the concentration camp) there is a monotonous, unbroken litany of undiscerning praise right across the sterotypical reality of the most varied ideologies, even up to the present. For what difference is there between, on the one hand, the bombastic literary effusions that immortalize the blossoming love between the young man in the *Hitler-Jugend* and the young woman who belongs to the *Bund deutscher Mädchen* in the ever-rustling forests or under fluttering flags and, on the other hand, the heterosexual mass of students gathered in the tear gas-filled corridors of the Sorbonne in May 1968 or the Chinese short story *The Role of Love*, in which the narrator describes how she fell in love with a young man?

> We began asking one another questions: "Did you see how Premier Chou's hearse drove down Changan Street to the funeral? Where were you standing? Did you catch part of the anthology of poetry in memory of Chou-en-Lai? [. . .] When did you first hear of the fall of the Gang of Four?" As we spoke, I saw that we had so much in common [39].

The lie inherent in the "be spontaneous" paradox has to be rendered credible; for that, propaganda and, above all, art that has been modified to fit the ideology must be mobilized. The impression has to be artfully created that there is actually a passionate enthusiasm trembling within all the others—and whoever does not feel this within himself had better recognize that something is wrong with him and not perhaps with the official definition of reality. Presumably one must cultivate these feelings *à la* Pascal so that they finally become spontaneous; then one can feel the same for Hua, Mao's successor, as a certain Yu Kuangh-Lee expresses in his poem:

> My pulsating heart
> Leaped into my throat;
> Tears of happiness
> Made me blind.

But through the sea of red flags,
Through the waves of flowers
I saw, I saw
Chairman Hua on the Tienanmen
in his green army uniform [64].

Not everyone succeeds with the trick of spontaneous enthusiasm. What the East German Thomas Brasch has to say in his ironic *Self-Criticism* sounds quite different, more probable, more human:

I admit it all. I do not stay on the topic. I do not take a stand. I only pick away the dirt from between my toes. I have never been active[. . . .] Hallelujah, the insurrection rots between my loose teeth. Hallelujah, the wind. It sweeps through our nationalized brains [9].

What has been said so far is only valid once power is in the hands of the ideologue. Until it has reached that point, the "be spontaneous" paradox has another function. This function results from the necessity of creating a revolutionary consciousness. The technique for this is called *consciousness raising*. Bringing about perfection presupposes an acute awareness of the imperfection of the world; yet it seems that one of the weaknesses of man is his ability to tolerate a great deal of this imperfection. Marx coined the term *mystification* both for the creation of this condition of blindness by the ruling class and for its continuing existence. The advocate of perfection, therefore, must, above all, demystify. It is not enough simply to uncover objectively and denounce the insufficiencies. To fulfill its purpose, the indignation may not be repeated mechanically; rather, it must be spontaneous. Not until then can the call for perfection be brought to a spontaneous resonance. Nothing is more aversive to the designs of these universal benefactors than the idea of limiting oneself to, and accepting the inevitable imperfection of, that which is feasible. Hence the more and more frantic search for burning problems, specifically in those countries enjoying a measure of freedom, security, and affluence unheard of in human history. But since this state of the world is largely the result of steeply increasing scientific progress, science—especially in our day—has more and more come into the ideologue's focus.

The Claim to Scientificity

> If the facts do not agree with the theory,
> so much the worse for the facts.
>
> Hegel, cited by Marcuse

With the growing trust in a total comprehension of reality on the basis of objective observations and experiments that can be repeated, science began to fill the ideological vacuum which in the last hundred years gradually developed through the fading of the great religious, ethical, and philosophical ideals. Admittedly there were early representatives of the doctrine of scientific salvation, for instance, Bacon and Descartes. Yet the utopian political expectations that have been removed from any context of divine revelation and attributed to science are relatively young.

The idea is seductive in its apparent simplicity and clarity: Whoever succeeds in comprehending nature's intrinsic order, in its existence independent of human opinions, convictions, prejudices, hopes, values, and so on, has eternal truth on his side. The scientist takes the place of the seeker after God; the objective truth takes the place of superstition:

> We ought then to regard the present state of the universe as the effect of its anterior state and as the cause of the one which is to follow. Given for one instant an intelligence which could comprehend all the forces by which nature is animated and the respective situation of the beings who compose it—an intelligence sufficiently vast to submit these data to analysis—it would embrace in the same formula the movements of the greatest bodies of the universe and those of the lightest atom; for it, nothing would be uncertain and the future, as the past, would be present to its eyes [33].

As early as 1840 Laplace used these words to outline the idea of a secularized eschatology. In all fairness it must be emphasized, however, that he takes into account its utopian character by using the conditional mood.

Competent minds since Giambattista Vico have emphasized again and again that no scientific theory (or interpretation) can be more than, at best, an image, a particular interpretation of the world, and not reality itself. It is in this sense that this volume was conceived as a contribution to the field of inquiry. At this point we only want to examine the practical consequences that follow the assumption that the world can be (or already has been) scientifically explained, or, in other words, to examine what happens when ideology attempts to derive its generally binding claim to truth from science.

What validity do scientific conclusions have? As far as the daily business of living is concerned, we may assume that they actually do have general validity. Observations of the free fall of a body in a vacuum at sea level—assuming it takes place under identical conditions—yields the same values every time. Here we can disregard the fact that this observation neither explains the causes of this phenomenon (the nature of gravity), nor does it establish more than a statistical probability that on the 1001th try the body will behave in the same manner (and not, for example, fly up away from the earth). Referring back to a distinction I have attempted to make elsewhere [59], there are two fundamentally different aspects of what we call *reality*. To start with, there are the properties of objects. Let us call this the reality of the first order. Accordingly, this reality would be the universe of all "facts" fitting in a particular framework, that is, that of observation or experiment (both of which, naturally, are constructs of the theories standing behind them), that is, the universe of "facts" which can be established objectively in as much as the repetition of the same experiment yields the same result independently of by whom, when, and where the experiment is being carried out.[7]

---

[7]At this point we shall not consider that this is, of course, only possible when all participants make use of the same linguistic and semantic communication system. The construction of the Tower of Babel ran aground when God commanded His angels "to go down there and confound their language."

It is then a great temptation to assume, with apparent logic, that the key to an ultimate interpretation of the world has been found, and with it, therefore the ultimate guidelines for man's proper attitude toward the world, his fellowman, and his own existence. For the truth would now be accessible to all men of good will, and only the insane, the obdurate, and the otherwise insidious would resist reason.

What the terrible oversimplification overlooks is that the facts of reality of the first order give no reference point for the meaning of human existence. As for what concerns us, the law of gravity teaches us nothing more than we already know: that a fall from great heights leads to death. Life's (or death's) meaning does not come from it. Shakespeare knew of no philosopher who could simply get over his toothache. And in the *Tractatus* Wittgenstein writes

> We feel that even when *all possible* scientific questions have been answered, the problems of life remain completely untouched. Of course there are then no questions left, and this itself is the answer [63].

Yet the reality that is addressed here (and which the ideology proposes to explain) is not the reality of scientific facts of the first order; rather here it has to do with that aspect of reality through which the first-order facts are given meaning, order, and value. A small child with normal vision can perceive a red light but does not already know that it prohibits his crossing the street or that it denotes a brothel. This meaning of the red light has absolutely nothing to do with its wavelength or the like; rather it is a human convention, an assignment of significance which, like every other sign—and more obviously—every word, has no other relation to that which is named by it (with the exception of onomatopoetic words, of course). As Bateson and Jackson have stated "there is nothing particularly five-like in the number five; there is nothing particularly table-like in the word 'table'," [4] thus giving a new form of expression to Shakespeare's remark, "There is nothing either good or bad, but thinking makes it so." The aspect of reality in the framework of which meaning, significance, and value are attributed is called reality of the second order. While it is sensible in the area of first-order reality to examine, in the cases of differences of opinion, whose opinions do justice to the concrete facts and who is wrong, in the sphere of second-order reality it is senseless to argue about scientifically established "truth" or to claim to have found it. Let us choose one of the innumerable possible examples of this. There is no "scientific," "objective" solution to the conflict between the Arab countries and Israel, just as there is no such solution for a conflict between two individual partners of a relationship. Relationships are not aspects of first-order reality, whose true nature can be determined scientifically; instead, they are pure constructs of the partners in the relationship, and as such they resist all objective verification. And with that the naive faith in reason based on scientific knowledge no longer can be the final authority. At the same time hope, for "man who is good by nature" (Rousseau), whose goodness grows out of his voluntary, spontaneous, and reasonable subordination to the so clearly recognizable, scientifically established value bases, and for whom, therefore, individual wishes and needs coincide completely with those of human society, is disappointed miserably.

Precisely this is the crux of the scientific utopias of a healthy, peaceful, selfless world: the claim to the scientificity of ideology, a claim that builds on the confusion between first- and second-order realities. Where this is the case, a construct of reality results that by no means needs to be similar to any other obligatory world of another "unscientific" ideology. In classical psychiatry it is naively assumed that there is a real reality, of which normal people (above all the psychiatrists) are more clearly aware than are the insane. In the sociological application of the doctrine of scientific world salvation there is faith in—as Andersson and Radnitzki have so poignantly noted in a reply [2]—a narrowing of the gap between what is and what should be, a hope for the fulfillment of man's century-old dream of a world in which undeniable facts and human wishes and hopes will be one and the same.

When a scientific theory is finally declared valid by political *fiat*, thus becoming a generally binding justification of the state's existence, the iron curtain of obscurantism comes down. Alfred Rosenberg's *Myth of the 20th Century* (a racial theory on account of which millions of human beings were declared worthless and killed) or Trofim Denisovitch Lysenko's theory of the genetic transmission of acquired characteristics (a theory that led to the arrest and death of colleagues who refuted it, and which for decades paralyzed the Soviet study of genetics) are particularly glaring examples—all the more glaring when one keeps in mind that even in both men's lifetimes these "theories" were preposterous nonsense. In the sublunar world of scientific ideologies there is no more place for further research, for questioning earlier assumptions, for creative doubt about what has already been established. What is a self-evident condition in the world of free science becomes of necessity treason and subversion when those in power imagine that they possess the ultimate truth.

Indeed, often the course of events itself is subversive by contradicting the ideology. The ideologues then usually make a jump that becomes a *salto mortale* only for those who cannot adjust quickly enough. Yesterday's truth becomes today's heresy. Those who have been murdered because of their errors are rehabilitated as geniuses.

Enantiodromy

> But where there is danger deliverance
> grows too.
>
> Hölderlin

Since Heraclitus, the great philosopher of change, we understand enantiodromy as the transition of things into their opposite. The forty-fifth fragment reads, "Changing into its opposite is the harmony which permeates the opposition." After Heraclitus numerous thinkers over the centuries have described and tried to explain this phenomenon in its most varied forms of appearance. It seems that finding a useful conceptual access to these processes that are illogical and therefore inexplicable in terms of a classical, linear understanding of causation is reserved for modern thought with its concept of systems and of systems' characteristics. The works of Nobel Prize winner Ilya Prigogine—technically difficult for the reader not schooled in biology, physics, and chemistry—are especially noteworthy in this context. In *From Being to Becoming* [49], dealing with *dissipative structures* as the interpretive principle of enantiodromy, Prigogine points out that the stabilizing and destabilizing functions of these structures can be demonstrated in social systems as well. Purely empirically, the impression forces itself upon us that enantiodromy can be expected most certainly where a certain attitude or orientation becomes extreme. This obviously applies to the realities created by ideologies. For there—as we have tried to demonstrate—everything that contradicts the ideology must be treated as nonexistent or brought to nonexistence. Even so the ideology entangles itself in the insidiousness of active negation. As Elster says in his analysis of atheism (p. 184), the negative faith of the atheist remains connected with God, as much as that of the believer (or even more so if the believer has no strong desire to proselytize); for "the inefficacy of atheism comes about precisely because it wants to achieve the impossible: to establish, by active negation, a state of passive negation."

As long as this dilemma takes place only in the ideologue's mind, the rest of humanity can dismiss it with a laugh or a shrug of the shoulders. But as soon as the enantiodromic component for the construction of the ideological reality is added not just in fantasy, but in actuality, it can no longer simply be shrugged off. The character Shigalov in Dostoevski's novel *The Possessed* offers such an example. Shigalov is the founder of a utopian system through which "the present form of society will be redeemed." As one might think, this system is very complex. He is ready to present it to his co-conspirers in its shortest form, but warns them from the start that this will

> occupy at least ten evening sessions, one for each of my chapters. (There was the sound of laughter) I must add, besides, that my system is not yet complete. (Laughter again) I am perplexed by

my own data, and my conclusion is in direct contradiction to the original idea with which I started. Starting from unlimited freedom, I arrived at unlimited despotism. I will add, however, that there can be no other solution of the social formula than mine. (The laughter grew.)

While Shigalov's personality is fictional, his dilemma is not; rather, it is the crass reality in many countries in which Shigalovism came to power. The more active the negation, the more powerfully the negated forces itself upon the person negating it. Freud spoke of the return to the suppressed; for Jung every psychological extreme contains "secretly its opposite, or stands in some sort of intimate and essential relation to it" [25]. Lenin, who thought he had "completely destroyed the bureaucracy," experienced enantiodromy as a bitter disappointment. Heinz Abosch reflects on this:

A new, much larger bureaucracy with more absolute control of power came out of the rubble of the old apparatus. Lenin filled his last years with complaints about this cancerous growth; he no longer praised the "destruction" of the bureaucracy, but rather regretted its complete triumph. In a secret memo in 1922 he admitted that the Soviet state "had simply been taken over from czarism and only very lightly anointed with Soviet oil" [1].

Not every ideologue takes the failure of the ideology so tragically. The terrorists who surface after years in the underground appear to have the inclination to aver naively and frankly that they are sorry, but to err is human. The President of Campuchea, Khieu Samphan, who with his Sorbonne dissertation gave the Khmer Rouge the ideological basis and justification for the murder of about 250,000 people and the gradual liquidation of another million by means of forced labor and privation, explained to *United Press International* on August 20, 1980,

We know now that there is no longer any possibility of a Socialist revolution for our generation. The only goal we can hope to realize in our lifetime is the survival of Cambodia [. . . .] People are still a bit afraid of us but we tell them we are nationalists before we are Communists and we now realize that we cannot fulfill our dream of socialism.[8]

The ideology's failure does not necessarily lead to insight into the fatal process of ideological constructivism. It only makes room for a new construct. For at best we know what reality is *not*. Or, as von Glaserfeld so clearly puts it in his contribution (p. 39),

> This means that the "real" world manifests itself exclusively there where our constructions break down. But since we can describe and explain these breakdowns only in the very concepts that we have used to build the failing structures, this process can never yield a picture of a world which we could hold responsible for their failure.

It is difficult to become aware of the enantiodromic fact that the dark side of an ideology that is to be found in praxis can be attributed neither to "industrial accidents" nor to the incapability of lower (or even higher) party functionaries nor to the intrigues of internal or external enemies. Stolzenberg shows us the reason for this, when he points out (p. 265 ff) that one can only escape the trap of a particular fundamental view by seeing this view no longer as a fact—existing independently of us and leading to certain conclusions (which, in turn, recursively "prove" the "veracity" of the view)—but, rather, by questioning the fundamental view itself.

Duverger poses precisely this question in his book *Les Orangers du Lac Balaton:*

> And what if Marx had not been betrayed? He did not desire the terrible regimes that claim to follow his teachings. They probably would have filled him with horror. But what if they are not an excrescence, an aberration, a deviation of his doctrine? What if they reveal the implicit logic of his doctrine, pushed to its ultimate conclusion? [14]

---

[8] A few minutes later in the same interview, Khieu accused the Vietnamese of "systematically creating famine conditions in Cambodia and purposely hindering the distributrion of international food aid to the people."

And in the course of his book Duverger masterfully shows that these abuses actually result from the nature of the ideology.

Today France's "nouveaux philosophes" are expressing clearly what Solzhenitsyn already said, and for which—less than ten years ago—he was accused of malicious distortion of the facts. Bernard Lévy, in his book *Barbarism with a Human Face* [36], states, "There is no worm in the fruit, no sin that came later, but rather the worm is the fruit and the sin is Marx." The same conclusion is found in André Glucksmann's *Master Thinkers* [18]: no Russian camps without Marxism. And Monique Hirschhorn summarizes this development with the following words:

> Having awoken from their dogmatic slumber, the new philosophers are discovering the truth in a strikingly simple thought. The connection between the Gulag and Marx is obvious. It is not an accident which can be explained by bureaucracy, Stalinist deviation or Lenin's errors. Rather it is a direct and ineluctable, logical consequence of Marxist principles. The classless society is not a messianic vision, but rather another name for terror [22].

One of the results of primitive causal thinking is that enantiodromy—in spite of all historical proofs to the contrary—remains unimaginable for the visionaries and ideologues, thus overtaking them completely unexpectedly. It makes matters worse that these two-dimensional thinkers have taken out their own lease on humanity, morality, and justice. What man of good will would not be willing to stand behind such catchwords as *classless society, freedom, equality, brotherhood,* and the like? For most, the sober realization comes too late— except for the rare Grand Inquisitor, who already knows. Neither the content nor the geographical location of the ideologies changes anything. Whether the condition of equality is created in a Marxist or capitalist sense makes no difference for the stereotypical result. The attempt to balance out the natural diversity of people unavoidably leads to totalitarian excesses of inequality. In a similar way the annihilation of freedom can result both from an unlimited overemphasis and from an all too anxious protection of freedom.

What the ideologue cannot accept in his search for perfection, even if he saw it, is the ancient truth that has been rediscovered again and again in more and more convincing forms in the last decades and in the most diverse disciplines. The truth is this: Complex systems—for example, human society—are homeostatic, that is, self-regulating, and deviations from the norm *themselves* lead to the correction of those conditions that endanger the system or limit its natural development. But everything that continues to develop is, for that very reason, imperfect—and the ideological reality cannot accept the imperfect. In complex systems, change and evolution result from factors that at first seem to be deviations and pathology; but without them the system would congeal into a hopeless sterility. Thus the apparent enemy must be recognized as an archetypical black sheep or demonic double rather than something to be liquidated.

The constructivist thinkers will strive to bring a better understanding of this complexity and of the logic that—although it cannot be comprehended by common sense—paradoxically both confirms and transcends itself. More about this vicissitude of constructivism shall occupy us in the Epilogue. Meanwhile Winston Churchill's wise maxim gives us a ray of hope: *Democracy is a lousy form of government, but I don't know a better one.*

REFERENCES

1. Abosch, Heinz. Karl Kautskys Kritik am Bolschewismus. *Neue Zürcher Zeitung*, 27-28. 11. 1976, 869.
2. Andersson, Gunnar, and Radnitzky, Gerard. Finalisierung der Wissenschaft im doppelten Sinn. *Neue Zürcher Zeitung*, 19./20.8. 1978, 33.
3. Bakunin, Michail A. Revolutionary catechism. In *Bakunin on Anarchy* (translated by Sam Dolgoff, ed.). A. Knopf, New York, 1972, p. 76.
4. Bateson, Gregory, and Jackson, Don D. Some varieties of pathogenic organization. In *Disorders of Communication*, Vol. 42 (David McK. Rioch, ed.). Research Publications, Association for Research in Nervous and Mental Disease, Williams and Wilkins, Baltimore, 1964, pp. 270–283.
5. Becker, Jillian. *Hitler's Children: The Story of the Baader-Meinhof Terrorist Gang.* Lippincott, Philadelphia, 1977, pp. 72, 159.
6. Bernheim, Roger. Der "kirchliche" Aspekt der sowjetischen KP. *Neue Zürcher Zeitung*, 16.8. 1970, 3.

7. Böckenförde, Ernst Wolfgang. *Der Staat als sittlicher Staat*, Duncker and Humblot, Berlin, 1978, p. 37.
8. Bolzano, Bernard. *Paradoxien des Unendlichen*. Mayer and Müller, Berlin, 1889.
9. Brasch, Thomas. Selbstkritik. In *Kargo: 32*. *Versuch auf einem untergehenden Schiff aus der eigenen Haut zu kommen*. Suhrkamp Taschenbuch 541, Frankfurt am Main, 1979, pp. 160–161.
10. Broch, Henry. Wunderrabbis. *Neue Zürcher Zeitung*, 4/5.10. 1975.
11. Castro, Fidel. Quoted *Neue Zürcher Zeitung*, 7./8. 11. 1978, p. 5.
12. Cohn, Norman. *The Pursuit of the Millennium*. Essential Books, Fairlawn, New Jersey, 1957, p. XIV.
13. Deutscher, Isaac. *The Prophet Unarmed*. Oxford University Press, London, 1959, p. 85.
14. Duverger, Maurice. *Les Orangers du Lac Balaton*. Le Seuil, Paris, 1980, p. 9.
15. Elster, Jon. *Ullysses and the Sirens: Studies in Rationality and Irrationality*. Cambridge University Press, London, 1979, pp. 47–54.
16. Freedman, Alfred. Quoted in *Monitor*, American Psychological Association, Vol. 4, No. 12, December 1973, p. 1, and United Press International, November 2, 1973.
17. Garaudy, Roger. *The Alternative Future: A Vision of Christian Marxism* (translated by Leonard Mayhew). Simon and Schuster, New York, 1974, pp. 169–171.
18. Glucksmann, André. *The Master Thinkers* (translated by Brian Pearce). Harper and Row, New York, 1977.
19. Gödel, Kurt. *On Formally Undecidable Propositions of Principia Mathematica and Related Systems I*. Oliver and Boyd, Edinburgh, 1962.
20. Goebbels, Joseph. Quoted by Schneider [52, p. 126].
21. Gregor-Dellin, Martin. Quoted by Schneider [52, p. 150] *Schriftsteller testen Politikertexte* (H. D. Baroth, ed.). Munich, 1967, pp. 75–87.
22. Hirschhorn, Monique. Les Nouveaux philosophes: L'Écume et la vague. *Stanford French Review* 2, 1978, 301–313.
23. Holstein, Walter. *Der Untergrund*, 2nd ed. Luchterhand, Neuwied, 1969, p. 67.
24. Jones, Jim. Quoted in *San Francisco Chronicle*, 15.3. 1979, 5.
25. Jung, Carl G. *Symbols of Transformation*. Bollingen Foundation, New York, 1952, p. 375.
26. Klemperer, Victor. *Die unbewältigte Sprache*. Melzer, Darmstadt, 1966.
27. Koestler, Arthur. *Darkness at Noon*. Modern Library, New York, 1941, p. 257.
28. Koestler, Arthur. *Le Zéro et l'infini*. Calmann-Levy, Paris, 1945.
29. Koestler, Arthur. *Sonnenfinsternis*. Artemis-Verlag, Zurich, 1946.
30. Koestler, Arthur. *The Invisible Writing*. Macmillan, New York, 1954, p. 357.
31. Korshavin, Naum. In *Kontinent*, Vol. 8 (Vladimir E. Maximov, ed.), Ullstein, Berlin, 1978. Quoted in *Neue Zürcher Zeitung* 1/2.7. 1978, p. 33.
32. Kraus, Wolfgang. *Die verratene Anbetung*. Piper, Munich, 1978, p. 49.
33. Laplace, Pierre Simon de. *A Philosophical Essay on Probability* (translated by Frederick W. Truscott and Frederick L. Emory). Dover, New York, 1951, p. 4.
34. Lenin, Vladimir I. What is to be done? In *Selected Works*, Vol. 2. Inter-

national Publishers, New York (undated), p. 53.
35. Lenin, Vladimir I. *Ibid.*, p. 53.
36. Lévy, Bernard-Henry. *Barbarism with a Human Face* (translated by George Holoch). Harper and Row, New York, 1979.
37. Lübbe, Hermann. *Ideologische Selbstermächtigung zur Gewalt. Neue Zürcher Zeitung*, 28./29. 10. 1978, pp. 65–66.
38. Lucas, J. R. *The Freedom of the Will.* Clarendon Press, Oxford, 1970, p. 114.
39. Mäder-Bogorad, Yvonne. Literatur als Zerrspiegel der Wirklichkeit. *Neue Zürcher Zeitung*, 5./6.5. 1975, p. 70.
40. Marx, Karl, and Engels, Friedrich. *The German Ideology.* International Publishers, New York, 1947, p. 22.
41. Meienberg, Niklaus. In *das konzept*, March 1979; quoted in *Neue Zürcher Zeitung*, 17./18.3. 1979, p. 33.
42. Michalkow, Sergej. In *Der Spiegel* 28, 4.2. 1974, p. 87.
43. Morin, Edgar, in collaboration with Bernhard Paillard and others. *Rumour in Orleans* (translated by Peter Green). Pantheon, New York, 1971.
44. Orwell, George. *1984.* Harcourt, Brace, New York, 1949, p. 258.
45. Orwell, George. Inside the whale. In *A Collection of Essays.* Doubleday, Garden City, New York, 1954, p. 235.
46. Popper, Sir Karl Raimund. *Conjectures and Refutations. The Growth of Scientific Knowledge.* Basic Books, New York, 1962, p. VI.
47. Popper, Sir Karl Raimund. *The Open Society and Its Enemies.* Harper, New York, 1963.
48. Popper, Sir Karl Raimund. Utopie und Gewalt. In *Utopie: Begriff und Phänomen des Utopischen* (Arnhelm Neusüss, ed.). Luchterhand, Neuwied, 1968, p. 322.
49. Prigogine, Ilya. *From Being to Becoming.* W. H. Freeman, San Francisco, 1980.
50. Reck-Malleczewen, Fritz P. *Tagebuch eines Verzweifelten.* Goverts, Stuttgart, 1966.
51. Revel, Jean-François. *La Tentation totalitarie.* Laffont, Paris, 1976, p. 320.
52. Schneider, Wolf. *Wörter machen Leute: Magie und Macht der Sprache.* Piper, Munich, 1976, p. 133.
53. Schneider, Wolf. *Op. cit.* p. 128.
54. Schnitzler, Arthur. *Flight into Darkness* (translated by William A. Donke). Simon and Schuster, New York, 1931, pp. 29–30.
55. Solschenizyn, Alexander, et al. *Stimmen aus dem Untergrund. Zur geistigen Situation in der USSR.* Luchterhand, Darmstadt, 1975.
56. Sontheimer, Kurt. Die Erweckung der Rassenseele. In *Bücher, die das Jahrhundert bewegten* (Günther Rühle, ed.). Piper, Munich, 1978, p. 113.
57. Sperber, Manès. Die Erben des Herostratos. *Süddeutsche Zeitung*, 20/21.9. 1975.
58. Stienstra, Tom. 400 Students Chant Ritual at Rain-Making Ceremony. *Palo Alto Times*, 18.12. 1977, p. 2.
59. Watzlawick, Paul. *How Real Is Real?* Random House, New York, 1976, pp. 140–142.
60. Watzlawick, Paul. Münchhausens Zopf und Wittgensteins Leiter. Zum Problem der Rückbezüglichkeit. In *Der Mensch und seine Sprache* (Anton Peisl and Armin Mohler, eds.). Propyläen, Berlin, 1979, pp. 243–264.
61. Watzlawick, Paul. *Op. cit.*, p. 253.

62. Whitehead, Alfred N., and Russell, Bertrand. *Principia Mathematica.* University Press, Cambridge, 1910–1913.
63. Wittgenstein, Ludwig. *Tractatus Logico-Philosophicus.* Humanities Press, New York, 1951, p. 186.
64. Yu Kuang-Lieh. Quoted in *Neue Zürcher Zeitung,* 12./13.3. 1977, p. 5.
65. *Zeitdienst.* Quoted in *Neue Zürcher Zeitung,* 17./18.3. 1979, p. 35.

PART 4

The Fly and the Fly-Bottle

PAUL WATZLAWICK

> What is your aim in philosophy?—
> To show the fly the way out of the fly-
> bottle.
> Ludwig Wittgenstein: *Philosophical
> Investigations I*, p. 309

*O*ld fashioned fly-bottles had a funnel-like opening whose large outer mouth made it appear safe for the fly to venture into the excitingly smelly (but gradually narrowing) interior. Once inside the inner chamber, the only way back out was through the same narrow inner opening of the funnel through which the fly had entered. But seen from the inside, this hole now appeared even more confining and dangerous than the chamber in which it found itself caught. Following Wittgenstein's metaphor, it would now be necessary to convince the fly that the only solution to its dilemma was the seemingly least likely and most threatening one.

How do we find the way out of the fly-bottle of an ill-fitting reality construction? And is there any hope of freeing ourselves if all conceivable solutions only lead to "more of the same" and enantiodromatic fatality seems to ordain that they only make worse what they are meant to improve?

Among the most ancient examples of this dilemma are the traps inherent in the apparently all-inclusive ordering of the world into truth and falsehood. For the purposes of the present chapter it is important to realize that since the days of antiquity an ominous creaking can be heard in the scaffold of this construction. A useful simplification traces the malaise back to the alleged statement by Epimenides, the Cretan, "all Cretans are liars" (in the professional literature usually condensed into "I am lying"). Upon *reflection it becomes obvious that Epimenides is truthful when he lies and lying when he tells the truth. This seemingly simple utterance therefore derails both Aristotelian logic and our sloppy everyday logic.*

The reason why this statement manages to create havoc must be sought in its self-reflexivity (self-reference), namely, in the fact that it declares something about itself but at the same time negates this declaration. Epimenides' (truthful) admission of his (all-inclusive) mendacity sets a true–false–true–false oscillation in motion and thereby makes him into the godfather of all paradox.

For centuries the paradoxes were considered of intriguing but marginal importance, or simply declared inadmissible. But like anything else that is dealt with through denial and repression, they have a disconcerting ability to cause insidious trouble. The painful dilemma of the scholastic theologians comes to mind: What did God say to the devil who challenged His omnipotence by inviting God to create a rock of such enormous size that not even God Himself could lift it? No matter how they looked at it, God could not fulfill one of the two conditions.

After June 1901, when Bertrand Russell discovered the famous paradox of the class of all classes that are not members of themselves, paradox was no longer just an ominous creaking in the girders of Aristotle's construction of our logical universe, but—to borrow Heinz von Foerster's pithy phrase—"the apostle of sedition in the kingdom of the orthodox." As will be shown in this chapter, paradox stands autonomously beyond the seemingly all-inclusive concepts of truth and falsehood. But first back to Bertrand Russell. In his autobiography he describes the personal consequences of his discovery:

> *At first I supposed that I should be able to overcome the contradiction quite easily, and that probably there was some trivial error in the reasoning. Gradually, however, it became clear that this was not the case. Burali-Forti had already discovered a similar contradiction, and it turned out on logical analysis that there was an affinity with the ancient Greek contradiction about Epimenides the Cretan, who said*

that all Cretans are liars [. . . .] It seemed unworthy of a grown man to spend time on such trivialities, but what was I to do? There was something wrong, since such contradictions were unavoidable on ordinary premises [7].

Russell then goes on to explain how this problem vexed him for years and how the two summers of 1903 and 1904 remained in his mind a period of complete intellectual deadlock.

For Russell, just as for his predecessors and followers, the problem was how to deal with this "apostle of sedition" that threatened to subvert the kingdom of orthodoxy. And it is as interesting as it is frightening to see that eventually even this great thinker found no better solution than to disallow the contradiction. In his monumental work Principia Mathematica, published in 1910 in co-authorship with Whitehead [13], self-referential propositions are simply delcared illegitimate. This principle of illegitimacy is a cornerstone of the Theory of Types.

Today we know that an involvement with the intricacies of paradox is by no means "unworthy of a grown man." Paradoxes invariably arise where the logical consistency of a reality construction has reached its limits and begins to lead itself ad absurdum. This phenomenon is not limited to mathematical logic and related esoteric problems of the philosophy of science: The publications of the so-called Palo Alto group [1,11,12] have shown that paradox is part and parcel of the schizophrenic disintegration of a personal world image, and essentially similar contradictions began to surface in supposedly consistent, self-contained theories. An example of the latter would be hitherto unknown problems related to the acceleration of acceleration, which space scientists have to deal with. Paradox is an epistemological warning light that begins to flash when—in von Glasersfeld's sense— a construction no longer fits or, in other words, when it becomes evident what reality is not.[1] And, as so often happens, at such a

---

[1]The interested reader will find a plethora of most interesting examples of paradoxical situations and problems in several recent publications, for example, by Hughes and Brecht [5], Smullyan [9,10], and Hofstadter [4].

critical point the stumbling block may turn out to be the corner-stone of a totally new and better-fitting construction.

A splendid example of this is associated with the British philoso-pher, logician, computer expert, psychologist, engineer, and author George Spencer Brown. In 1967, after years of grappling with the problems of self-reference in logic and their conse-quences for computational procedures, he presented "with some trepidation" to Bertrand Russell a logical calculus [3] *that no longer stood under the fatality of unresolved paradox and the consequent need to "disallow" it. In Brown's own words, Betrand Russell "was delighted. The Theory* [of Logical Types] *was, he said, the most abitrary thing he and Whitehead had ever had to do, not really a theory but a stopgap, and he was glad to have lived long enough to see the matter resolved"* [3, p. ix]. *When Brown's book was published, Russell said, "In this book Mr. Spencer Brown has succeeded in doing what is very rare indeed. He has revealed a new calculus of great power and simplicity. I congratulate him."*

This book is Laws of Form, *a calculus that in spite (or perhaps precisely because) of its "great simplicity" is accessible only to readers trained in logic and mathematics. It is a modern logic no longer constructed on the Aristotelian categories of true, false, and the excluded middle, but on the concepts of inside and out-side, that is, on the separation of physical or conceptual space which arises the moment we draw a distinction.*

It is of interest to note that Brown takes as one of his starting points the liar paradox. In the preface to his book he points out that the paradoxes of self-reference (which, it will be remem-bered, had to be declared illegitimate in the Theory of Types) "are no worse than similar self-referential paradoxes which are con-sidered quite acceptable in the ordinary theory of equations" [3, p. ix]. *Greatly—perhaps excessively—simplified, the reason is approximately the following.*

All numbers are either positive, negative, or zero. Conse-quently, any number that is neither positive nor zero is negative; and any number that is neither negative nor zero must be posi-

tive. Now what about the seemingly harmless equation $x^2 + 1 = 0$? *If we transpose the 1 to the other side of the equation, we obtain* $x^2 = -1$ *and, further, that* $x = \sqrt{-1}$. *But in a conceptual universe that is constructed such that any number can only be positive, negative, or zero, this result is unimaginable. For what number multiplied by itself (raised to its square) can possibly yield* -1? *The analogy of this impasse with the above-mentioned paradoxical dilemma arising in a world based on the concept of truth, falsehood, and the excluded middle is obvious. But, imaginable or unimaginable as the square root of* -1 *may be, mathematicians, physicists, and engineers have long since accepted it with equanimity, have assigned to it the symbol* i *(meaning imaginary), have included it in their computations just as the other three (imaginable) number categories (positive, negative, and zero), and have obtained practical, concrete, and perfectly imaginable results from it. But for our lay thinking, the imaginary number* i *remains of a fantastic irreality. The Austrian novelist Robert Musil expresses it in the words of one of his characters, young Törless. Finding himself for the first time confronted with the enigmatic properties of* i, *Törless says to a fellow student,*

> Look, think of it like this: in a calculation like that you begin with ordinary solid numbers, representing measures of length or weight or something else that's quite tangible—at any rate, they're real numbers. And at the end you have real numbers. But these two lots of real numbers are connected by something that simply doesn't exist. Isn't that like a bridge where the piles are there only at the beginning and at the end, with none in the middle, and yet one crosses it just as surely and safely as if the whole of it were there? That sort of operation makes me feel a bit giddy, as if it led part of the way God knows where. But what I really feel is so uncanny is the force that lies in a problem like that, which keeps such a firm hold on you that in the end you land safely on the other side [6].

But even for the mathematician it may be difficult to find the way out of the fly-bottle of a seemingly self-evident given and to unmask it as something whose "objective reality" is due only to the fact that it has never been questioned, indeed blindly accepted as true and evident. (*An obvious example, albeit from the field of astronomy, is the apparently simple and self-evident assumption of the simultaneous occurrence of two events in different parts of the universe. Only when the whole concept of time was questioned did the idea "at the same time" become untenable.*) In his contribution to the present chapter, the mathematician Gabriel Stolzenberg shows how such a process of entrapment, as he calls it, can take hold of the mathematician's mind; he also shows how one can find the way out of this trap. We mathematical laymen may find it surprising that even the Queen of Sciences tends to disallow and suppress some questions that, if admitted, might cause sedition in her realm. Thus even here, in the supposedly most impersonal and objective scientific context, we can see the mind-boggling structures of self-fulfilling, reality-creating premises. This point, namely, the contention that mathematical givens are not discovered but invented, is one of the most fascinating aspects of Stolzenberg's essay.

In the pursuit of his analysis, Stolzenberg, like Elster, arrives at a reexamination of the apparently self-evident concept of negation. To define it unequivocally, it is necessary to step outside the frame of the primitive yes–no thinking and to question the entire domain of classical mathematics. But from within this frame this procedure is wrong; seen from within, Stolzenberg's negation (being a passive negation in Elster's sense of the term), is "false."

Although Stolzenberg does not refer to Spencer Brown, the perspectives of the two authors are similar. Brown's is a logic based on the concepts of "inside" and "outside." Putting it in very dilettante terms, one might say that Brown shows how a reality construction may transcend its own limits, look at its totality from the vantage point of being outside the frame, and eventually "reenter" its limits with the information gained about itself. Stolzenberg shows that some apparently definitive, self-evident mathematical findings turn out to be traps as soon as the mathematician manages to step outside the frame of that particular orientation. From the outside, the frame then reveals itself as a trap, while within the limits of the frame, the system appears

*to be a consistent universe, free of contradictions. (That Stolzen-
berg calls some features of this universe "incorrect" should not
give the impression that what can be found outside the frame is,
at long last, eternal truth. "Incorrect," as I interpret this term, is
equivalent to "not fitting" in von Glasersfeld's sense.)*

*Even the layman can appreciate that all this goes well beyond
pure mathematics. What Stolzenberg tells us about the process of
entrapment is essentially what Rosenhan has shown to be the
case in the clinical realm. To become aware of this analogy one
can substitute the term* mathematical problems *for* human
problems, *and* mathematics *for* therapy *throughout Stolzenberg's paper. Though this may seem far-fetched, the semantic
substitution satisfies our intuition. For he who suffers from his
being in the world is caught in his own fly-bottle; the attempted
solution is his problem [11]; and only by stepping outside the
vicious circle of problem—"solution" and "solution"—caused problem can he discover that reality can be constructed differently
[12]. Of course, this other reality is again precisely this: a construction, but a construction that, if it fits better, will not only be
less painful to live in but will convey that undefinable feeling of
being "in tune" without which man cannot survive psychologically.*

*The properties of this construction, which is ultimately as uni-
maginable as the number i and yet—very much as i—leads to
concrete, practical results, are the subject of the last contribution.
In it the Chilean biologist Francisco Varela presents a concise
synthesis of virtually all the themes of this book, from cell repro-
duction to the paradoxes of logic (and therefore also of our thought
processes) to the self-referential mechanisms of our perception of
the world, until he eventually arrives at the central concept of
autonomy that stands beyond the true—false oscillation of paradox.*

REFERENCES

1. Bateson, Gregory, Jackson Don D., Haley, Jay, and Weakland, John H.
Toward a theory of schizophrenia. *Behavioral Science* 1, 1956, 251–264.

2. Berger, Milton M. (ed.). *Beyond the Double Bind*. Bruner/Mazel, New York, 1978.
3. Brown, George Spencer. *Laws of Form*. Bantam Books, New York, 1973.
4. Hofstadter, Douglas R. *Gödel, Escher, Bach: An Eternal Golden Braid*. Basic Books, New York, 1979, and Vintage Books, New York, 1980.
5. Hughes, Patrick, and Brecht, George. *Vicious Circles and Infinity*. Doubleday, Garden City, New York, 1975.
6. Musil, Robert. *Young Törless* (translated by Eithne Wilkins and Ernst Kaiser). Noonday Press, New York, 1958, pp. 106–107.
7. Russell, Bertrand. *The Autobiography of Bertrand Russell*, Vol. 1. Little, Brown, Boston, 1951, pp. 221–222.
8. Sluzki, Carlos E., and Ransom, Donald C. (eds.). *Double Bind*. Grune and Stratton, New York, 1976.
9. Smullyan, Raymond M. *What Is the Name of This Book?* Prentice-Hall, Englewood Cliffs, New Jersey, 1978.
10. Smullyan, Raymond M. *This Book Needs No Title*. Prentice-Hall, Englewood Cliffs, New Jersey, 1980.
11. Watzlawick, Paul, Weakland, John H., and Fisch, Richard. *Change*. W. W. Norton, New York, 1974, pp. 31–39.
12. Watzlawick, Paul. *The Language of Change*. Basic Books, New York, 1978.
13. Whitehead, Alfred N., and Russell, Bertrand. *Principia Mathematica*. Cambridge University Press, Cambridge, Massachusetts, 1910–1913.

GABRIEL STOLZENBERG

Can an Inquiry into the Foundations of Mathematics Tell Us Anything Interesting About Mind?*

For the moment I must ask you to disregard the title question of this chapter. At the end, I shall return to it and explain how the body of my remarks may be regarded as constituting an affirmative answer, albeit one of a nontraditional sort.

It is my view, a view that I share with the rest of the so-called "constructivist" mathematical community, that during the latter part of the nineteenth century, in the course of an attempt to rigorize itself and establish proper foundations, the science of pure mathematics fell into a certain intellectual trap; and that, since that time, mathematicians, with the help of logicians, have been going along digging themselves in deeper and deeper. I want to show what this trap is like: how it is built up out of certain structures of logic and language, why it is so easy to fall into it, and what happens when one does. As a mathematician, I also would like to do something to get my discipline out of this trap. But that is another matter. It should be understood that what I am calling "a trap" is seen by most other pure mathematicians, who look at it only from within, as more like an intellectual paradise; and, really, there is no contradiction. But so much already has been said elsewhere about mathematics as paradise; here I shall talk about traps. Why? In part, simply because I find the sub-

---

*This contribution is excerpted from a longer article by the same author.

ject intellectually fascinating. But also because I believe that there is a significant piece of practical knowledge to be gained by other scientists who familiarize themselves with the case of contemporary pure mathematics. At issue here are certain fundamental questions about the proper form of sciencitic inquiry. And an understanding of what went wrong in the case of pure mathematics may help other scientists to avoid the same kind of mistakes elsewhere.

What did go wrong in the case of pure mathematics? What is the trap into which it has fallen?

In order to answer these questions I should first explain, in reasonably general terms, what I mean by "a trap" or by "being trapped." In addition, I must specify those particular institutionalized attitudes, beliefs, and habits of thought of contemporary pure mathematics that I claim constitute such a trap. Finally, I must give my reasons for making this claim. In my view, the case that can be made on the basis of a careful examination of existing mathematical theory and practice is far stronger than it is possible to indicate here. But I believe that even in this nontechnical discussion I can make out a prima facie case that is strong enough to leave a substantial burden of explanation on those who may wish to dispute it.

Use of the Term *Trap;* Considerations of Standpoint

The conditions I impose upon the use of the term *trap* are very stringent: in order to justify its use in the case at hand one must show, for the institutionalized attitudes, beliefs, and habits of thought referred to above, not merely that they constitute a closed system but also, and more significantly, that certain of these beliefs are demonstrably incorrect; and (2) that certain of the fixed attitudes and habits of thought prevent this from being recognized. And in order to carry out such a demonstration, or merely to recognize one when it is presented, one first must establish a standpoint from which those givens of contemporary mathematics that are to be called into question are no longer givens but merely hypotheses or proposals which, as it stands, are neither accepted nor rejected.

This raises the crucial question of how such a standpoint may be established. Any adequate answer must take into account the particular position from which one begins; and that may vary significantly from person to person. Also, if one's starting point is inside the system, then what is required is a procedure for getting out; and that will entail the "undoing" of certain seemingly fundamental beliefs and habits of thought.[1] While such procedures are available, it takes considerable discipline to follow them correctly.

Having said this much, and having already observed that what I am calling here "a trap" is seen from within as something completely different, it should not be too surprising that I say also that the basic methodological errors that landed pure mathematics into this trap and that, even now, contribute to keeping it there, consist chiefly in ignoring basic considerations of standpoint. What we have, in case after case, is a failure to take into account how certain of the givens of one's particular standpoint may be contributing both to the way in which a question is construed (e.g., by construing it as being equivalent to some other question) and, also, to the way in which certain answers to it are judged. In some cases, the relevant givens are beliefs or hidden assumptions, including "nonfactual" assumptions about the meaningfulness of certain modes of discourse; but they may also be attitudes, habits of thought, as well as other social and psychological phenomena.[2]

---

[1]In particular, the belief that one possesses a concept of "truth independent of knowledge" of the sort that is needed to support the practice of "excluded middle" type reasoning.

[2]For example, in certain cases, a relevant given is that one simply is unable to take seriously a particular answer to some question, even though it may be seen "from without" that, in fact, the answer is correct. There is an amusing instance of this in Imre Lakatos' *Proofs and Refutations* [4]. One of the characters in this play about pure mathematicians at "work" has what in fact is a perfectly good counterexample to the conjectures that the others are continually putting forward. However, even though there are many other counterexamples that they do take seriously, to this one they invariably respond, "Quit kidding around!"

I hope it is quite clear that, when I stress the importance of taking into account considerations of standpoint, I am not preaching any brand of relativism. I do not say that there is your truth and my truth and never the twain shall meet. On the contrary, in order to be truly objective—in order to give one's answer to some question an objective basis—it often is necessary to pay attention to how the givens of one's particular standpoint may be influencing the way in which the question is being answered. And, sometimes, the result of paying such attention will be to recognize the need, for the sake of really answering the question adequately, to give up one's own standpoint temporarily and adopt a completely different one. However, when psychological factors are involved (and they very often are), when some of the givens that have to be relinquished, at least for a while, are beliefs and habits of thought, then carrying this through in practice may be extremely difficult. On the other hand, nobody ever promised us that doing science would be easy.

The Process of Entrapment: A Brief Description in General Terms

Thus far, I have characterized a trap as a closed system of attitudes, beliefs, and habits of thought for which one can give an objective demonstration that certain of the beliefs are incorrect and that certain of the attitudes and habits of thought prevent this from being recognized. In this formulation, the "methodological errors" are those failures to take into account considerations of standpoint that have the effect of *maintaining* the system. But nothing is said of its *origin;* of how such a trap may be formed. So I now would like to give a very brief description of what might be termed "the process of entrapment," still in very general terms but mindful of some of the distinctive features of the case of pure mathematics.

The *process of entrapment* consists, first, *in being taken in* (1) by certain uses of language that have the appearance, but only that, of being meaningful; and (2) by certain modes of reasoning that have the appearance, but only that, of being self-evidently correct; second, *in being locked in* as a result of the psychological act, or process, of accepting these appearances as being "really so." Somehow, by a process that may be quite complex, they become so thoroughly woven into the very fabric of what we take to be our web of reality that it no longer seems possible to adopt a standpoint from which the question of their correctness may be entertained seriously as a "mere" hypothesis. What were, originally, assumptions have now become givens and the idea of calling them into question is no longer intelligible.

Notes

i. For the case of contemporary pure mathematics, when I speak about being taken in by certain uses of language and modes of reasoning, I have in mind specifically (1) the use of a "present tense" language "of objects and their properties" in a manner that presupposes a literal interpretation of it; and (2) the practice of reasoning according to the so-called "law of excluded middle."

ii. The term *process of entrapment*, as I am using it here, may be taken to refer either to something that the entire discipline of pure mathematics went through from about 1870 to 1930 in the course of an attempt to "do itself over right" after producing a literal confusion of riches over the preceding 200 years or, with equal validity, to a process that each new student of pure mathematics goes through, even today, in the course of what nowadays is called "learning to think like a pure mathematician."

The Concept of an Act of Acceptance as Such

Falling into a trap is something that can happen in the course of scientific activity. But, *in* science, what sort of things *happen?* What acts are performed in the activity of science? Certainly, a part of the answer is that questions are raised and investigations are carried out. But there also are those acts by means of which, intentionally or not, there is "built up" the "structure" of the very system (of beliefs, practices, habits of thought, attitudes, language use, etc.) within which the activity of a science is carried out (including the activity of building up the structure of the system within which the activity is carried out). And these are not merely acts "of construction" but, also, "of acceptance." Or, rather, I should say, "of acceptance as such." Let me elaborate on this very important point.

In general, to "accept" something—an experience or an object—"as such" consists in taking it for what it appears, or is purported, to be, *and proceeding on that basis*. Despite a certain superficial similarity, there is all the difference in the world between (1) *accepting* something as being what it appears to be and proceeding (in life, as an experiencing being) on that basis; and (2) merely exploring the consequences of *the assumption* that some thing is what it appears to be. When I wake up in the morning and "find" that the sun is shining, it is not that I have a certain sensory experience and, on the basis of it, make the assumption that "the sun is shining." Of course, there *are* mornings when I do that; but I am talking about ones for which, when I wake up, I simply see that the sun is shining. I do so because that is how my experience is constituted for me. Now, my waking up in the morning and finding that the sun is shining is a typical instance of what I am calling here "an act of acceptance as such." Notice: It is not deliberate and, in fact, from the standpoint of the "performer," there is no such act. On the contrary, it is only if I had chosen to question the authenticity of my "seeing that the sun is shining" that there would be, from my standpoint, any recognizable act. Nevertheless, with hindsight or from the standpoint of an outsider observer, it does make sense to say that an act of acceptance as such has been, or is being, performed. This may be seen in various ways. For example, the observer may have conned me by setting up some artificial source of light that makes it appear, from my standpoint, that the sun is shining. Then, from this observer's standpoint, what I experience as "seeing that the sun is shining" consists in my *accepting* what appears to be "seeing that the sun is shining" *as such*. From that standpoint, but not my own, I am being taken in by certain appearances. Falling into a trap is something that can happen in the course of a scientific activity as a result of being taken in by appearances; in other words, it is something that can happen as the result of certain acts of acceptance as such.

Therefore, let me now demonstrate the ubiquity of such acts of acceptance as such in the activity of building up the structure of the system in which the activity of a science is carried out. I think the following example should suffice. The structure of the system in which pure mathematicians operate is, in part, built up by acts which are accepted as establishing a new theorem or introducing a new concept; and the qualification "which are accepted as" is an essential part of the account. For, how is a new theorem established? From within the system, the answer is simply: by constructing a proof. But, from the standpoint of an outside observer, any such act "of constructing a proof" may be recognized as that of constructing what appears to be a proof—that is, what, so far as one sees, is a proof—and accepting it as such. Let us examine the matter a little more closely. The experience of constructing a proof is basically this: A mathematical argument is made which is then checked out step by step and found to be correct. However, the experience of checking out a mathematical argument and "finding it to be correct" is not different in kind from the experience of waking up in the morning and "finding that the sun is shining." In each case, there is an implicit act of acceptance as such that may be recognized only with hindsight or from the standpoint of an outsider observer. In the case of checking out a mathematical argument, this may be shown by the following.

Suppose that a "great authority" announces that there is something wrong with the argument. In that case, my experience upon checking over the argument may be quite different from what it was before this announcement was made. Instead of having the experience of "seeing that the argument is correct, that it checks out," my experience may now be that of "finding that I cannot see what, if anything, is wrong with it." (And, if I truly accept the "authority's" authority, we may also delete the "if anything.") Just as before, I find that the argument *appears* to be correct; only this time I do not accept it *as being* correct. And there we have the difference between the two situations; in the first, there is an act of acceptance as such while, in the second, there is instead an act of questioning something that appears to be correct. If I do find the argument to be correct, then the theorem is established and may then be used to do other things, for example, to establish other theorems or to disprove certain conjectures. But, so long as I am trying to see what is wrong with the argument, my energies are engaged otherwise. I may recheck the argument again and again, looking for an error or a gap. Am I overlooking something? Or, am I, perhaps, reading into the argument something that is not there? It may happen that the "great authority" publishes an explanation of what is wrong with the argument. That ought to help; however, I may find that, as it stands, I am unable to follow this explanation. [To pursue this fantasy just a little bit further, here are three possible "outcomes": (1) I finally manage to grasp the "great authority's" explanation and can see what is wrong with the argument. (2) The situation remains unresolved. (3) I decide that the "great authority" is not such a great authority after all and that, in fact, the argument is "obviously" correct.]

I believe that this single example makes it abundantly clear how, in general, acts of acceptance as such enter into each and every step of the building up of the structure of the system in which the activity of any science is carried out. I remarked earlier that the presence of such acts may be recognized by an outside observer or sometimes, with hindsight, by the performer himself. And, indeed, for the case of acts "of mathematical proof," mathematicians themselves often discover with hindsight that some act of acceptance as such has been made. And, within the limitations imposed by their unquestioning acceptance of what they take to count as a proof, they are open both in principle and in practice to doing whatever may be required in order to attempt to eliminate any errors which may have resulted from such acts. By contrast, for those more fundamental acts of acceptance as such of the kind that landed mathematics into its trap, there is no such tradition of critical reexamination; nor is there any provision for introducing one. On the contrary, the accepted attitude is that *these* issues need not be reconsidered and that, although a mathematician is free to carry out his own private investigation into such matters, any substantive claims he puts forward can simply be ignored. I shall return to this subject later on when I get into the specifics of the case of contemporary pure mathematics.

For us, the three most important facts about acts of acceptance as such are

1. From the standpoint of the "performer," there is no recognizable act at all, only an absence of questioning.
2. Such acts are potential sources of error; that such an error is being made may sometimes be seen from the standpoint of an outside observer.
3. The significance of accepting something as such is that one then treats it, and everything else, accordingly.

Thus, in any given case, accepting and not accepting may lead one down very different roads. By accepting something as such and integrating this belief into how one then sees the world, one may, in some cases, effectively lose the capacity for going back and calling it into question. And, by not accepting it as such but instead choosing to question it, one may be led eventually to the recognition that it, as well as certain of its consequences, is in fact incorrect.

Acts of Acceptance as Such in the Domain of Language Use

Acts of acceptance as such are ubiquitous; unavoidable. That simply is how things are.[3] Therefore the proper question to be considered is not how such acts may be avoided but, rather, how the knowledge that they can and do occur needs to be taken into account in the conduct of science. My own answer to this question is that we need to adopt an activist policy concerning the invention and following of procedures that entail the undoing of accepted beliefs and habits of thought; and we ought to regard the invention of

---

[3]Indeed, even the recognition that some thing is "in fact incorrect" quite obviously entails its own act of acceptance as such; and so it too might be "found to be incorrect."

such procedures as one of the fundamental means by which scientific knowledge may be increased.

I say this for two reasons; first, because, as scientists, our interests is in the world, not merely in the world as seen from within one particular system of beliefs; and second, because, for any of the particular beliefs or habits of thought that we ourselves now possess, we have to allow for the possibility that it is held by us not for the reasons we suppose but, rather, on account of our having performed, unwittingly, certain seemingly innocuous acts of acceptance as such in a domain that, conceptually, is far removed from that of the belief or habit of thought.[4] I have in mind, particularly, acts of acceptance as such that take place strictly in the domain of language use and yet produce beliefs about matters "of fact." Indeed, I believe it is a matter of common experience that people sometimes come to "see" certain things, for example, some "fundamental truth about the nature of reality," solely as a result of having been taken in by some use of language that has the appearance, but only that, of making sense. Moreover, it seems clear that the main reason such things can and do occur is that we all are taught, when we learn to use language, to attribute both to ourselves and others much more of a command of language use than actually has been established. In ordinary language use we almost never look for more than an appearance of sense.

To make these ideas more concrete let us consider for a moment one particular belief about a matter "of fact" that is produced by an act of acceptance as such, performed unwittingly in the domain of language use.

Story of a Definition That Was Too Good To Be True

Some people "learn" in high school that "π is, by definition, the ratio of the circumference of a circle to its diameter." I have found that if you ask such a person how one

---

[4] I claim that we have no difficulty in observing this to be the case for beliefs that *other* people hold; it remains only to learn how to apply the lesson of these observations to ourselves.

might prove that, for any two circles, the ratios of circumference to diameter are equal, you are likely to be told that "of course they are equal; they are both equal to π." Many years ago, I had the interesting experience of attempting, without success, to convince a group of such people that it simply is not obvious that if you take a big circle, measure its circumference and diameter, form the ratio, and then do the same for a small circle, that (to within the accuracy of the measurements) the results will be equal. To them, it *was* obvious because what they "saw" is that "both are measurements of π." I tried to instill some doubt in them by pointing out that what they were telling me was really remarkable: that through a mere act "of learning a definition," an act that takes place strictly in the domain of language use, they had come into possession of a nontrivial piece of "factual" knowledge. And they agreed that it *was* rather remarkable; but, instead of this arousing their suspicions, it merely confirmed their opinion of what a "good" definition it was.

My own position was that they did not know what they were talking about and, more specifically, that what they mistakenly took to be "a definition of π" depended for its validity upon it first being established that, in fact, the ratio of the circumference to the diameter *is* the same for all circles. To me, it was obvious that such a proof had to precede the definition (and I was prepared to show them the beautiful demonstration based on inscribed polygons and the proportionality theorem for similar triangles). But, to them, their "definition" was obvious. As they saw it, they knew "what definitions are" and could recognize one when they saw one.[5] I questioned this. They saw no need to do so. And we left it at that.

In this particular case, what would it have taken to arrive at a mutual understanding? Certainly, if we had been operating in a system with accepted canons of definition, we could have settled the matter simply by checking whether their

---

[5]Very likely, this belief was reinforced throughout their mathematical education. At a more advanced level, the pseudo-definition for π does get corrected; but much worse ones, such as those given for "the square root of 2" and "real number," do not.

purported definition was, in fact, correct. But obviously we were not operating in such a system; they had their canons and I had mine. We might have settled the matter anyway if I had managed, somehow, to show them on their own terms that their ideas about "definition" were, in fact, defective; and with hindsight I see how this might have been accomplished. But, in the absence of these alternatives, it seems to me that mutual understanding could have been achieved only if those within the group had been willing to do something that they otherwise saw no need to do: namely, to refrain, at least temporarily, from taking their purported "knowledge of definitions" as a given.

In this example, we have a very transparent case of standpoint-dependent reasoning that is seen as being "objective." Without its being realized, the conclusion is, in effect, built in to the standpoint from which the question is being considered. But notice how it is built in. It is *not* that the people in the group were *assuming* the conclusion to be true. That might have been the case if what they had been told in high school was that mathematicians had proven that, for any two circles, the ratios of circumference to diameter are equal; and the definition of π had been presented on that basis. However, in that case they would have understood that the conclusion is not obvious; that it requires proof. And this is precisely what they could not see. The problem was not that certain assumptions had been made but, rather, that certain acts of acceptance as such had been performed.

The situation just described exhibits some, but not all, of the features of a trap. The two main reasons it would not be correct to call it a *trap* are, first, that it was an isolated encounter; so, despite the students' unwillingness at that time to reconsider their apparent grasp of "what definitions are," there is no reason to suppose that they really were wedded to this position. Second, even though they did believe their position to be secure and were not threatened by what I said (they took me to be a crank), in fact, their position was not secure. For example, by using their own "acceptance criterion" for definitions, I could have introduced a new "number," Π, as "the ratio of the area of a circle to its diameter" and, on the basis of what else they knew, they would have been forced to the conclusion "that Π is not constant." But then they would have been open to the question, "How do you know that π is constant?"

Belief Systems; Attitudes about Undoing Accepted Beliefs

It should now be quite clear that the question of whether one might *ever* fall into a trap depends fundamentally on what attitude one adopts toward the idea of undoing accepted beliefs and habits of thought. Thus, once again, we find ourselves having to confront this basic issue. It is true that acts of acceptance as such are unavoidable; and there also is no avoiding the possibility that as a result of such acts we may come to hold certain beliefs that someone else is in a position to see are incorrect. However, what can be avoided and what, on strictly scientific grounds, should be avoided is the adoption of a methodology that effectively prevents one from coming to share in this knowledge. From one standpoint, it is obvious that no scientist would knowingly adopt such a methodology; the idea of being locked into a belief that someone else is in a position to see is incorrect is, for the scientist, intolerable. Nevertheless, such methodologies *are* adopted and sometimes the resulting system does become a trap.

The underlying attitude that gives rise to such a methodology is the desire for a system, a world-view, that can be maintained and that one will want to maintain. This is what Maturana likes to call "the sin of certainty." Any system that is informed by such an attitude will be called here a "belief system." And any belief system that, in fact, can be maintained will be called a "self-justifying," or "irrefutable," belief system.

A belief system may be like a genuinely scientific system in every other respect, but it has this one distinguishing feature: All acts of observation, judgment, etc., are performed solely from the particular standpoint of the system itself. Therefore, once any belief or operating principle has been accepted, that is, is seen as "being so," any argument for not accepting it will be rejected unless it can be shown that there is something "wrong" with it from the standpoint of the system itself.[6] Thus, it may be the case that, from the standpoint of not having accepted a certain principle, say the law of excluded middle, a very good reason for not accepting it is simply that one sees no reason *to* accept it; whereas, if this is an accepted principle within a belief system, such a consideration will have no force at all.

This way of operating does not, by itself, provide a system with any principles or procedures governing the acceptance of beliefs; that is, with procedures for coming to see that something "is so"; that is, with canons of "proof." However, it does suggest accepting, as a fundamental methodological principal, that the "acceptance criterion" for any other belief or methodological principle is that it can be shown that once it is accepted and incorporated into the system it cannot be shown to be incorrect in the terms of the system itself. This is essentially the approach that the pure mathematicians took in establishing the canons of "proof" for the belief system in which contemporary pure mathematics is practiced; and it is what they are referring to in their well-known slogan that "in pure mathematics, the only criterion for correctness is consistency—the consistency of the system itself."

Descriptive Fallacies Produced by a Failure to Respect Considerations of Standpoint

It is important to bear in mind that being inside a belief system means seeing things a certain way, for example, that "the sun is shining," or that "π is, by definition, the ratio of the circumference of a circle to its diameter," or that "every mathematical statement is either true or false," but without

---

[6] In particular, the only way that one could show that there is something wrong with the accepted methodology of the system would be by using that very same methodology. And any such demonstration would collapse as soon as it had been given because its force would depend upon the correctness of the very methodology that had just been found to be incorrect. Of course, the entire system would also collapse.

any awareness of how this way of seeing things is standpoint dependent. One simply takes for granted that everyone else sees things this way too; and, because of this, one is almost guaranteed to get a seriously mistaken understanding of the beliefs and experiences of others who, in fact, do not see things that way.

For example, the chapter entitled "Deviant logics" in W. V. Quine's *Philosophy of Logic* [6] is marred by errors of this kind, and they result in factually incorrect conclusions about matters to which the author attaches considerable significance. Quine's position is interesting in that, at least in one respect, he would appear to be a counterexample to a claim I made above; for, even though he operates only from within a particular belief system (classical logic and the world-view it produces), he does not regard it as being "God given." In fact, he agrees that it is something that is acquired as a result of (or, along with) acquiring what we take to be "a mastery" of language use. Furthermore, Quine emphasizes that the test of a good system is in how it functions as a way of "seeing the world" and, most importantly, as a way for scientists to "see the world." He lists convenience, simplicity, and also beauty among the criteria that are to be used in comparing competing systems. On the basis of this account it seems quite clear what needs to be done in order to carry out such a comparison in any particular case: namely, each of the competing systems must be tried out in order to see how well it works. However, this is not what Quine does. Instead, he remains squarely inside his own system as he attempts to see what it is like to operate within a different one. It is no wonder that he finds it confusing to try to do this. Moreover, he treats this experience as if it shows, somehow, that actually operating in the other system is confusing, even though, of course, it shows nothing of the sort. Nevertheless, on the basis of such "evidence," Quine draws the significant conclusions that what he calls "our logic" is simpler, more convenient, and even more beautiful; none of which is correct. Note that my objection is not that these are value judgments and, therefore, are subjective. My point is that Quine himself cannot know which "logic" he would find to be simpler, more convenient, or more beautiful because he has failed to do what is necessary to really find out.

The basic error in Quine's methodology is revealed most clearly by his talk about the price of having to think in what he calls "a deviant logic." One might as well talk about the price that a Chinese has to pay for using a "foreign" language. Throughout Quine's entire discussion, there is no sign of awareness that, for "the deviant," the "deviant" logic is not deviant.

To sum up, a belief is a system in which all acts of observation and judgment are made solely from within and in which all other considerations are subordinated to the maintenance of the system itself. When an outside observer is in a position to see that such a system contains an incorrect belief and also that no proof of its incorrectness can be given in the terms of the system itself, then he is in a position to say that this system has become a trap. In such a situation, the outside observer will see those within as being dogmatic while those on the inside will see the observer as someone who refuses to accept what is "obviously so." And, in fact, both will be right.

The Case of Pure Mathematics:
The Contemporary Mathematician's Attachment to His Beliefs

One point not in dispute is that the system in which the contemporary mathematician operates is, indeed, a belief system. We know that the contemporary mathematician does have a fixed way of "seeing" mathematics; for example, he sees that, given any "set" and any "mathematical object," that object either does or does not "belong to" that set (and he sees also that whichever of these is the case will remain so). Moreover, we know from the mathematician's own account that he is deeply attached to this particular way of seeing mathematics, that he has no experience of seeing it any other way, and that he belongs to a community of fellow practitioners who participate with him in the experience of seeing it this way. And, finally, we know how the contemporary mathematician responds to the idea of being, perhaps only temporarily, in a state of not seeing mathematics in this way—of undoing the basic givens of his particular mathematical world-view. He finds it disturbing—in fact, disruptive—and the occasional suggestions that, for strictly scientific reasons, one ought to do so anyway have been responded to with such epithets as "utterly destructive" and "the Bolshevist menace."

The contemporary mathematician is very impressed by the "reality" of his mathematical experience; and the fact that it is a shared experience—shared by a worldwide community of mathematicians—greatly reinforces his belief in its "objectivity." But in what does this objectivity really consist? First, in the use of an objective mode of discourse and, second, in there being a well-known and widely employed "learning process" by means of which apparently anyone can come to "see" mathematics in this particular way. The latter fact is not without interest. However, because the contemporary mathematician has no experience, not even in the imagination, of standing outside the system and looking in, he attributes far more significance to what is "seen" from inside than what actually is warranted on the basis of more objective considerations. This is true both with respect to the *mathematical* significance he attaches to certain of his "findings," for example, that some mathematical structure is what he calls "finite dimensional" or that some equation has the property that he calls "having a solution," and also with respect to what is perceived to be the significant *methodological* advantages of doing things this way, for example, that it is "simpler" and that "you can do more." There is absolutely no awareness of the extent to which these perceptions and value judgments are merely by-products of the same acts of acceptance as such (in the domain of language use) out of which the system itself is created.

In particular, there has been no end to the talk about how much more "complicated" mathematical reasoning becomes when one does not accept the law of excluded middle as a given. It also is said that when one refrains from accepting this "law" one limits what can be accomplished. David Hilbert merely was expressing the general sentiment when he said that it would be like denying the astronomer his telescope or the boxer the use of his fists. It is remarkable how obvious this appears to be when one is standing inside the contemporary mathematician's belief system and yet how utterly naive and wrongheaded it is seen to be when one steps outside and checks.

From within the system, there is no recognition of *how* the acceptance of the law of excluded middle as a given contributes to the construction of that very same "mathematical reality" about which one then "discovers truths" by using, among other things, the law of excluded middle. Instead, the contemporary mathematician imagines his task of proving theorems to be rather like that of a lawyer whose job is to attempt to establish things in court. On this view of the matter, by "disallowing" appeals to the law of excluded middle one is, in effect, restricting the "legal" means by which a case can be made; that is, the means by which a mathematical theorem can be proved. Hence, one expects that, in general, there will be fewer successes and that what ones there are will be always no easier and in some cases much harder to achieve. But this is an incredibly naive conception of mathematics; it simply takes for granted that, when one undoes one's acceptance of excluded middle reasoning for mathematics, the "reality" of mathematics remains the same while the "allowable" methods of proof are reduced in number. In fact, nothing could be farther from the truth.[7]

A View from the Edge of the System: The Tug of Language That Pulls One Inside

Let me now present some of the defining characteristics of the belief system in which the contemporary mathematician

---

[7]On the contrary, when one views mathematics from a standpoint that does not have excluded middle reasoning "built in," one finds that the effect of introducing it is to make it impossible to maintain certain important discriminations. As a result, the structure of mathematics is "flattened" and much of its pattern and internal organization is rendered opaque.

operates. To this end, instead of starting off either with a picture of mathematics as seen from *inside* the system, or with a view of the system itself as seen from the *outside* looking in, I shall take the unorthodox approach of heading directly for what might be regarded as "the edge." This strikes me as being as good a way as any of gaining an understanding of the system's "defining" features. Furthermore, from such a position, it will be relatively easy for us to shift a little bit in either direction and thus acquire some firsthand experience at doing and undoing the basic acts of acceptance as such by means of which the "reality" of the contemporary pure mathematician's system is actually constructed.

To get to the edge of the system, we can follow a route that Michael Dummett took several years ago and which he reported upon in a brilliant essay entitled "The philosophical basis of intuitionistic logic" [1]. The discussion that follows is based upon the latter part of that work. Dummett was investigating the force of various arguments that someone in my position might offer to a mathematician inside the system to get him to see that certain of his accepted beliefs about mathematics are, in fact, incorrect. And, while developing a complex line of reasoning designed to show why a certain approach would not necessarily succeed, Dummett was led to focus his attention upon the following question.

Suppose that we have two mathematical assertions, S and T, and also a computational procedure, P, which has the property that by carrying it out either S or T (and possibly both) is established. (Example: S is the assertion that more than a million terms of the sequence $s(n) \equiv$ the fractional part of $(\frac{2}{3})^n$ lie in the interval from 0 to $\frac{1}{2}$; T is the corresponding assertion for the interval from $\frac{1}{2}$ to 1; and P is the procedure of computing two million and one terms of the sequence, keeping count of how many fall into each of the two intervals.) Suppose also that the procedure has not been carried out. Question: In such a case, is it correct to say that what we possess is either a procedure for establishing S or a procedure for establishing T (and possibly both)? When T is the negation of S, the question being asked is whether, without having carried out the procedure, we are nevertheless in a position to say that we now possess either a way of proving

S or a way of disproving S, although we are not in a position to say which.

Now, one reaction to such a question might be that it has only to do with terminology; that all the facts were laid out before the question was posed and that we can "say" whatever we like so long as it is understood that by so doing we are merely introducing a paraphrase of what we said in the beginning. If that is your reaction then you are standing outside the system at this point. However, at the time he wrote that essay, Dummett was clearly standing a bit inside the system; and, as a result, for him the matter was not nearly so simple as I have just made it out to be. Indeed, the position I have just stated is one that he continually refers to as "hardheaded"; and he suggests that it takes a significant act of will to be so hard-headed. (In fact, as he told me later, at the time he wrote the essay he did not believe that anyone was actually capable of holding such a position.) Why? Because, so we are told, "It is very difficult for us to resist the temptation to suppose that there is already, unknown to us, a determinate answer to the question of which of the two disjuncts we should obtain a proof of, were we to apply the decision procedure" [p. 36]. Thus, from where Dummett stood at the time he wrote these lines, there is a certain temptation that is difficult to resist. This temptation is part of the "reality" of that standpoint; let us now attempt to find out where it comes from.

Note

In the discussion that follows, it is important to try to keep in mind what one's own position is at any given point. My aim is to shift back and forth so as to give one the experience of what it is that creates the "reality" of the contemporary mathematician's system along this particular part of its "edge." This means, on the one hand, being completely on the "outside" so as to feel no temptations of the sort to which Dummett refers and, on the other hand, also allowing ourselves to experience the tug that pulls one "inside." In addition, we shall have to attempt to act as observers of ourselves in the course of having these experiences.

Anyone who experiences the temptation to which Dummett refers must, first of all, attribute to himself an understanding of the expression "there is already, unknown to us, a determinate answer" to a certain question. In other words, such a person must suppose of himself, correctly or not, that he has participated in an establishment of language use that specifies, at least implicitly, what is entailed in "supposing that there is already, unknown to us, a determinate answer" to a certain question. I contend that this is the fundamental act "of acceptance as such"—one taking place strictly in the domain of language use—that creates the conditions that produce the temptation. Let me now attempt to support this contention as best I can.

Consider first my own position. When I take Dummett's statement in the straightforward way that it is presented in his essay, my response to it is this: Let him first explain to me what he means by it and then I might have something more to say. No matter that the expression "there is already, unknown to us, a determinate answer" is suggestive; that I have a number of associations to it; and that I find myself thinking that I understand what sort of things prompt Dummett to say what he does. All of this is relevant. But let us recall the context in which we are operating; it is a scientific context, the science being pure mathematics. And we have focused our attention upon a class of cases whose description has been given with admirable clarity: Two mathematical statements and a procedure by means of which at least one and possibly both can be established. Therefore, however suggestive one may find the language use, "there is already, unknown to us, a determinate answer to the question of which of the two statements we should obtain a proof of, were we to carry the procedure out," unless we have provided a clear account of what we mean by "supposing" that "this is so," we would simply be mucking up our scientific discourse and also our conceptual framework to "accept" such a "supposition" without any further ado. As I see it, on this ground alone, the temptation is highly resistable.[8]

---

[8]However, it would be quite proper for anyone who feels so inclined to attempt to produce an account of the required sort. Should one be produced, it might then be possible to discuss these matters in a very different way. Also, by attempting to provide such an account and not succeeding one might be led to reconsider one's position.

Let us take this as a sign that one who finds the temptation
difficult to resist feels that the meaning of the expression *is*
quite clear; and let us attempt to figure out in what this
meaning might consist. We could of course take the meaning
of "there is already, unknown to us, a determinate answer"
to be "there is already, known to us, a determinate procedure for getting the answer but the procedure has not been
carried out." In fact, this is the meaning I myself assign it,
and I believe that many other people do too. But if one takes
this approach, then there is no temptation, no resistance;
there is merely a paraphrase of what has already been said.
Therefore, someone who feels such a temptation must mean,
or believe that he means, something more than this. What
could that possibly be? Perhaps what is meant is that,
although the answer is unknown to us, it is known to someone else. This way of attaching a meaning to the expression
does go beyond the data; however, it clearly is not what is
intended in the case at hand. When Dummett says "unknown
to us," he means to all of us. Of course, someone else *might
have* carried out the procedure and determined the answer;
it is just that in most cases there is no particular temptation
to suppose that this is the case.

By the way, it also is clear that, whatever the expression
"there is already, unknown to us, a determinate answer" is
supposed to mean, it is not going to be something that we
are capable of knowing, only of supposing. (This is true even
in the case where what we mean is that somebody else has
determined the answer.) Therefore, what we need an account
of is not what is required in order to know such a thing but
rather of what is entailed in supposing it; that is, in accepting it "as so."

Dummett's own discussion of this matter is based on a
consideration of the adjective "determinate." He asks: Is this
a case in which it is correct to say that there is a "determinate" answer? And he argues, quite successfully in my opinion, that it is. As he sees it, the situation we are considering
is of the following sort: we know that if an act of type A is
performed, then the outcome will be either of type B or type
C. But, in many such cases, the answer to the question of

which of the two outcomes we would get, were the act to be performed, is "indeterminate" in the sense that it may depend upon other factors. For example, we know that if the Red Sox and the Yankees play a complete game, then either the Red Sox or the Yankees will win; but on different occasions it may be one team or the other. However, the mathematical case is definitely not of this kind; the answer to the question of which of the two statements would be established if the procedure were to be carried out cannot vary from one act of carrying it out to another.[9] In this sense, it is not "indeterminate." As Dummett says, "since at each step the outcome of the procedure is determined, how can we deny that the overall outcome is determinate also?"

Dummett's point is well taken. And yet, notice that if we accept it, it still does not take us beyond the level of a mere paraphrase of "we have a determinate procedure that has not been carried out." So there is no temptation and no resistance. Therefore, we still have to look elsewhere.

I believe that I know where to look. "There is already . . . an answer." Certainly, if we were to carry the procedure out, we would come to know the answer and we would be able to say either "The answer is S" or "The answer is T." Also, even before the procedure has been carried out, we may wonder: Is the answer S? Is it T? Or both? Hence, it may appear that what we are talking about is a certain "thing," the answer; that is, that "there is," at least in the realm of potentiality, this "thing," the answer, about which we would acquire a certain piece of information were we to carry out the procedure. Similarly, when we discuss the case that T is the negation of S and remark that by carrying out the procedure we would establish either that S is true or that it is false, it again may appear that we are talking about a certain "thing," the statement S. In this case, what is at issue is whether this "thing," the statement S, "already" possesses a certain property. What property? Answer: That one of the

---

[9]Why? Answer: because we do not allow it. Thus, were we to perform two acts, each of which we accept as an instance of "carrying out the procedure," and find afterward that they yield two different answers, we would say "An error must have been made."

two properties, "being true" and "being false," that we would discover it to possess, were we to carry out the procedure.

As soon as we allow ourselves to accept that talk "about answers" and "about statements" is, in some literal sense, about "things" that stand in some relationship to us—more specifically, to accept that, in the cases under consideration, being in a state of "knowing the answer" (as a result of having carried out the procedure) constitutes a recognition of "its" existence—it also appears to make sense to ask whether "knowledge of the answer" is a *necessary* condition for "the existence of the answer." And it is precisely here that we may feel an irresistible temptation to say "No, it is not." By accepting that at least *after* we have carried out the procedure there is a "thing," the answer, that we then confront, we find ourselves faced with the question of whether the act of carrying out the procedure is one of "creation" or "discovery." By carrying out the procedure, do we actually "make" either S or T (or both) "be" the answer or do we merely "find out" which of them "is" the answer? Is there already, unknown to us, a determinate answer or does it only come into being by the act of carrying out the procedure? In a case that T is the negation of S, by carrying out the procedure do we actually "make" S have the property of "being true" or of "being false," or do we rather "find out" either that S "is" true or "is" false?

Once we have, unwittingly, committed those acts "of acceptance as such" concerning language use that make these pseudoquestions appear to be genuine ones, it does indeed seem to be hard-headed, and perhaps even solipsistic, to refuse to accept that the act of carrying out the procedure is one of discovery and not of creation. Why? One reason is that, whereas the act of carrying out the procedure is obviously repeatable, that "thing" we call "the answer" is unique. If the act of carrying out the procedure literally produced the answer, then by carrying it out twice we would get two answers; and we see this as being plainly counterfactual. By contrast, the explanation that we "find" the answer seems to fit the situation very well because an act of finding some thing is one that can be repeated again and again, and by different people.

Also, to someone who has already accepted this much, the thought of somebody maintaining that the act of carrying out the procedure is what "makes" there be an answer is likely to conjure up other images of an apparently similar sort; for example, that of someone insisting that his act of finding an old pair of shoes in the closet is what "made" those shoes "be" in the closet. We are conditioned to find this position repugnant.[10] We can see that it is incorrect but it also seems to be irrefutable. Why is it incorrect? We might say that it is because the shoes were already in the closet before we found them there; however, that would not be right because, for all we know, the shoes were *not* in the closet before we found them there. It is rather that, however and whenever the shoes did get into the closet, it was not by an act of perception. In case you are playing the devil's advocate here and asking "But how do you know that?" let me take the trouble to put this in the proper way. I am not pretending that we can literally *rule out* the possibility of it being established that, at least in some cases, an act of perception "makes" that which is perceived "be." I am merely observing that, as it stands, we have no grounds for supposing this to be so. All we know is that the position of maintaining that it is so appears to be irrefutable. But it certainly is not something that we "see" to be so; our experience is not constituted for us that way.

On Not Being Taken in by Language

The question of why we find the idea of solipsism so repugnant is an interesting one. But for us, it is enough to recognize that it is a position that need not be maintained. And we need not maintain the position that "the answer did not exist until the procedure was carried out." On the other hand, we also need not maintain the position that "the answer

---

[10]And, unfortunately, this repugnance tends to spill over onto other positions which, when looked at superficially, seem to be close to this one.

did exist before the procedure was carried out." So long as we do not allow ourselves to be taken in by language, we do not have to maintain either position; and, as I shall argue, there are very good reasons why we should not.

In this discussion I have tried to use language in a way that allows one to experience the tug that pulls one "inside" the system. It is a way of using language that seems to force us to choose between what in fact are two metaphorical descriptions of the manner in which pure mathematical knowledge is acquired: discovery or creation. And it strongly compels us to accept that the "correct" answer is "discovery" and not "creation." If one yields to this compulsion—or temptation, call it what you will—then, in the absence of any pull in the opposite direction, one will be drawn almost immediately to a completely Platonistic conception both of mathematical statements and also of the activity of mathematics; that is, of the relationship between the mathematician and his domain of inquiry. However, we have seen that the source of this tug is to be found in certain unexamined acts of acceptance as such that take place strictly in the domain of language use. So long as we do not fall for the idea that talk "about statements" and "about answers" must be taken literally as being about "things" that stand in a certain relationship to us, there is no temptation and no choice to be made. Nor does this way of talking have to be abandoned; on the contrary, by providing a strictly operational account of what constitutes correct usage, it can be made into an extremely precise and efficient means for the expression of pure mathematical knowledge. Let me now elaborate on this point of view.

Statements as Signals: Using Language to Make Knowledge Sharable

In a science, the chief function of language is to make knowledge sharable. For example, if I know that no square of a rational number can be equal to 2, then by an appropriate use of language I may be able to "share" this knowledge with you; I may be able to "prove it" to you. Of course, in order for us to be able to participate in such a "sharing" of an experience of knowing something, we must already share an understanding as to how language is to be used for such a purpose; we have to be able to "read" each other's signals. But the conventions of language use are something that we ourselves have to establish; and, among these conventions, there must be ones that specify the conditions under which it is correct to assert such and such. In a scientific context, the conditions under which it is correct to assert such and such are precisely those that constitute being in a state of knowing that such and such; for example, of knowing that no square of a rational number can be equal to 2 or that some odd numbers are prime. Thus, a "statement," or "assertion," is nothing more (nor less) than an announcement, or signal, that one is in possession of a certain piece of knowledge. Also, at least in the case of pure mathematics, it is understood that this is knowledge that one is in a position to share; for example, by using language to specify certain procedures that are to be followed in order to attain this knowledge.

From this standpoint, to inquire about some statement whether "it might be true, independent of our knowing it" is merely idle talk, devoid of substance. For there are not literally such "things" as "statements"; only acts "of stating." And, in a scientific context, the idea that one "might be" speaking "the truth" without knowing it is at best a confused way of attempting to pose a question.

In other words, what is called for here is not an attempt to define some notion of a statement S "being true" or "being correct" but rather an account of what one has to know, as an observer of one's own states of knowing, in order that it be correct to assert S; or, equivalently, that it be correct to assert that "S is true." Since such an assertion is supposed to be a signal that one knows that S is true, it is correct to assert it when one does know that S is true and it is incorrect when one does not. In the same spirit, a question of the form "Is S true?" ought to be construed as signaling, literally, a quest: a quest after knowledge that S; for example, a quest after knowledge that no square of a rational number equals 2. And

284   GABRIEL STOLZENBERG

such a quest is successful when it results in the attainment
of the desired state of knowledge; in a state that one recognizes as "knowing that S."

Two Mathematical Statements and a Procedure
for Getting into a Position
to Make at Least One of Them

Now let us reconsider the type of situation in which it was
said to be "very difficult for us to resist the temptation to
suppose that there is already, unknown to us, a determinate
answer to the question of which of the two disjuncts we
should obtain a proof, were we to apply the decision procedure." We have a computational procedure P and we know
that by carrying it out either S or T, and possibly both, would
be established. This is a type of situation in which what we
possess knowledge of is a means for acquiring other knowledge of a particular sort; more specifically, we are in a state
of knowing that if we were to carry out the procedure we
would get either into a state of "knowing that S" or else into
a state of "knowing that T," and possibly into both.

But so far we have been talking only about a hypothetical
situation; therefore, let us now consider a specific case of this
type, the one that was mentioned earlier parenthetically. S is
the assertion that more than a million terms of the sequence
$s(n) \equiv$ fractional part of $(\frac{3}{2})^n$ lie in the interval from 0 to $\frac{1}{2}$; T
is the corresponding assertion for the interval from $\frac{1}{2}$ to 1;
and P is the procedure of computing the first two million
and one terms of the sequence, keeping count of how many
fall into each of the two intervals and noting at each stage of
the procedure whether at least one of the two counts exceeds
a million. We know that, were the procedure to be carried
out, the sum of the two totals would (be found to) exceed 2
million and also that each individual total either would or
would not (be found to) exceed 1 million. But we know also
that if neither of the two totals were (found) to exceed 1 million, then their sum would not (be found to) exceed 2 million. So we now know that, were the procedure to be carried
out, at least one of the two totals would (be found to) exceed

1 million. Hence, this is a particular case in which we now know that, were we to carry the procedure through to completion, we would be either in a state of "knowing that S" or else in a state of "knowing that T." And there is nothing more to it than that.

We saw earlier that when we allow ourselves to be taken in by superficial characteristics of language use, we may find ourselves forced to choose between two metaphorical descriptions of the act of carrying out the procedure P: "discovery" or "creation." Now, from the present standpoint, S and T serve as signals to be made when one is in a certain state of knowing; and the function of the procedure P is to get one either into one state or the other. Therefore, in the absence of any other way of getting into one of these states, it is definitely *not* correct to assert either S or T *before* the procedure has been carried out. In this sense, the actual state of affairs is operationally, if not conceptually, more accurately captured by the "creation" metaphor than by the "discovery" one; note that this is exactly the opposite of what we found when we allowed ourselves to be taken in by the metaphorical use of a language "of things." From a scientific standpoint, what counts is knowledge not talk. Thus, in the present case, what would constitute something significant would be to get either into a state of knowing that S or else into a state of knowing that T.[11] And, as it stands, we know only one way of doing this: namely, by carrying out the procedure P.

In this case, we may say that the act of carrying out the procedure "creates" or "produces" a certain state of knowledge: either knowledge that S or knowledge that T. However, it does not follow that it produces any thing called "the answer to the question of which of these two states of knowledge would be produced, were the procedure to be carried

---

[11]So far as I have been able to determine, neither S nor T has been established. To anyone who enjoys tackling such questions I recommend the following policy: Attempt to establish both statements by proving more generally that for each positive integer k there is a $N \geq 2k$ with the property that among the first N terms of the sequence "fractional part of $(\frac{3}{2})^n$" there are at least k in each half of the interval from 0 to 1.

out." If we want to continue to talk metaphorically about things called "answers," then we still do better to speak about "finding" the answer, rather than "making it," by carrying out the procedure. But if we are going to maintain such a metaphorical use of language in a scientific context, we at least ought to recognize it as such.

Understanding Mathematical Statements

In using language the way we did in the preceding illustrative example, the seemingly "present tense" statement "more than a million terms of the sequence 'fractional part of $(\frac{3}{2})^n$' lie in the interval from 0 to $\frac{1}{2}$" is not presumed to refer to anything that, literally, "is now the case." What we have to bear in mind is that, from the present point of view, being in a state of what would be called "understanding this statement" consists in nothing more or less than understanding, in strictly experiential terms, the conditions under which, according to the conventions that we have established, it is correct for someone to perform the act of making this statement in order to signal a certain state in which he finds himself. However, we really have not yet explained just what these conditions are. And anyone who still is inclined to think that the expression "terms of the sequence" *must* somehow refer to "things" that are "already there" in the interval may suppose also that these conditions must consist in "finding out" something that "is already the case."

Thus, in a sense, we are back in a situation in which we found ourselves earlier; only now, instead of talking "about answers" and "about statements," we are talking about what certain of these statements are about. By carrying out the appropriate computation, do we "find" that a certain term of the sequence lies in the interval between 0 and $\frac{1}{2}$? Or do we "make it" be there? When I compute $(\frac{3}{2})^5 = 243/32 = 7 + 19/32$ and thereby come to know that the fifth term of the sequence equals 19/32, which is between $\frac{1}{2}$ and 1, am I "finding out" something that "was already the case" or am I "making it be so"? As before, once we allow ourselves to accept that there really is such a choice to be made, we feel compelled to accept also that the correct answer is "find" and not "make."

However, our previous remarks about the use of a language "of things" for talk "about answers" and "about statements" apply equally well to its use within the statements of mathematics themselves: to talk "about numbers," "about functions," "about sets," etc. When we approach this way of using language uncritically, it does exert a powerful influence upon us; and we do find ourselves feeling compelled to suppose that, in some unexplained (and apparently unexplainable) way, such statements as "7 is odd," "19/32 is between $\frac{1}{2}$ and 1" and "more than a million terms of the sequence 'fractional part of $(\frac{2}{3})^n$' lie in the interval between 0 and $\frac{1}{4}$" are, in some literal sense, "present tense" assertions "about objects and their properties." Therefore, this way of using language should *not* be approached uncritically; for, as scientists, we simply have no business playing guessing games about the meaning of our scientific language, in this case the language of pure mathematics.

On the contrary, if we want mathematical language to function as a vehicle for signaling, recording, and communicating mathematical *knowledge*,[12] then we must take the position that an "understanding" of mathematical language that is, an understanding of "what the statements of mathematics are about," can consist in nothing more nor less than an understanding of the conventions that do, in fact, govern the use of mathematical language for precisely those purposes. But, as I have already remarked, these conventions must be established by *us*; and until we have done so they do not exist.

Note

It cannot be emphasized too strongly that I am writing here about conventions governing the use of language for the purpose of

---

[12] And, moreover, in such a way that those acts of mathematical language use that we call "proofs" are precisely the acts of acquiring such knowledge.

signaling, recording, communicating, etc., certain experiences of
knowing, those that we label "mathematical," and not (or, more
precisely, not only) about rules of some formal "language game"
in which one is allowed to make certain utterances, or marks on
paper, on the condition that certain other ones already have been
made. We are concerned here with mathematics as knowledge
acquired by acts of mathematical proof and with mathematical
language as a means of communicating that knowledge. [13]

One Way of Making Mathematical Language Work

Let me now give substance to the preceding discussion by
indicating how the traditional language "of counting numbers," including statements "about the operations of addition and multiplication," can be and to a considerable extent
already is used for the purpose of signaling, recording, communicating, etc., knowledge about acts "of counting." In fact,
more will be shown; for we shall see how this language is
used also for the purpose of *acquiring* mathematical knowledge, and not only knowledge about acts of counting (which
are themselves acts of mathematical language use) but also
about acts of mathematical language use that provide us with
knowledge about acts of counting; for example, acts "of performing a computation." (And not only knowledge about acts

---

[13] In contemporary mathematics, there are precise definitions stipulating
the form that a succession of utterances or marks on paper must display
to be a "formal proof" of a "formal mathematical statement" S. Since
mathematicians sometimes work for years, even decades, attempting to
produce either a formal "proof" or "disproof" of some particular "statement," obviously the construction of such formal entities does, in this
one sense, provide us with new and often highly nontrivial knowledge.
But in and of itself the construction of such formal entities does not—and
cannot—provide us with any knowledge of the sort that is traditionally
taken to be "mathematical": knowledge of the laws of arithmetic that we
use in daily life, of the theory of proportions, elementary geometry, and
so on. In particular, it does not and cannot provide us with any knowledge about the results of performing arithmetic (or any other) computations—for example, that if one adds a column of figures from the top
down or from the bottom up the results will be equal. (So that if we find
that "they are not equal" an error must have been made.) Knowledge of
this sort *can* be acquired by acts of mathematical proof, but not within
the context of a strictly "formal game" approach to mathematics.

of mathematical language use of that sort but also about acts of mathematical language use that provide us with knowledge about acts of mathematical language use of that sort, etc.)

To begin, we must distinguish between "recitational" counting, say in base 10 notation, and what, for want of a better term, will be called here "real" counting; for example, tallying a vote or counting the number of primes less than 100. We do not have to attempt to explain what, in general, constitutes an act "of real counting" because in pure mathematics we carefully prescribe the context in which such acts are performed; and this permits us to give an account of them that is special to that context.

Once we have learned how to recognize and perform acts of recitational counting (which consist in making one after another, in a specialized order, certain distinguishable utterances or marks on paper), and have learned the general rule of formation, we may also learn how to recognize and perform acts of the type "counting B numbers after A." For example, counting five numbers after 7 is done as follows: 8 is 1, 9 is 2, 10 is 3, 11 is 4, and 12 is 5. In this context, we make the convention that a statement of the form "$A + B = C$" is to be used to signal being in a state of knowing that were one to count B numbers after A one would end up with "C is B." Thus, with apologies to Kant, on the basis of our just having counted five numbers after 7 and having ended up with "12 is 5" we are now in a position of knowing that $7 + 5 = 12$.

In addition to the "standard" base 10 system for recitational counting, 1, 2, 3, 4, 5, 6, etc., we may also introduce ones of the type "counting in blocks of B"; for example, counting in blocks of three could be taken to be 1, 2, 3, 1, 2, 3, 1, 2, 3, etc., except that in this notion the marks (or utterances) are not all distinct. So we correct for this by using instead some notation like (1,1), (1,2), (1,3), (2,1), (2,2), (2,3), (3,1), (3,2), (3,3), (4,1), etc. Once such systems have been introduced, one is in a position to perform (and to talk about) acts of the type "counting up to A in blocks of B"; for example, counting up to 7 in blocks of 3 is done as follows: 1 is

(1,1), 2 is (1,2), 3 is (1,3), 4 is (2,1), 5 is (2,2), 6 is (2,3), 7 is (3,1). And we make the general convention that a statement of the form "$A = C \cdot B$" is to be a signal for knowing that were one to count up to A in blocks of B one would end up with "A is (C,B)." Thus, by what we have done above, we are in a position to make the assertion that $6 = 2 \cdot 3$.

By continuing in this manner, we may readily establish conventions of a similar sort governing all the rest of the traditional language of arithmetic (and, for that matter, analysis, algebra, etc.). This includes notation like "N^k"; statements of the form "$A = B$" and "$A < B$"; talk "about negative numbers," "about integers," "about rational numbers," "about real numbers"; the use of predicates, as in statements of the form "A is odd" or "A is prime"; and so forth.

Statements involving predicates have the superficial appearance of being "present tense" assertions "about objects and their properties"; consider, for example, "7 is prime," "There is a number greater than a million that is prime," "For every positive integer, there is a number greater than it that is prime," and "Every positive integer is either prime or composite." However, according to the conventions that we establish in order to use such statements for signaling knowledge about acts of counting, acts of acquiring knowledge about acts of counting, and so on, this mode of expression is strictly metaphorical. (Nor do we know of any other way of establishing conventions governing its use according to which it is otherwise.) For example, a statement of the form "A is prime" is, by convention, a signal for being in a state of knowing that were one to perform certain acts of mathematical language use, that is, certain "computations," they would display a certain specified form. The computations are these: For each value of B that is greater than 1 and less than A, count up to A in blocks of B, ending up in each case with an utterance (or mark on paper) of the form "A is (D,E)." Then check whether E is less than B or equal to B. We use the statement "A is prime" to signal knowledge that were one to carry out these computations one would get in each case that E is less than B. We also make the convention that "A is composite" to be used to signal knowledge that were one to perform these same computations, one would get some value of B for which E is equal to B (in which case $A = D \cdot B$). Evidently, by carrying out these computations for any particular value of A we get into one of the following two states: knowing that A is prime; knowing that A is composite. And we signal our knowing this by the statement "Every positive integer is either prime or composite."

For the purpose of the present discussion, I have now said enough (and perhaps somewhat more than that) about how "present tense" talk "about mathematical objects and their properties" can be made to function as a vehicle for signaling, recording, communicating—and acquiring—knowledge of a particular kind.

The Contemporary Mathematician's Unfulfilled Task: Making Mathematical Language Function the Way He Wants It To

Whether or not one happens to "like" the particular conventions of mathematical language use that I talked about in the preceding section, the fact remains that they do the job that is required of them. Namely, once they are adopted, pure mathematics does become a genuine scientific discipline in which acts of mathematical proof are, in the traditional sense, acts of acquiring knowledge; in other words, the proofs really do prove something and we can say just what that something is. By contrast, despite appearances, the contemporary pure mathematician's way of "using" mathematical language is not governed by *any* set of conventions that make it function in such a way. To my mind, this is a devastating criticism of contemporary mathematical practice. On the other hand, from within the system, this particular criticism has no force whatsoever. It takes the form of a question that the contemporary mathematician has learned he does not have to answer.

That the contemporary mathematician does not accept the particular conventions I have outlined in the preceding section is, in itself, no criticism of his position. He may prefer to establish conventions according to which the statements of pure mathematics will be about something *other* than acts

of counting, acts of acquiring knowledge about acts of counting, etc. Indeed, we know that he does have such a preference and we also know why. He feels that to say that pure
mathematics is about such acts as counting is as wrongheaded as saying that astronomy is about acts of looking
through a telescope rather than about "what one sees" when
one looks through a telescope. And, in this spirit, he wishes
to insist that a statement such as "$7 + 5 = 12$" is not about acts
of counting but rather about "a relationship among numbers" that may be discovered by means of certain acts of
counting. Fine; but in that case he faces the task of establishing conventions of mathematical language use that will make
mathematical language function that way. However, no such
thing has ever been done; nor is there the slightest reason to
suppose that it ever could be done.

Notes

i. During the nineteenth century, the founders of the contemporary system attached great importance to the task of establishing the requisite conventions of mathematical language use; and,
for a good while, they believed that they had in fact accomplished this by explaining all pure mathematical discourse as
being "about sets." One fundamental error that they made was
to allow themselves to be taken in by the notion that talk "about
sets" is, in some literal sense, talk about certain things called
"sets." It is instructive to reread, with a critical eye, those traditional (and also contemporary) accounts that are supposed to
produce in us knowledge of "what sets are" and, in particular,
of referents for such terms as "the set of all odd positive integers
less than 10," "the set of all primes," and so on. Despite appearances, these accounts do not succeed even in establishing what
sort of thing a set is supposed to be; that is, in telling us what
special properties a thing must possess in order to be a set.[14]
ii. I am not criticizing talk "about sets" as such but only attempts to construe it as being talk about certain "things" (conceptual or otherwise) called "sets." Talk "about sets" has a straight-

---

[14]We are told that a set is "made up" out of its elements; however, as it
stands, this use of language is strictly metaphorical.

forward operational interpretation in terms of acts of declaring type and, as such, has a proper and very significant role in pure mathematical discourse.

iii. Eventually the inadequacy of the purported accounts of "what sets are" was recognized even within the contemporary mathematician's system; but the attitude that was taken had the effect of leaving the situation basically unchanged. Thus, the contemporary mathematician still feels that he has some intuition of "what sets are" but, since he finds himself unable to make it precise, when pressed he will take the position that his mathematical language use is strictly formal, that his mathematical statements are not *really* about anything but that the structure of his formal language is intended to "model" (whatever that means) his "intuitive idea of set." However unsatisfactory such a response may appear to an outside observer, for the contemporary mathematician it serves the important purpose of enabling him to stay inside his system. And he can rationalize what he describes as his inability to make precise his "intuition of what sets are" by attributing it to the inherent imperfection of the human mind as "an organ" for "seeing into" the realm of pure mathematics.

iv. An even more fundamental error that the nineteenth-century founders of the contemporary system made was to take for granted that making mathematical language use precise necessitates taking talk "about mathematical objects" literally; so that, for example, talk "about the square root of 2" must be explained as being about some thing, "a real number" having a certain specified property. Why is it that in pure mathematics the use of a language "of objects" can exert such a tug upon us, a tug to take it literally, whereas in so many other regions of discourse we use such a mode of expression to communicate complex pieces of information precisely and efficiently but without feeling any such tug whatsoever? Certainly, had the founders of the contemporary system given the matter any thought, they would have seen from the most trivial considerations that talk "about objects" can be completely precise without being, in any literal sense, about objects. And had they done so, they might also have recognized that a rigorization of mathematical language use need not, and perhaps should not, entail giving "present tense" talk "about objects and their properties" a meaning that is in accord with its surface form.

A Pseudomystery About the Nature of Mathematical Knowledge and the Manner in Which It Is Acquired

Thus, one manifestation of the trapped state into which I claim that pure mathematics has gotten itself is that, although it is supposed to be and appears to be a scientific activity, that is, a discipline in which research is conducted and knowledge is acquired, it is committed to a position for which there is no intelligible account of what, if anything, the statements of pure mathematics are about (and hence of what, if anything, one is acquiring knowledge about when one conducts pure mathematical research). Moreover, this is the case even for such seemingly well-understood statements as "Every positive integer is a sum of four squares" or "π is between 3 and 4." Of course, these statements may be understood operationally, that is, according to the particular conventions that were sketched out before. But, as I have pointed out, the contemporary mathematician explicitly rejects the operational account even though he is not in a position to replace it with any other. He knows what he wants and if he cannot have it he is prepared to do without.

Hence, for the contemporary mathematician, the nature of mathematical knowledge—what it is knowledge of and by what "faculty of mind" one obtains it—is a great and apparently unresolvable mystery. And yet, from the standpoint of an outside observer, there is no mystery as to how this pseudomystery is created. The basic acts of acceptance as such by means of which one enters into the system, that is, by means of which one learns to think "like a pure mathematician," consist chiefly in attributing to oneself (and others) knowledge (that one does not possess) of conventions (that do not exist) according to which "present tense" talk "about the truth or falsity of unproven statements" and "about mathematical objects and their properties" does have a meaning that is in accord with its surface form. Therefore, it really is not surprising that afterwards, when the contemporary mathematician attempts to locate this knowledge that he "knows" that he possesses, he discovers that it is, or at least appears to be, inaccessible to him. But instead of taking this as evidence that he might do well to review the grounds on which he attributes to himself such knowledge, he prefers to treat it as evidence of certain inherent limitations to human understanding. And, in this fashion, by building up fantasy upon fantasy, the contemporary mathematician's world view is expanded to encompass not only mathematics but also the human mind.

Note

Furthermore, as is well known, certain technical results in the theory of formal systems are interpreted as providing more rigorous proof of such limitations to human understanding. The principle is very simple. Suppose that, in the basis of an analysis of possible ways of making proofs, one is able to give a reasonably convincing argument that, for a particular mathematical statement S, both S and its negation are unprovable. From a strictly operational point of view, this is no more evidence of any limitation upon our "capacity" for acquiring knowledge than is, say, our manifest inability to acquire knowledge that $2 + 2 = 3$. However, if one attributes to oneself a mastery of conventions governing the use of "true" and "false" according to which it is correct to say that every mathematical statement is "either true or false, independent of our knowledge of which," then it will indeed appear to be the case that, of the two statements S and *not* S, at least one is a "truth" that is unknowable to us. But if one recognizes that, despite appearances, no such conventions have been established, then the entire picture collapses and one is left only with an empty piece of phraseology, "true or false, independent of our knowledge of which," and a technical result in the theory of formal systems.

The Decisive Influence of Language Use on the Conduct of Mathematical Research

Thus far I have talked mainly about how, by certain acts of acceptance as such taking place in the domain of language use, the contemporary mathematician acquires certain beliefs

that may be described as beliefs "about mathematics."[15] I
have criticized these beliefs, the grounds upon which they
are based, and also the inability of the contemporary mathematician to reconsider the process by which they are
acquired. But I have not yet established any connection
between the holding of these beliefs and the day-to-day conduct of mathematical research; and, because of this, one may
be tempted to dismiss what I have said so far by contending
that my criticism is directed not against the activity of contemporary mathematical research, nor against the product of
that activity, but only against certain admittedly metaphysical beliefs about the nature of that activity and its product.

On this view, that body of "theorems and proofs" that is
to be found in contemporary mathematical textbooks and
journals has a significance, an intellectual value, that somehow manages to be above the criticism I have presented here.
It is easy to see why this may appear to be so, especially from
the standpoint of someone who holds the beliefs that have
been criticized.[16] Nevertheless, to take such a position is to
overlook completely the fact that much, perhaps most, of what
the contemporary mathematician takes to be the activity of
"acquiring mathematical knowledge"—e.g., knowledge about
continuous functions or partial differential equations—is seen
by him as such *only* because of his holding these beliefs. In
performing this activity, the contemporary mathematician
relies on certain "principles of reasoning" that appear to him
to be self-evidently correct. But this perception is completely
standpoint dependent; the principles will appear to be self-

---

[15]If I did not use quotation marks here it might appear that I am accepting
that a statement like "I believe that mathematical objects are discovered
and not created" expresses a belief about the nature of certain things
called "mathematical objects." But it is rather the belief that it does not
express such a belief that I am calling here a belief "about mathematics."

[16]Thus, the contemporary mathematician knows well enough that his
account of what mathematics is about is somewhat incoherent. But the
lesson he learns from "the reality" of his everyday mathematical experience is that it simply does not matter. Also, even when one takes contemporary mathematical research to be "only a formal game," there is no
gainsaying the extraordinary technical virtuosity that sometimes is displayed in the construction of a formal "proof" or "disproof" of a formal
mathematical "statement."

evident to anyone who has been taken in by the use of a "present tense" language "of objects and properties" and they will not appear that way to anyone who has not. A brief consideration of what Errett Bishop has called "the principle of mathematical omniscience" should suffice to make this point clear.

The principle is that, whenever one is in a position to make an assertion of the form "Every x is either of type A or type B," one is also in a position to assert "Either every x is of type A or some x is of type B." In other words:

If every x is either of type A or type B, then
either every x is of type A or some x is of type B.

Notice how the use of a "present tense" language "of objects" makes this appear to be, somehow, true "by definition."[17] It is therefore no wonder that the contemporary mathematician accepts it as such and operates with it accordingly; nor is it any wonder that by means of it he is able to "obtain" a great many "significant results" that he would not otherwise be able to establish. To the contemporary mathematician, the principle of omniscience[18] is a self-evidently correct principle of mathematical reasoning. He sees it this way because in fact the principle *would* be true "by definition" if one *were* able to establish conventions of mathematical language use according to which "present tense" statements "about mathematical objects and their properties" do have a meaning of the sort that the contemporary mathematician *anyway* attributes to them.

On the other hand, no such conventions have been established; nor, as the very name of the principle suggests, is there any reason to expect that they ever could be.[19] Further-

---

[17]One almost is tempted to say that it must be by definition of "true."

[18]Which he does not call by that, or any other, name.

[19]The name "principle of omniscience" is suggested by a consideration of those cases in which the range of the variable x is a potentially infinite domain such as the domain of positive integers. In case the range of the variable is finite, we do have a procedure—namely, checking for each value of x whether it is of type A or B—which, were we to perform it, would put us either into a state of knowing that every x is of type A or that some x is of type B. But we do not have any such general procedure

more, according to the only set of conventions that *have* been established, those described in my sketch of an operational account of mathematical language use, the principle of omniscience is demonstrably incorrect; for, in particular cases, one can see by inspection that one *is* in a position to make an assertion of the form "Every x is either of type A or type B" and yet one *is not* in a position to assert "Either every x is of type A or some x is of type B."[20]

Note

However, it does not follow from this that all the "significant results" that are based upon the principle of omniscience also are incorrect. Some are; others are not.[21] As a matter of fact, despite the widespread use of the principle of omniscience (and others like it), contemporary mathematical theories do contain a good deal of significant operational content. On the other hand, even though much of it can be extracted fairly mechanically, the overall job of digging it out has proved to be fundamentally a salvage operation. Thus, direct experience has shown it to be only a myth that the contemporary system is, in any sense, a convenient framework for producing mathematics that is operationally significant. On the contrary, it is a handicap: a very serious one. Not only are so many of the "theorems" of contemporary mathematics operationally incorrect; it is the theories themselves that are, almost always, fundamentally off-base from an operational point of view. What may appear to be the main result or a

---

for those cases in which the domain is potentially infinite. There is a much quoted remark by Bertrand Russell to the effect that the lack of such a procedure by the pure mathematician, and by the mathematical logician, is a "merely medical" impossibility that he should feel free to disregard. To me, this witty remark of Russell exhibits one of the distinctive features of contemporary pure mathematics: Namely, a failure of "that feeling for reality" that Russell himself declared "ought to be preserved even in the most abstract studies" [7].

[20] For example, I am in a position to make the assertion "For each positive integer k, either no more than a million of the first k terms of the sequence 'fractional part of $(\frac{3}{2})^n$' lie between 0 and $\frac{1}{2}$ or more than a million of them do" but I am not in a position to assert "Either for all k no more than a million of the first k terms lie between 0 and $\frac{1}{2}$ or for some k more than a million of them do."

[21] And, of those that are, some are only "a little bit" wrong while others are almost entirely so.

key concept from one standpoint need not be anything of the sort from the other.

The Influence of Talk "About Statements Being True"

In the preceding illustrative example, I showed how the use of a "present tense" language "of mathematical objects and their properties" can make the principle of omniscience appear to be true "by definition." However, in the essay by Michael Dummett [1] to which I referred earlier, the point is made that it is possible to separate the contemporary mathematician's beliefs about what constitutes correct mathematical reasoning from his belief that the statements of mathematics are in some literal sense about certain things called "mathematical objects." To see how this can be so, consider the following reformulation of the principle of omniscience wherein talk "about mathematical objects and their properties" is eliminated (or, rather, suppressed).

If, for each x, either statement $A(x)$ or $B(x)$ is true, then either all the statements $A(x)$ are true or some statement $B(x)$ is true.

Notice that, as before, it is the use of a "present tense" language "of objects and their properties" that makes the purported principle appear to be true "by virtue of its meaning." However, this time the objects are "statements" and the purported property is "being true." In a similar manner, all the rest of the contemporary mathematician's "principles of correct reasoning"—his laws of logic—can be framed in such a way that all talk "about mathematical objects" is eliminated and it is only his beliefs about the meaning of talk "about statements being true" that make him see these purported principles as being self-evidently correct.

By acts of acceptance as such in the domain of language use the contemporary mathematician acquires the belief that he knows "what it is like" for a mathematical statement "to be true without anyone knowing or being able to know that it is true."[22] As a consequence, he sees himself as being in a position to regard talk "about mathematical statements" not merely as talk about signals that we agree to use (according to conventions that we establish) to announce that we are in a certain kind of state "of knowing" but, more fundamentally, as being about things that stand in the following kind of relationship to us[23]: there is a property called "being true" that each of these things, unchangingly, either does or does not possess and it does so irrespective of whether any of us knows or is capable of knowing that it does.[24]

This is the "present tense" aspect of mathematical talk and we experience it most vividly at those moments in which we find ourselves wondering about some mathematical statement,[25] not whether we can prove it, or disprove it, but "whether it is true." For the contemporary mathematician, it is experiences like these—ones in which he sees himself as being in possession of a concept of "truth independent of knowledge"—that constitute the unstated justification for the practice of excluded middle reasoning: that practice that the contemporary mathematician would describe as "reasoning according to the principle that every mathematical statement either is or is not true, independent of our knowledge of which."

At bottom, it is this one belief "about mathematics"—a belief that one possesses a concept of "truth independent of

---

[22]See Note ii at the end of this section.

[23]Who, on this account, also are things: ones constructed in such a way as to be capable of "acquiring knowledge about" other things.

[24]It is interesting to observe how this conception of mathematical statements, each residing permanently in one of the two cateogries "true" or "false," leads the contemporary mathematician to adopt a "definition" of "S implies T" that does not entail T in any sense "following from" S. From an operational standpoint, it is appropriate to use "S implies T" or "If S then T" to signal possession of a procedure for *getting from* a state of knowing that S into a state of knowing that T. By contrast, the contemporary mathematician "sees" four possibilities: S and T both true; S and T both false; S false and T true; S true and T false. And he "defines" the expression "S implies T" to "mean" that one of the first three cases "holds," which for him is equivalent to the fourth case "not holding."

[25]For example, the statement that for every value of N, no matter how large, each half of the interval from 0 to 1 contains at least N terms of the sequence "fractional part of $(\frac{3}{2})^n$."

knowledge" of a sort that makes the principle of excluded middle be "true by definition"—that makes all the rest of the contemporary mathematician's operationally incorrect "principles of reasoning" seem to be self-evidently correct. And, however innocuous the holding of this belief may appear to someone who does already hold it, it nevertheless is fair to say that no other belief "about mathematics" occupies nearly so central a role either in the construction or in the maintenance of the contemporary mathematical world view.[26]

Notes

i. From the standpoint of an outside observer, one of the most significant consequences of adopting the practice of excluded middle reasoning is an inversion of the natural relationship between "truth" and "proof." Instead of "*S* is true" being a signal to announce a state of knowing which one has attained by means of an act of proof, the very notion of an act of proof is to be explained in terms of a prior notion of "truth independent of knowledge" which may then be appealed to in the course of performing such an act. On this account, an act of proof is an act of reasoning about things called "statements," each of which "is already" either true or false, in order to discover *for a particular one of them* either that it is true or that it is false. But this is a description of an activity that is radically different from anything that would constitute an act of proof on *any* operational account of conventions of language use.

ii. In my earlier account of what I referred to as "the edge" of the system I described how, by certain acts of acceptance as such taking place in the domain of language use, one may acquire a

---

[26]Its role in maintaining this world view is manifested most clearly by the manner in which the contemporary mathematician, or logician, comprehends and responds to criticism of the sort that has been present here: criticism that has no force unless one *first* undoes the basic belief that is being called into question. He responds to it with the observation that when one considers this belief only from the standpoint of holding it, there does not appear to be any good reason for rejecting it. And since he is operating within a belief system, to him this is an entirely adequate response. Moreover, he may argue *from* the belief to the conclusion that any such criticism of it must be misguided. See, for example, p. 85 of Quine [6], where Quine talks about what *he* calls "a confusion between knowledge and truth."

belief that an act of mathematical proof consists in finding out something that "is already the case"—in other words, that any mathematical statement that can be proved "is already true"—and in this way come to hold a belief that one knows "what it is like" for a mathematical statement "to be true without anyone yet knowing it." But a belief of this sort *may be* entirely compatible with the view that "is true" means nothing more than "is provable," and if it is then it does not support either the practice of excluded middle reasoning or the use of any of the other operationally incorrect "principles of mathematical reasoning" that the contemporary mathematician finds self-evident. The holder of such a belief will find it correct to assert that a mathematical statement "either is or is not true independent of our knowledge of which" provided that he has a procedure by means of which the statement can be either proved or disproved. But for him to see no need to have such a procedure in order to make the assertion, to see himself as being in a position to say that *every* mathematical statement "either is or is not true independent of our knowledge of which," it is necessary that he hold the more obscure belief that he knows "what it is like" for a mathematical statement "to be true without anyone being able to know it."

No account has been given here of how this "stronger" belief is acquired, but I claim that, in fact, it is a product of the same acts of acceptance as such that, in my earlier discussion, were shown to produce the more modest, if also unwarranted, belief that one knows "what it is like" for a mathematical statement "to be true without anyone yet knowing it." Recall that these are acts of acceptance as such that are performed not in the course of actually having an experience of "seeing that some mathematical statement is true" but rather in the course of thinking about, and using a "present tense" language "of objects and their properties" for talking about, what such experiences are like. The distinction is crucial; when one carefully examines the experience of proving a mathematical statement S and thereby getting into a state "of seeing that S is true," one finds that the conclusion of an act of proof is indeed an act of recognition, of "seeing" something.[27] However, when one merely reflects in a general way upon what such experiences are like, it is possible to lose sight of what

---

[27] For example, if S is the statement "There is a prime number greater than 10," an act of proof might consist in representing 11 in the form $11 = QB + R$, with Q a positive integer, for each positive integer value of B from 2 through 10 and *seeing that* in each case the value of R is positive.

it is that one does "see" and to confuse it with the sign that one uses to signal that one has seen such a thing. And one product of that confusion may be a belief that one knows "what is it like" for "a mathematical statement to be true without there being any way of proving it."

What one "sees" or "discovers" at the conclusion of an act of proof is that a certain structure (which is constructed in the course of the proof) displays a certain form: a form of the type that, according to the conventions of mathematical language use that have been established, entitles anyone who observes it to say "*S* is true."[28] But "*S* is true" is merely what one *says*, not what one *sees*; the expression itself is merely the "brand name" for *the type* of thing that one sees at the conclusion of the proof. And it is a type of thing that may be seen only by constructing a proof—not because we need to use the proof as "a ladder" to get ourselves into a position to see it but rather because what one sees is "in" the structure that is created by the act "of making the proof."

Evidently, when one views things in this way, the idea of "a statement being true without there being any way of proving it" is a contradiction in terms. However, if one has not made the observations just described, the usual way of talking "about statements being true" makes it all too easy, when thinking in a general way about what acts "of proving that a statement is true" are like, to confuse what one does discover at the conclusion of a proof with the sign, or signal, one uses to announce the discovery: "that *S* is true." And if one does make this confusion— if one does fail to recognize that the actual discovery is, of necessity, always about the form of structures that are constructed in the course of the proof—and accepts instead that what one discovers is simply "that *S* is true," then it will indeed appear to be the case that the possibility of constructing a proof is not a necessity for "a statement to be true." And that, in essence, is the belief "about mathematics" that is needed to make excluded middle reasoning seem right.

iii. While the contemporary mathematician certainly is not alone in his belief that he possesses a concept of "truth independent of knowledge," there does not seem to be any other contemporary scientific discipline that requires such an absolute

---

[28] I am ignoring, for the moment, the "predictive" aspect of the knowledge that is provided by an act of proof: knowledge that *were* one to make certain computations they *would* display a certain form. However significant this aspect may be, it has no bearing upon the present discussion.

commitment to this belief as does pure mathematics.[29] There are
some philosophers of science, such as Karl Popper [5], who think
otherwise and say that physics is such a discipline, whether or
not the physicists themselves are aware of it. However, those
whom I have read invariably arrive at this conclusion by confusing what it actually is like not to believe that one possesses a
concept of "truth independent of knowledge" with what it
appears to be like from the standpoint of someone who does
believe that he possesses such a concept.[30] Quite predictably,
what these authors come up with as an account of what it is like
for someone not to hold this belief is the well-known picture of
a solipsist: a person who says that "the world is my dream." And
they consider this to be a damning criticism. However, from the
very standpoint they are criticizing, their own position appears
to be that of someone who says "my dream is the world." Is that
also a damning criticism? No? Yes? How do we decide? By failing to take into account the standpoint-dependent nature of their
own view of other views, the so-called "realist" or "objectivist"
philosophers end up committing the very error of which they
accuse others; namely, that of seeing other sentient beings *only*
as projections of one's own self.

Concluding Remarks

I am only too aware of the major respects in which this
account is incomplete. That no point has been argued even
nearly adequately is, I think, too obvious to require further
comment. What concerns me more, however, is that I have
had to leave out significant portions of the total picture.
For example, I have not managed to say anything, until

---

[29]Furthermore, in contemporary science, a belief in a concept of "truth
independent of knowledge" need not consist in anything more than a
belief that one knows "what it is like" for an event to occur—a tree to fall
in the forest, or Icarus from the sky—without anyone being there to
observe it. And in the context of pure mathematics a belief of this sort
does not produce anything more than the "modest" one, discussed above,
that is too weak to support the "self-evident correctness" of the principle
of excluded middle.

[30]Moreover, they sometimes compound this confusion by failing to make
a decision between the "more modest" and "stronger" forms of this belief
that were discussed above in the context of pure mathematics. They do
this by treating their criticism of what they take to be the position of not
holding the more modest belief as if it constitutes an argument in support of the stronger one.

now, about the bizarre situation that has been created by the insistence that even the activity of mathematical construction[31] be carried out *within* the contemporary mathematician's belief system. On the subject of mathematical construction the contemporary literature is so unreliable that when an author asserts that he has constructed an X he may just as well have constructed an X', or nothing at all; and when he asserts that he has *not* constructed an X he may well have constructed one anyway.[32] In my view, the travesty that contemporary mathematics has made of the activity of mathematical construction is, in a practical if not in a legalistic sense, the reductio ad absurdum of the position upon which it is based. However, this is but one of a number of equally important subjects that have not been dealt with here.

Also, no attempt has been made to examine how well the arguments presented in the latter part of the chapter support the claim that the contemporary mathematician's belief system really is a trap according to the precise meaning I gave this term earlier. My own view is that when the whole case is laid out the only point about which there is some doubt is whether the contemporary mathematician's basic position really is, on its own terms, irrefutable. Certainly it appears to be[33]; moreover, I believe that a good case can be made out that it is. However, if I should be proved to be wrong on this particular score, then so much the better!

The Title Question Answered

The title question of this chapter is: Can an inquiry into the foundations of mathematics tell us anything interesting

---

[31]That activity that the contemporary mathematician would describe as "the activity of finding mathematical objects of a given type or of constructing rules, algorithms, and explicit formulas for so doing."

[32]He may say, in such a case, "I have proved that there exists a such and such, but I don't know any way of finding one," whereas, in fact, his proof does provide a way of "finding" one. A notable instance of this is Littlewood's proof of the existence of a sign change for the function $\pi(x) - Li(x)$; see Ingham [2] and also Kreisel [3].

[33]As is evidenced by the traditional response that is given by the contemporary mathematical community to Brouwer's "constructivist" critique, and also to more recent variations on it.

about mind? There is a tradition of answering this question
in the affirmative, usually by constructing an argument that
our capacity for obtaining pure mathematical knowledge can
be accounted for only by the existence of some special faculty
of mind. Anyone who shares the mathematical world-view
of the contemporary mathematician is bound to feel at least
some temptation to answer the question with an argument
of this sort because he does not have any other way of
explaining how it is that we are able to know of and to obtain
nontrivial knowledge about a domain of nonphysical "objects" whose existence is "independent of us." Nor does he
have any other way of explaining how it is that the beginning student of pure mathematics invariably finds the law of
excluded middle, as well as the other logical "laws," to be
self-evidently correct. It certainly is not knowledge that is
acquired in any ordinary way, that is, by observing the world
or by having it demonstrated.[34] Therefore—so this particular
line of reasoning goes—it must be knowledge that is somehow "given" to us as part of the basic structure of our faculty
of understanding.

But, of course, there is another explanation available:
Namely, that this purported knowledge does not exist and
that the contemporary mathematician's impression that both
he and the entering student do possess such knowledge (or,
at least, the capacity for possessing it) is merely an illusion—
albeit a very powerful one—arising from certain unfounded,
and also unarticulated, beliefs "about mathematics" which
themselves are the product of certain unwittingly performed
acts of acceptance as such in the domain of ordinary language use. Such is the explanation that has been offered in
this chapter and, if it is right, the contemporary mathematician's way of answering the title question in the affirmative
is nothing more than a fantasy produced by language.[35]

---

[34]Indeed, if a student were to fail to assent to the "self-evident correctness"
of the law of excluded middle—if, say, he were to request a much fuller
account of the matter on the grounds that he has never used such terms
as "is true" with the kind of exactness that seems to be called for here—
there would be nothing that could be done. There is no "fuller" account.
Everything depends upon the student's immediate assent.

[35]Moreover, even as a fantasy it is rather thin.

Furthermore, if one examines the positive part of the account I have presented here—that is, my little sketch of the nature of pure mathematical knowledge and the process by which it is acquired—one will find that, according to it, there is nothing special, nothing peculiarly "nonempirical," about those states of knowledge that we label "mathematical."[36] To put the matter as plainly as I can, in the course of my own investigation into the foundations of mathematics—the one I have reported on here—I have found no evidence to support the view that pure mathematics, or for that matter logic, is in any respect, like language, a "mirror of mind."

And yet I have asserted, at the beginning of this chapter, that I do see the body of my remarks as constituting an affirmative answer to the title question, albeit one of a radically nontraditional kind. I am referring here to the remarkable phenomenon of mind being acted upon by language and producing a "reality," or world view, of the sort that was described in this chapter.

That language can affect us so powerfully is itself nothing new. We do not need to conduct an inquiry into the foundations of mathematics in order to make the observation that people—all of us—are capable of being taken in by talk, of being carried away by it, of reading into what someone says more than is actually there. Indeed, it is just because experiences of this kind are so familiar—so ordinary—that it may be considered illuminating to discover how much of the contemporary mathematician's perception of an "objective" mathematical reality is actually a product of experiences of this kind. But the case itself is not an ordinary one, except for someone who is strictly in the position of an outside observer. To anyone who starts off inside the contemporary mathematician's belief system, the discovery that an entire component of the "reality" of one's experience is produced by acts of acceptance as such in the domain of language use is not merely illuminating. In a literal sense, it is shattering:

---

[36]On the other hand, there does appear to be something peculiarly nonempirical about what I termed before, somewhat inaccurately, the "predictive" aspect of mathematical knowledge. However, that is a subject for another discussion.

Once a mathematician has seen that his perception of the "self-evident correctness" of the law of excluded middle is nothing more than the linguistic equivalent of an optical illusion, neither his practice of mathematics nor his understanding of it can ever be the same.

REFERENCES

1. Dummett, M. The philosophical basis of intuitionistic logic. In *Studies in Logic and the Foundations of Mathematics*, Vol. 60, H. E. Rose and J. C. Shepherdson (eds.). North-Holland, Amsterdam, 1975.
2. Ingham, A. E. *The Distribution of Prime Numbers*. Cambridge University Press, Cambridge, 1932.
3. Kreisel, G. On the interpretation of non-finitist proofs, part II. *Journal of Symbolic Logic 17*, 1952, 43–58.
4. Lakatos, I. *Proofs and Refutations: The Logic of Mathematical Discovery*. Cambridge University Press, Cambridge, 1976.
5. Popper, K. *Objective Knowledge: An Evolutionary Approach*. Oxford University Press, Oxford, 1972.
6. Quine, W. V. *Philosophy of Logic*. Prentice-Hall, Englewood Cliffs, New Jersey, 1970.
7. Russell, B. *Introduction to Mathematical Philosophy*. Allen and Unwin, London, 1919, p. 169.

FRANCISCO J. VARELA

The Creative Circle: Sketches on the Natural History of Circularity

A HAND RISES OUT of the paper, groping into a larger world. When we believe it is hopelessly beyond the flatness of its origin, it plunges back onto the flat surface, sketching its own emergence from the white sheet. A loop is completed whereby two levels are collapsed, intercrossed, entangled. At this point, what we wanted to hold in separate levels is revealed as inseparable, our sense of direction and foundation seems to falter, and a sense of paradox sets in (Figure 22).

Traditionally such circularities were called vicious circles; they were the epitome of what had to be shunned. But I suggest that they be called virtuous and creative circles. In their apparent strangeness, there are keys to the understanding of natural systems, their cognitive phenomena, and a rich world of forms. Here I shall offer some sketches of this world of strange loops from three fundamental perspectives: empirical, formal, and epistemological.

The Empirical Perspective

In the Escher engraving we see that the two hands mutually draw themselves. That is, they mutually specify their conditions of production.

They bootstrap themselves out of the engraving to consti- tute a separate entity. More precisely, their mutual specifi-

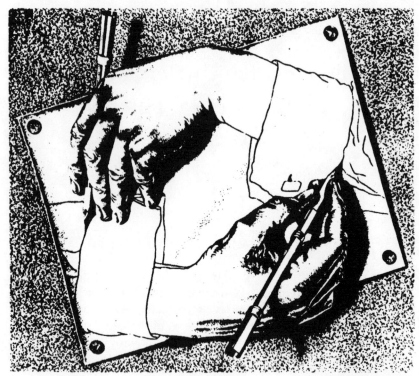

Figure 22   (M.C. Escher, "Hands")

cation sets them apart from the rest of the drawing to
constitute a *unity*. Their operation (mutual drawing) specifies the conditions under which they can be distinguished,
setting them apart from a background.

To find that a unity sets itself apart from a background by
its operations is an ordinary experience we normally associate with living things. Since antiquity, *automony* served to
designate this experience. If I observe a dog walking on the
street and it suddenly changes direction and moves toward
me, I generally impute an intention in the dog to greet me.
Whether or not such an imputation of mentality is valid is
not so interesting to me as the fact that it is *tempting* to impute
intention on the basis of what the dog does. That is, the dog's
behavior is difficult to account for unless I observe that the

dog confronts its environment not as if it were receiving instructions from this environment for particular outcomes but, rather, as if these instructions were mere disturbances that the dog interprets and constructs according to *its* sense of regulation and balance. This is again that peculiar quality we call autonomy. In fact, should my car not start one morning, I would be tempted to say it was mad at me; but since I am civilized, I realize that such an imputation is impossible, given that the machine was designed by men in the first place.

Perhaps the trouble begins precisely there: We did not design the dog, nor does it seem to be there for any purpose about which we can easily agree. The sharp contrast between living systems that exhibit autonomy and many other natural and man-made artifacts has fascinated biologists since the time of Aristotle and until the nineteenth century, and only the fascination with the diversity of the living could compete in attraction [11]. Interestingly, the theme of autonomy gradually disappeared into the fog of nondiscussion with the rise of genetics and molecular biology by the turn of the century, and, in parallel, the fields of engineering and design developed rapidly, giving rise to cybernetics and control theory. As a consequence, today not only do we not think about autonomy in natural systems, but we simply do not even recognize that such a name could apply to anything that could be made precise. Autonomy's conceptual counterpart, control, can surely be made exact, but not autonomy.

There is, of course, no more intrinsic mystery to autonomy than there is to control. The key is to see that autonomy is an expression of a peculiar kind of *process* that is profusely found in nature in many concrete forms [13]. This kind of process is precisely the one portrayed by Escher—parts that mutually specify themselves.

It is through this kind of articulation, in the molecular domain, that life specifies itself and acquires its autonomous quality. A cell stands out of a molecular soup by defining and specifying boundaries that set it apart from what it is not. However, this specification of boundaries is done through molecular productions made possible through the boundaries themselves. There is, therefore, a mutual specification of chemical transformation and physical boundaries; the cell draws itself out of a homogeneous background. Should this process of self-production be interrupted, the cellular components no longer form a unity and gradually diffuse back into a homogeneous molecular soup [8].

The backbone of the cellular organization (Figure 23) can be drawn as follows:

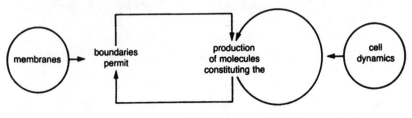

Figure 23

This configuration is the key: *closure* of operations whereby products are in the same levels as productions. In fact, within this organization, the usual distinctions between producer and product, beginning and end, or input and output cease making sense.

Little can be said about how cells originated, but a substantial amount of recent evidence is consistent with the idea that the closure just sketched is a necessary condition [3]. Once such autonomous unities are established, a whole new *domain* is generated: life as we know it today. Indeed, on this basic theme of tangled loops of molecular productions, many variations can be played, many different specific configurations, and thus a host of different cells.

In fact, it is possible that modern cells arose out of the symbiosis of units that were themselves autonomous and are now only vaguely remembered as mitochondria, chloroplasts, and other organelles [6]. Or even today, algae and fungi mutually satisfy their individual environments for maintenance and form a lichen. Thus cells can interact among themselves so as to constitute new autonomous unities; all multicellular organisms arise under similar circumstances.

In all such cases, the basic phenomenon is always the same:

operational closure of elements in separate levels inter-crossed to constitute a unity. When such level crossings and tangledness are interrupted, the unity vanishes. Autonomy arises at this point of intercrossing. The origin of life is no meager example of this general law.

The Structural Perspective

"Yields falsehood when apprended to its own quotation" yields falsehood when appended to its own quotation. This Quine [10] koan is a colorful way of presenting a pervasive knot that has been present in the study of language and mathematics for a long time. In fact, ever since the Cretan Epimenides had the odd idea of saying, "All Cretans are liars," the odd quality of self-reference has been a permanent headache [4]. This oddity springs from the assumption that what we say about something should not enter into the con-stitution of that something. Epimenides–Quine-type phrases explicitly violate this assumption.

In all such cases of linguistic tangledness, the family resemblance with both the Escher engraving and the emer-gence of cells and autonomy is apparent. There is the same move whereby that which should have stayed separate (in the Quine or Epimenides case, levels of meaning) is inter-crossed and two levels collapse into one, yet remain distin-guishable.

What is interesting, however, is that what seemed com-plex but understandable at the molecular domain acquires a sense of *paradox* in this linguistic domain. It is harder to leap out of the need to stay at a given level of meaning and simply look at the whole sentence as a unity. Paradox is exactly that: that which cannot be understood unless we examine it by leaping beyond both levels tangled in the structure of the paradox. In the Quine or Epimenides case, the phrases remain a paradox unless I am willing to let go of the need to choose between true or false, and see the sentence's circularity as its own way of specifying its meaning. That is, the sentence sits in a larger domain and only becomes paradoxical when pro-jected to the flatter domain of either true or false.

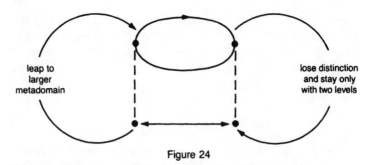

leap to
larger
metadomain

lose distinction
and stay only
with two levels

Figure 24

(I suppose this is why paradox appears over and over again in situations such as Zen training, where the learning is precisely that of leaping out to a larger domain where one can consider one's thoughts and values with detachment. To the extent that the student is fixed on one level or another, with one preference or judgment—good or bad, positive or negative, spiritual or mundane—the aim of the teaching is not achieved. A good teacher, I suppose, is one who can convey the unity or circularity, the tangledness of the situation, so vividly that the student is forced to leap out of it).

Perhaps the most interesting and illustrious evidence of the richness of self-reference in language and mathematics is Gödel's theorem, which I shall use as an example to trace some further consequences of closure.

The spirit of Gödel is (again) well represented in the Escher engraving. He and others of his time were interested in examining whether formal languages could examine themselves, whether the very inside of mathematics could talk to itself. For this purpose we must concentrate on those mathematical languages that can at least refer to and deal with numbers. Now numbers are not mathematical statements; they are mathematical objects that can be referred to in mathematical language adequate to that task. The genius of Gödel was to intercross these two levels, numerical language and numbers: a strange loop. To make the cross, he chose a correspondence between every symbol in the language and a number, in such a way that strings of symbols (thus statements *about* numbers) could also correspond to a number.

The details need not concern us here [9], but this is the general gist of the language thus constructed by Gödel.

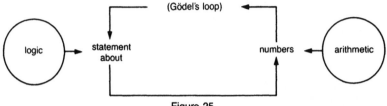

Figure 25

Once this intercrossing of domains is firmly established, it is easy to generate circular sentences like Quine's. In Gödel's case it takes the form, "This sentence has no proof" (it cannot be proved either true or false). Now the very existence of such a statement shows that all formal systems rich enough to contain numbers and arithmetic have perfectly well-defined and sensical things that cannot be decided right or wrong; thus, it is said, they are *incomplete*.

That undecidable statements could be thus produced at the very heart of such a central portion of mathematics sent waves of dissatisfaction among mathematicians. From our point of view, however, it is possible to understand Gödel's result rather differently: Not one of limitation, but as yet another instance of how closure can lead to the constitution of an autonomous domain, where out of a background a unity emerges and specifies a larger domain. In Gödel's case, once the loop is completed and the levels entangled, we have the emergence of a unity in the linguistic universe. The comparison with the biological case is evident:

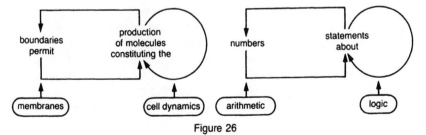

Figure 26

Let us consider for a moment the *inside* of any of these strange loops. In the Epimenides case, if we assume the statement is true, then it is consequently false; if it is false, then it must be true. Its fine structure is one where there is an oscillation between parts that were previously separate. We can write it thus:

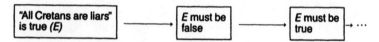

Or, in the cellular case, we can unfold the circle and obtain also an infinitely growing pattern:

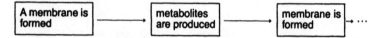

In a unit with operational closure, what appears as *coherent* or *distinguishable* behavior (whether in the domain of meaning or in the domain of molecular structures) has a peculiar nature indeed. On the one hand, it appears as a single property of the unit itself; on the other hand, when we attempt to examine the origin of such a property through its own properties, we find that there is nothing but an indefinite iteration of the same; it starts nowhere and it ends nowhere. The coherence is *distributed* through an ever-repeating circle that is infinite in its circulation, yet finite, since we can see its effect or results as a unit's property.

Let me give a more tangible illustration of this same idea. Consider a triangle. Break each side of it in three so as to produce a six-pointed star. Take each side of the star and break these in the same fashion. Repeat the process with every new side, *ad infinitum*. The resulting figure, somewhat like a snow crystal, is immediately graspable; it has coherence as a shape. Yet what we perceive is like a mythical ancestor that can never be fully drawn or described, but only stated as a trend of uninterrupted iteration. Interestingly enough, because of this self-referential geometrical construction, figures such as this have dimensions that are in between the traditional ones (besides having other peculiar properties). In the case of the triangle, the dimension of the final product is greater than 1, but less than 2—it is exactly 1.2618. Because of their fractional dimension, such figures are called *fractals* (Figure 27) [5].

In the example of a fractal we have all the ingredients, in a visual form, to see how closure in a process can lead (1) to a coherence that is always distributed and thus never fully present, but graspable as a "mythical ancestor" and (2) to properties which are emergent, and not simply added from the component elements that participate in the process.

Figure 27

Figure 28

The Cognitive Perspective

We have been discussing two instances—whether they be cells and the living, or formal systems and undecidability—where operational closure generates a whole new domain in the apparently harmless act of curling onto itself. At this point, we must take the next step in our examination of the natural history of circularity and explore the next fundamental case where closure changes the picture completely: our *own* descriptions, our *own* cognizing.

In fact, in considering our own cognizing, we put *together* the essentials of the two previous instances discussed. On the one hand, our cognition is in our biological substrate as body; on the other hand, our descriptions are fully capable of self-descriptions at indefinitely many levels. Through the nervous system, these two modes of closure are superimposed so as to constitute that closest and most elusive of all experiences: ourselves.

It is apparent that the nervous system is a part of our unity as biological beings, an autonomous unit in its own right. What is not so apparent is that the nervous system *itself* is curled on itself in several fundamental ways [7].

First, there is no effect or action of the nervous system (motility, glandular secretion) that does not have a direct effect on a sensorial surface. Just as a neuron acts on another by a close apposition of their surfaces in a synapse, a set of muscles acts on the sensorium of the body through recurrent action or sensorimotor synapse. A knee jerk is produced because a tendon is stretched, proprioceptors are pulled, and the activity of motor neurons in the spinal cord is changed, leading to muscles contracting in the opposite direction of the stretch. Motor actions have sensorial consequences, and sensorial actions have motor consequences. This reafference principle is of universal validity.

But there is still another essential sense in which the nervous system has operational closure. Once we pass the threshold of the sensorium or motorium, the effects of such organs in the nervous system are not like a one-way street or channel where traffic is clearly routed. Rather, it resembles

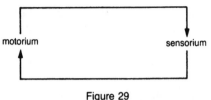

Figure 29

the addition of one new voice on the floor of the stock market. For example, if we were to travel with the nerve activity originating at the retina into the cortical area (of the occipital lobe), we would find that for each fiber from the retina entering this piece of cortex, 100 other fibers enter at the same spatial location from all over the brain [1]. Thus the activity of the retina at best sculpts or modulates what is going on internally in the high interconnection of the neural layers and nuclei.

But there is still more. Although electrical impulses travel along in only one direction, many other chemicals travel in the opposite direction in the cell's axon, so that routes in the nervous system are always two-way. For example, regulatory metabolites can be taken up at the axon's terminal end, travel toward the cell body, and go across a synapse to act on the preceding neuron with respect to the electrical flow. There are many such mutual effects in the nervous system that are just beginning to be charted [2]. A diagram may help to visualize this organization:

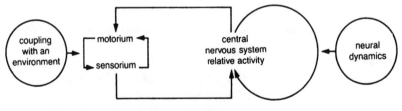

Figure 30

In this view of the nervous system we see a behavior when there is some particular *coherence* attained by the closure of this whole pattern of interconnections. One can analyze this coherence by breaking the process into its parts. We could start, say, with vision as originating in the eye, and then consider all the pathways that lead from the eye into the cortex, and then from the cortex to the thalamus and the forebrain, and so on. Eventually, we would end up in a full circle, and, indeed, we could loop around indefinitely. As in the illustration of a fractal, behavior is like the mythical ancestor of this infinitely recurring process, looping on itself repeatedly.

Subject / Object

If we are thoroughly consistent with what we have said about the nervous system, we must see our own experience arising in the same manner. And if we do so, there are two paramount consequences to consider.

First, that we cannot *step outside* the domain specified by our body and nervous system. There is no world except that experienced through those processes given to us and which make us what we are. We find ourselves in a cognitive domain, and we cannot leap out of it or choose its beginnings or modes.

Second, and equally important, we cannot trace a given experience to its *origins* in a unique fashion. In fact, whenever we do try and find the source of, say, a perception or an idea, we find ourselves in an ever-receding fractal, and wherever we choose to delve we find it equally full of details and interdependencies. It is always the perception of a perception of a perception. . . . Or the description of a description of a description. . . . There is nowhere we can drop anchor and say, "This is where this perception started; this is how it was done."

In finding the world as we do, we forget all we did to find it as such, entangled in the strange loop of our actions through our body. Much like the young man in the Escher engraving "Print Gallery," we see a world that turns into the very substratum which produces us, thereby closing the loop and intercrossing domains. As in the Escher engraving, there is nowhere to step *out* into. And if we were to try, we would

find ourselves in an endless circle that vanishes into an empty
space right in its middle (Figure 31).[1]

Figure 31   (M.C. Escher, "Print Gallery")

[1]Editor's note: Escher's biographer, Bruno Ernst, explains this print as
follows:

> At the lower right-hand corner we find the entrance to a gallery in
> which an exhibition of prints is being held. Turning to the left we
> come across a young man who stands looking at a print on the wall.
> On this print he can see a ship, and higher up, in other words in the
> upper left-hand corner, some houses along a quayside. Now if we
> look along to the right, this row of houses continues, and on the far
> right our gaze descends, to discover a corner house at the base of
> which is the entrance to a picture gallery in which an exhibition of
> prints is being held. . . . So our young man is standing inside the
> same print as the one he is looking at! [*The Magic Mirror of M. C.
> Escher*, Random House, New York, 1976, p. 31]

Tradition[2] would have it that experience is either a subjective or an objective affair, that the world is there and that we either see it as it is or we see it through our subjectivity. However, when we follow the guiding thread of circularity and its natural history, we may look at that quandary from a different perspective: that of *participation* and *interpretation*, where the subject and the object are inseparably meshed. This interdependence is revealed to the extent that nowhere can I start with a pure account of either one, and wherever I choose to start is like a fractal that only reflects back precisely what I do: to describe it. By this logic, we stand in relation to the world as in a mirror that does not tell us how the world is: neither does it tell us how it is not. It reveals that it is *possible* to be the way we are being, and to act the way we have acted. It reveals that our experience is *viable*.

That the world should have this plastic texture, neither subjective nor objective, not one and separable, neither two and inseparable, is fascinating. It points both to the *nature* of the process, which we can chart in all of its formality and materiality, as well as to the fundamental *limits* about what we can understand about ourselves and the world. It shows that reality is not just constructed at our whim, for that would be to assume that there is a starting point we can choose from: inside first. It also shows that reality cannot be understood as given and that we are to perceive it and pick it up, as a recipient, for that would also be to assume a starting point: outside first. It shows, indeed, the fundamental *groundlessness* of our experience, where we are given regularities and interpretations born out of our common history as biological beings and social entities. Within those consensual domains of common history we live in an apparently endless metamorphosis of interpretations following interpretations [12].

It reveals to us a world where "no-ground," "no-foundation" can become the basis for understanding that the age-old ideal of objectivity and communication as progressive

---

[2]One should qualify the various alternative traditions that are dissident. A very important one in this regard is phenomenology, and many of its side branches, but we speak here of the dominant common sense.

elimination of error for gradual attunement is, by its own scientific standards, a chimera. We should do better to fully accept the notoriously different and more difficult situation of existing in a world where no one in particular can have a claim to better understanding in a universal sense. This is indeed interesting: that the empirical world of the living and the logic of self-reference, that the whole of the natural history of circularity should tell us that ethics—tolerance and pluralism, detachment from our own perceptions and values to allow for those of others—is the very foundation of knowledge, and also its final point. At this point, actions are clearer than words.

REFERENCES

1. Braitenberg, V. *The Texture of Brains*. Springer-Verlag, Berlin, 1978.
2. Dismukes, R. K. *The Brain and Behavioral Sciences* 2:409, 1979.
3. Eigen, M., and Schuster, P. *The Hypercycle*. Springer-Verlag, Berlin, 1979.
4. Hughes, P., and Brecht, G. *Vicious Circles and Infinity*. Doubleday, New York, 1975. Also see Hofstadter, D. *Gödel, Escher, Bach; An Eternal Golden Braid*. Basic Books, New York, 1979.
5. Mandelbrot, B. *Fractals: Form, Chance, Dimension*. Freeman, San Francisco, 1978.
6. Margulis, L. *The Evolution of Eucaryotic Cells*. Freeman, San Francisco, 1980.
7. H. Maturana, The biology of cognition. In Maturana and Varela, *op. cit.*
8. Maturana, H., and Varela, F. *Autopoiesis and Cognition*. Boston Studies in Philosophical Science, Vol. 42. D. Reidel, Boston, 1980.
9. Nagel, E., and Newman, J. *Gödel's Proof*. New York University Press, New York, 1965. See also Hofstadter, *op. cit.* [4].
10. Quine, W. O. *The Ways of Paradox and Other Essays*. Harvard University Press, Cambridge, Massachusetts 1971.
11. Schiller, J. *La Notion d'organization dans l'histoire de la biologie*. Maloine, Paris, 1978.
12. The closest philosophical expression of this conclusion I have found is the Madhyamikan school of medieval Indian philosophy. See for example, the helpful introduction by F. Streng, *Emptiness: A Study in Religious Meaning*, Abingdon Press, New York, 1967.
13. Varela, F. *Principles of Biological Autonomy*. North Holland, New York, 1979.

Epilogue

We shall not cease from exploration,
and the end of all our exploring
will be to arrive where we started
and know the place for the first time.
T. S. Eliot: *Little Gidding*

One thinks that one is tracing the outlines of nature over and over again, and
one is merely tracing round the frame
through which we looked at her.
A picture held us captive. And we
could not get outside it, for it lay in our
language and language seemed to repeat
it to us inexorably.
Ludwig Wittgenstein: *Philosophical
Investigations I*, pp. 114–115

FOR THE READER who has followed the gradual unfolding
of constructivist thinking throughout these pages, an
obvious question arises: What *practical* conclusions, if any,
can be drawn from all of this? Is constructivism a new perspective that may perhaps bring about changes in the philosophy of science but which has as little relevance for one's
private life as, say, the theory of relativity has for the construction of a shed? What does it have to offer modern men
and women in a bewildering world where the time-honored
ideas and ideals have lost their meaning and their comfort?

For many, constructivism is another name for nihilism.
Whoever is convinced that life cannot be lived without ultimate meaning must see in constructivism the forerunner of
despair and chaos. For this person, the idea that all reality is
invented appears to leave only one conclusion: suicide. "I
am bound to show my unbelief," says the suicide Kirillov in
Dostoevski's *The Possessed:*

I have no higher idea than disbelief in God. I have all the history
of mankind on my side. Man has done nothing than to invent
God so as to go on living, and not kill himself; that's the whole
of universal history up till now [3].

The suicide searches for the meaning of life, then somehow convinces himself that the world is senseless, and therefore kills himself—not because the world or life *as such* has
revealed itself as unlivable, but because it does not satisfy *his*
demand that it should have a final and conceivable sense. With
this demand the suicide has constructed a reality that does
not fit and therefore leads to his extinction. Nothing could
be more alien to the inventor of this fatal reality than the
wise moderation of the King in *Alice in Wonderland* who, upon
reading the poem of the White Rabbit, finds it nonsensical
and concludes in relief, "If there is no meaning in it, that
saves us a world of trouble, you know, as we needn't try to
find any" [2]. Wittgenstein expresses essentially the same
thought in his *Tractatus* (6.521): "The solution of the problem
of life is seen in the vanishing of this problem" [11].

The counterpart of the suicide is the seeker; but the difference between them is slight. The suicide arrives at the conclusion that what he is seeking does not exist; the seeker
concludes that he has not yet looked for it in the right place.
Whereas the suicide thus introduces zero into the existential
"equation", the seeker has introduced infinity. For the seeker
any such quest is, in Karl Popper's sense, self-sealing and
therefore endless, there are an infinite number of possible
"right" places in which to look.

The charge of nihilism leads itself *ad absurdum:* It proves
what it wants to disprove, namely, that to postulate a sense
provides the precondition for the "discovery" of a senseless
world.

But all of this still tells us nothing about what reality is
constructed by constructivism *itself.* In other words, what
would the world of a person be like who managed to accept
reality fully and totally as his or her own construction?

First of all, as Varela has stated on p. 323, such a person
would be *tolerant.* If we come to see the world as our own

invention, we must apply this insight to the world of our fellow creatures as well. If we know that we do not or cannot know the truth, that our view of the world is only more or less *fitting*, we will find it difficult to ascribe madness or badness to the world views of others and to remain caught in the primitive Manichaean conviction that "whoever is not for me is against me." The realization that we know nothing as long as we do not know that we shall never know the ultimate truth is the precondition for one's respect for the realities others have invented for themselves. Only if those realities become intolerant can we then—again in Karl Popper's sense—"claim, in the name of tolerance, the right not to tolerate the intolerant" [8].

Secondly, such a person would feel *responsible*, in a very deep ethical sense, responsible not only for conscious decisions and actions, not only for dreams, but—in a much wider sense—even for the reality created by individual self-fulfilling prophecies. Our cozy expedient of attributing blame to others or to circumstances would no longer be available to this person.

This total responsibility would mean total *freedom*. Whoever is conscious of being the architect of his or her own reality would be equally aware of the ever-present possibility of constructing it differently. In the truest sense of the word, this person would be a heretic, that is, one who knows that choice is possible. Such an individual would be where the *Steppenwolf* finds himself at the end of the novel: in the Magic Theater, which his *psychopompos* Pablo explains to him with these words:

> This little theater of mine has as many doors into as many boxes as you please, ten or a hundred or a thousand, and behind each door exactly what you seek awaits you. It is a pretty cabinet of pictures, my dear friend; but it would be quite useless for you to go through as you are. You would be checked and blinded at every turn by what you are pleased to call your personality. You have no doubt guessed long since that the conquest of time and the escape from reality, or however else you may choose to describe your longing, means simply the wish to be relieved of your so-called personality. That is the prison where you lie. And

EPILOGUE

if you were to enter the theater as you are, you would see everything through the eyes of Harry and the old spectacles of the Steppenwolf" [4].

But the Steppenwolf is unable to take off his spectacles, and he is therefore "condemned to eternal life." This inversion of the meaning of life and death is much more than a clever play on words. Most reports by people who have escaped from life-threatening danger [7] have this one element in common: the experience of "breaking through" into a reality that is much more real than anything experienced before, whose immediacy defies description, and which is later remembered as being "more I than myself." When all constructions have collapsed, when all spectacles are discarded, then we are "at the end of all our exploring" and shall "arrive where we started and know the place for the first time."

Dostoevski, the epileptic, has his Prince Myshkin in the *Idiot* describe the *aura* (the seconds preceding a *grand mal* attack) by saying, "At that moment I seem somehow to understand that extraordinary saying that *there shall be no more time*." Arthur Koestler, in the death cell of a Francoist prison in Seville, obviously had an identical experience during what he calls the Hours by the Window:

> Then I was floating on my back in a river of peace, under bridges of silence. It came from nowhere and flowed nowhere. Then there was no river and no I. The I had ceased to exist[. . . .] When I say "the I had ceased to exist," I refer to a concrete experience that is verbally as incommunicable as the feeling aroused by a piano concerto, just as real—only much more real. In fact, its primary mark is the sensation that this state is more real than any other one has experienced before [5].

Countless soldiers have had similar experiences during combat. Robert Musil, whose protagonist, the young Törless, in vain implored his mathematics teacher to explain to him the significance of the imaginary number i, must have had a similar experience and described it in his narration *Der Fliegerpfeil*. [1] However, from his description it is not possible

---

[1] *Fliegerpfeil* means "fléchette," a small steel dart, dropped in clusters from airplanes on enemy troop concentrations during World War I.

to conclude whether or not Musil was aware of the possibility that hidden in this experience there was an answer to Törless' question:

> [The whizz of the falling *fléchette*] was a thin, singing, simple high-pitched sound, as when the rim of a glass is made to vibrate; but there was something unreal about it; you have never heard this before, I told myself. And this sound was directed at me; there was some connection between this sound and myself, and I did not have the slightest doubt that something decisive was about to happen to me. Not one of my thoughts was of the kind that is supposed to occur at the moment of departing from life, but everything I felt was directed into the future; and, to put it simply, I was certain that in the next minute I would feel God's presence close to my body[. . . .] My heartbeat was firm and calm; and not for the fraction of a second can I have been frightened; there was not an atom of time missing from my life[. . . .] At this very moment an intense feeling of gratitude came over me and I think I blushed all over my body. If somebody had said that God had entered into me I would not have laughed at it. But I also would not have believed it [6].

But all the foregoing anthological references and possible parallels, all these ultimately vague and subjective descriptions, sound exalted and "mystical" in the bad sense of the word, and yet their mystical character cannot be altogether denied if by this term we mean those brief moments during which, inexplicably, subject and object merge into what may be called their primordial unity. The problem is their description. The so-called mystics either fall silent—as Wittgenstein recommends—or they are forced to use the language of the great symbols governing their era: religion, mythology, philosophy, and the like. But in doing this they are "merely tracing around the frame" through which they looked at the world and they again become captives of the particular reality constructed through the use of these symbols. In the incomparable simplicity of his style, Lao-Tsu expressed this paradox in the first chapter of the *Tao Te Ching*: "The Tao that can be expressed is not the real Tao; the name that can be named is not the real name." Whoever is capable of writing a sentence like this knows about the relativity and the subjective origin of all meaning and naming. He knows that all attribution of sense and significance creates a particular reality. But to arrive at this knowledge he had to catch himself, so to speak, in the very act of constructing that reality; in other words, he had to discover how he first created a world "in his own image," how he remained unaware of this act of creation, how he then experienced that world "out there" as being independent of himself, and how, finally, he constructed—self-reflexively—himself in relation to the "suchness" of this supposedly objective world. The inevitability of this quest makes its senselessness meaningful. The wrong track must be taken in order to reveal itself as wrong. Wittgenstein must have had this in mind when he wrote the following:

> My propositions are elucidatory in this way: he who understands me finally recognizes them as senseless, when he has climbed out through them, on them, over them. (He must so to speak throw away the ladder, after he has climbed up on it.) [11]

We now see that the question that this epilogue attempts to answer ("What reality is constructed by constructivism itself?") is a fundamentally wrong question. But we also see that this mistake had to be committed in order to reveal itself as a mistake. Constructivism does not create or explain any reality "out there"; it shows that there is no inside and no outside, no objective world facing the subjective, rather, it shows that the subject–object split, that source of myriads of "realities," does not exist, that the apparent separation of the world into pairs of opposites is constructed by the subject, and that paradox opens the way into *autonomy*.

Since these thoughts have already been expressed more competently and rigorously by others, it may be useful to quote from some of these sources. In his book *Mind and Matter* Schrödinger wrote as early as 1958,

> The reason why our sentient, percipient and thinking ego is met nowhere within our scientific world picture can easily be indicated in seven words: because it is itself that world picture. It is identical with the whole and therefore cannot be contained in it as part of it [9].

These words have an almost mystical sound, but the reader should remember that they were written by a physicist who was honored for his work by receiving the Nobel Prize. Speaking of the physicist's world image, Spencer Brown has this to say in the concluding remarks of *Laws of Form:* "The world we know is constructed in order (and thus in such a way as to be able) to see itself." And he goes on to say the following:

> But *in order* to do so, evidently it must first cut itself up into at least one state which sees, and at least one other state which is seen. In this severed and mutilated condition, whatever it sees is *only partially* itself. We may take it that the world undoubtedly is itself (i.e., is indistinct from itself), but, in any attempt to see itself as an object, it must, equally undoubtedly, act so as to make itself distinct from, and therefore false to, itself. In this condition it will always partially elude itself [1].

And in his *Calculus for Self-Reference,* which starts from, but goes beyond Brown's logical system, Varela arrives at analogous conclusions:

> The starting point of this calculus [. . .] is the act of indication. In this primordial act we separate forms which appear to us as the world itself. From this starting point, we thus assert the primacy of the role of the observer who draws distinctions wherever he pleases. Thus the distinctions made which engender our world reveal precisely that: the distinctions we make—and these distinctions pertain more to a revelation of where the observer stands than to an intrinsic constitution of the world which appears, by this very mechanism of separation between observer and observed, always elusive. In finding the world as we do, we forget all we did to find it as such, and when we are reminded of it in retracing our steps back to indication, we find little more than a mirror-to-mirror image of ourselves and the world. In contrast with what is commonly assumed, a description, when carefully inspected, reveals the properties of the observer. We, observers, distinguish ourselves precisely by distinguishing what we apparently are not, the world [10].

REFERENCES

1. Brown, G. Spencer. *Laws of Form*. Bantam Books, Toronto, 1973, p. 105.
2. Carroll, Lewis. *Alice in Wonderland*. Dutton, New York, 1934.
3. Dostoevsky, Fyodor. *The Possessed*. Modern Library, New York, 1936, p. 628.
4. Hesse, Hermann. *The Steppenwolf*. Bantam Books, Toronto, 1963, p. 201.
5. Koestler, Arthur. *The Invisible Writing*. Macmillan, New York, 1969, p. 429.
6. Musil, Robert. "Der Fliegerpfeil." *Der Monat* 3, 1950, 193–195.
7. Noyes, Russell, and Kletti, Roy. "Depersonalization in the face of life-threatening danger: A description." *Psychiatry* 39, 1976, pp. 19–27.
8. Popper, Karl. *The Open Society and Its Enemies*. Harper Torchbooks, New York, 1963.
9. Schrödinger, Erwin. *Mind and Matter*. Cambridge University Press, Cambridge, Massachusetts, 1958, p. 52.
10. Varela, Francisco. "A calculus for self-reference." *International Journal of General Systems* 2, 1975, 5–24.
11. Wittgenstein, Ludwig. *Tractatus Logico-Philosophicus*. Humanities Press, New York, 1951.

The Authors

The biographical notes that follow have been furnished by
the contributors.

Rolf Breuer, born in 1940 in Vienna, studied English, French,
and philosophy at Bonn and at Göttingen, where he received
his Ph.D. After several years as assistant professor of English
at Regensburg University, he worked as associate professor
in various places, including the University of Massachusetts
at Amherst. He is now full professor at the recently founded
University of Paderborn. His main interests are English
Romanticism, modern English literature, and the theory of
literature. Among his publications are *Die Kunst der Paradoxie: Sinnsuche und Scheitern bei Samuel Beckett* ("The Art of
Paradox: Quest and Failure in Samuel Beckett," Wilhelm Fink,
Munich, 1976), *Das Studium der Anglistik* ("The Study of
English," with R. Schöwerling, C. H. Beck, Munich, 1980),
*Literatur—Eine kommunikationsorientierte Theorie des sprach-
lichen Kunstwerks* ("A Communication-Theoretical Approach
to Literature," Carl Winter, Heidelberg, 1983).

Jon Elster, born in 1946, teaches philosophy and history at the
University of Oslo. He is also responsible for a Working
Group on "Rationality and Society" at the Maison des Sciences de l'Homme (Paris). His publications include *Leibniz et
la formation de l'ésprit capitaliste* (Paris, 1975), *Logic and Soci-*

ety (London, 1978) and *Ulysses and the Sirens* (Cambridge, 1979). He is currently working on a critical study of Karl Marx and is pursuing the work on irrational behavior on which the article in the present volume is based.

Heinz von Foerster was born 1911 in Vienna. After completion of his studies (M.S., Physics, Institute of Technology, Vienna; Ph.D. Physics, University of Breslau) he worked in various industrial research laboratories in Germany and Austria. In 1949 he moved with his family to the United States and joined the staff of the Department of Electrical Engineering at the University of Illinois, Urbana, Illinois, and, at the same time, became secretary of the Cybernetics Conference Program of the Josiah H. Macy, Jr., Foundation in New York. In this connection he edited five volumes of the proceedings of these conferences: "Cybernetics: Circular Causal and Feedback Mechanisms in Biological and Social Systems."

With colleagues of the department of physics, he established the Department of Biophysics and Physiology in 1957, and in 1958 the Biological Computer Laboratory, an international and interdisciplinary research laboratory for the study of the physiology, theory, technology, and epistemology of cognitive processes.

Professor von Foerster was a Guggenheim Fellow (1956/1957 and 1963/1964), President of the Wenner-Gren Foundation for Anthropological Research (1963/1965), President of the Society for General Systems Research (1976/1977), is a Fellow of the American Association for the Advancement of Science (since 1980), and directed the Biological Computer Laboratory from 1958 until his retirement in 1976. The list of his publications has approximately 100 entries.

Heinz von Foerster is now Professor Emeritus of the Departments of Electrical Engineering and of Biophysics and Pysiology of the University of Illinois and lives in California.

Ernst von Glasersfeld born in 1917 of Austrian parents, went to school in Italy and Switzerland, briefly studied mathematics in Zurich and Vienna, and survived the war as a farmer in Ireland. In 1948 he joined the research group of Silvio Ceccato and subsequently became a permanent collaborator of the Center of Cybernetics in Milan. During this period he also worked as a professional journalist. In 1963 he received a contract from the U.S. Air Force Office of Scientific Research in the area of computational linguistics, and in 1966 he and his team moved to Athens, Georgia. Since 1970 he has taught cognitive psychology at the University of Georgia. His principal interests are conceptual analysis, epistemology, and, recently, the development of number concepts in children. He is currently writing a book on the constructivist theory of knowledge.

Rupert Riedl, born in Vienna in 1925, studied anthropology and biology at the University of Vienna. After undertaking marine biological expeditions from 1948 to 1952, he received his Ph.D. in 1952. In 1956 he became associate professor of the Department of Zoology at the University of Vienna; in 1966, visiting professor and since 1967 Kenan professor for Zoology and Marine Sciences at the University of North Carolina (Chapel Hill); and in 1971, director at the Department of Zoology at the University of Vienna. Today he is full professor at the biocenter of the University of Vienna, head of the Department for Marine Ecology and Ultrastructure and Theoretical Biology, and substituting director of the Institute of Anthroplogy at the University of Vienna. His books include *Order in Living Organisms; Systems, Conditions in Evolution* (German and English versions, 1975 and 1978), *The Strategy of the Genesis* (German, 1976), *Biology of Cognition* (German, 1979, English version by Wiley, London, in preparation), and *Evolution and Cognition* (German, 1982).

David L. Rosenhan has been professor of psychology and law at Stanford University since 1970. Prior to 1970, he taught at Swarthmore College, Princeton University, Haverford College, and the University of Pennsylvania. His present research activities deal with the influence of context on perception, especially the perception of social situations; the influence of emotional factors on behavior and cognition; and the overlap between psychology and law.

Gabriel Stolzenberg was born in New York City in 1937. He was graduated from Columbia College in 1958 and received his Ph.D. in mathematics from M.I.T. in 1961. He taught at Harvard University (1961–63) and at Brown University (1964–68) while doing mathematical research in the fields of several complex variables and algebras of functions. He has been professor of mathematics at Northeastern University since 1969. For the past decade and a half, his main work has been on the constructive development of mathematics and the constructivist critique of classical mathematics, but in recent years the scope of this work has been broadened to include questions about language, cognition, communication, and the methodology of science. Professor Stolzenberg has been a fellow of the National Academy of Sciences (1963–64), the Alfred P. Sloan Foundation (1967–69) and the John Simon Guggenheim Foundation (1977–78).

Francisco J. Varela was born in 1946 in Chile. He studied medicine and sciences at the University of Chile in Santiago and received his Ph.D. in biology from Harvard University in 1970. Since then he has taught and conducted research at the Universities of Chile and Costa Rica and the Medical Schools of the University of Colorado and New York University, and has been guest lecturer on numerous occasions in the United States, Europe, and Latin America. He is presently professor of natural sciences at the University of Chile and New York University, and author of some 40 research papers dealing with neurobiological, mathematical-cybernetic, and epistemological subjects, as well as four books on these subjects (the latest being *Principles of Biological Autonomy*, Elsevier-North Holland, New York).

Paul Watzlawick, born in 1921 in Austria, received his Ph.D. in modern languages and philosophy in 1949 at the University of Venice. From 1950 to 1954 he trained at the C. G. Jung Institute for Analytical Psychology, Zurich, and obtained an analyst's diploma. From 1957 to 1960 he was professor of psychotherapy at the University of El Salvador; since 1960 he has been a research associate at the Mental Research Institute,

Palo Alto, California; and since 1976 also clinical associate professor at the Department of Psychiatry and Behavioral Sciences, Stanford University Medical Center. He is the author of seven books (in 33 foreign editions) and over 40 articles in professional journals, and he has given numerous courses and guest lectures in university departments, clinics, and training institutes in North and South America as well as Europe.

Name Index

Subject Index

Printed in the United States
95206LV00002B/42/A

9 780393 333473

1940179

Made in the USA